Praise for *Beyond Success*
by Randall J. Ottinger

More than any other book on the intersection of wealth, family, charity, and personal fulfillment, Randy Ottinger's *Beyond Success: Building a Personal, Financial, and Philanthropic Legacy* convincingly illuminates the challenges faced by all who struggle with how best to transform their material success into lives that will bring personal fulfillment to themselves, their families, and their heirs, as well as benefit to the wider world around them. It provides an entirely new framework for thinking about how, at the prime critical junctions over a wealth-generator's lifetime, he or she can confidently deal with those challenges in ways that bring lasting satisfaction. In lucid and highly readable prose, informed by the wisdom and experiences of hundreds of real-life individuals, the names of many of whom are widely known, Ottinger has succeeded in producing the best available how-to-do-it playbook for those with any substantial amount of wealth who are grappling with some of the toughest questions anyone ever faces—how and how much to allocate to themselves, their spouses, and their children, as well as how, how much, and how best to devote to efforts that benefit society at large. This book proves that difficult challenges do not require complicated, complex, difficult-to-read manuals, but can be resolved by fresh, clear-headed, evidence-based ideas communicated in the simplest language. I recommend it with great enthusiasm.

Joel L. Fleishman
Author of *The Foundation: A Great American Secret—*
How Private Wealth Is Changing the World
(PublicAffairs Books, 2007), and Professor
of Law and Public Policy, Duke University

Randy Ottinger is entitled to speak and write about journeys. He has been through a long one himself getting to this final, well-done version of *Beyond Success*. . . . Randy Ottinger has committed the last several years of his life to creating a framework that illustrates many more choice points than people take advantage of, or perhaps even understand. Many future generations stand to benefit greatly from the work Randy has done to raise the possibility of better journeys.

Christine Letts
Associate Dean of Executive Education
Harvard's Kennedy School of Government

Beyond Success by Randy Ottinger analyzes many of the personal and family issues that I deal with every day in estate planning for my clients. The book provides an invaluable road map for individuals to think through their personal, family, and philanthropic goals. This should be required reading for anyone who advises wealthy families.

Bill Zabel
Partner, Schulte, Roth & Zabel,
leading estate and trust attorney,
winner of American Lawyer
Lifetime Achievement Award

Randy Ottinger in his book, *Beyond Success*, provides great wisdom about how to turn financial and corporate success into a philanthropic legacy. He has clearly thought through the issues that successful individuals face when they turn their attention from building a company or family business to building a personal and family legacy. This book is very timely and insightful, and should be on any successful individual's reading list.

Jeff Brotman
Chairman of Costco

Beyond Success by Randy Ottinger provides incredible insights for how to make the same kind of social impact with one's time and money as we did with The Body Shop. His book offers a road map that will benefit individuals, families, and society. This is a must-read for executives and philanthropists who want to apply their talents, passion, and fortune to make a real difference.

Anita Roddick
Founder and CEO of The Body Shop

Randy Ottinger in his book, *Beyond Success*, has captured the philanthropic mindset of donors. He provides great insights for how to make a philanthropic impact and to achieve passion and fulfillment from giving. This should be mandatory reading for all philanthropists, advisors, and not- for- profits.

Mr. Charles Raymond
Former President of the Citigroup Foundation
and currently a Philanthropic Advisor

BEYOND SUCCESS

TO my GOOD FRIEND
DAN. FOR ALL
GOOD THINGS !

BEYOND SUCCESS

Building a Personal, Financial, and Philanthropic Legacy

RANDALL J. OTTINGER

New York   Chicago   San Francisco   Lisbon   London
Madrid   Mexico City   Milan   New Delhi   San Juan
Seoul   Singapore   Sydney   Toronto

ISBN-13: 978-0-07-149676-6
ISBN-10: 0-07-149676-9

This publication is designed to provide accurate and authoritative information in regard to the subject matter covered. It is sold with the understanding that the publisher is not engaged in rendering legal, accounting, or other professional service. If legal advice or other expert assistance is required, the services of a competent professional person should be sought.
>   —*From a declaration of principles jointly adopted by a committee of the American Bar Association and a committee of publishers.*

McGraw-Hill books are available at special quantity discounts to use as premiums and sales promotions, or for use in corporate training programs. For more information, please write to the Director of Special Sales, Professional Publishing, McGraw-Hill, Two Penn Plaza, New York, NY 10121-2298. Or contact your local bookstore.

This book is dedicated to my parents,
Betty Ann Ottinger and Richard L. Ottinger,
who modeled my values;
to my wife, Lea Anne,
who is my closest companion on my life's journey;
and to my children,
Lauren, Michael, and Ryan,
who are my most important legacy.

Don't forget until too late that the business of life is not business, but living.

B.C. FORBES

CONTENTS

FOREWORD

Randy Ottinger is entitled to speak and write about journeys. He has been through a long one getting to this final, well-done version of *Beyond Success*. When Randy visited me back in 2003, he had an idea for an in-search-of-excellence study that he felt would be useful for successful people and family business owners. He had been researching best wealth, family, and philanthropy practices but could not find an integrated framework of best practices. He felt there was an opportunity to apply wealth management portfolio theory to the arenas of family and philanthropy so that people could potentially achieve better "returns." At the time I was skeptical. Unlike many other people who visit me to pitch ideas, however, Randy really listened to my many questions, and worked really hard over the next three years to develop what has become a valuable framework for family business owners, philanthropists, and people of means.

There are several ideas that Randy presents in *Beyond Success* that make this work distinctive and valuable. The first is that the many industries that serve the affluent (lawyers, accountants, investment advisers) are not very well equipped to help people navigate and integrate the issues associated with building and managing wealth, philanthropy, and family. There are legions of advisers in fairly narrow silos, which create gaps in information. Their advice is expensive, and the gaps are cumbersome to overcome. Perhaps this book will help to create demand for more integrated services.

The second big idea is that it makes sense to understand the pitfalls and opportunities of each of the three areas more fully throughout one's life. Randy and I had many interesting conversations about the predictable patterns in the lives of people who build significant wealth. Randy's interviews with such people, reported across the chapters, reinforce the limitations of focusing on one thing at a time. Since the first thing is primarily wealth-building and this is sustained for a long time, the value of learning new habits associated with establishing the family and social spheres of life is less understood and simply put off for too long.

One thing is inevitable for all of us. The years will pass. What is not inevitable is how we spend those years. Randy Ottinger has committed the last several years of his life to creating a framework that illustrates that there are many more choices than people take advantage of or perhaps even understand. Many future generations stand to benefit greatly from the work Randy has completed, which supports the possibility of better journeys.

CHRISTINE W. LETTS

PREFACE
More Than "Just Passing Through"

On a warm summer's day in Washington, DC, surrounded by his extended family, my grandfather, Sam Schneider, rose to address his loved ones. Dressed in a suit and tie, with his signature hat in place, Grandpa Sam's eyes viewed the admiring crowd.

It was his ninety-fifth birthday, and like most patriarchs closing in on that coveted century mark, he was thinking back on his life. "Grandpa Sam," as he was commonly referred to by his family, was a gentleman from Louisville, Kentucky. He lived a good life, was married once, and had three healthy, successful children to show for it. All his children graduated from college, which in the first half of the twentieth century was an unusual accomplishment, especially for women.

While many of his contemporaries settled into comfortable lives and watched history from a distance, Sam volunteered for the military in World War II, proudly serving alongside his two sons even though he was far beyond the age requirements for the draft. For Sam there was a higher call to duty than that which his own government required of him.

Over the years Sam made a solid, middle-class living. He raised his children in a modest home in Louisville, Kentucky, and provided a comfortable life for his family. His wife and children were always well fed and neatly dressed. He enjoyed the simple things in life—to read the morning paper on the front porch, to track the price of his favorite stocks, and, of course, to attend the horse races. He lived with integrity and was universally loved by friends and family. For Sam that was enough.

In fact, for Sam, that was more than enough.

On his ninety-fifth birthday, surrounded by his adoring children and grandchildren, after he had blown out the candles on his birthday cake—angel food cake with chocolate frosting (a family weakness)—Grandpa Sam gave a brief speech. It went something like this:

Thank you for your love and celebration of my life. After 95 years, you might guess that I have seen a few things, and have something to say about them. Yet, the truth is that I am a man who is just passing through.

My life is not notable for having created a great invention for the benefit of humanity or for saving lives in battle or for building an enduring business. Nor have I created great wealth. My life has been a modest life, lived like so many others, with friends and family. That is what I will leave behind when I am gone . . . and that is enough for me.

With these words, this simple, humble man from Louisville returned to his seat and let us all enjoy the party. That moment at Grandpa Sam's birthday party helped me understand that each individual has to define significance in his or her own way. For

Grandpa Sam it was his family, his duty to his country, and the lives he touched on a daily basis.

For many, like my grandfather, their legacies are a result of simple, daily acts, such as raising and educating their children, or providing a caring ear for friends, or supporting the schools and charities that are personally meaningful to them. They could no more put a price tag on raising a healthy, happy family than they could on serving their country.

Most people live their lives by surviving and striving to leave their children the hope of a better life than their own. Their legacies, like that of my grandfather, are less tangible than mere assets or ledgers. Their legacies are their families, the lives they touch every day through just plain living, the time they give to their community, and often their strong commitment to their faith of choice. To put a price tag on such values is to measure the very achievement such priceless legacies leave behind.

By contrast, my other grandfather, Lawrence Ottinger, had a different life story and defined significance in another way. Grandpa Larry was a great entrepreneur amassing a small fortune by growing a company called US Plywood. He was often seen on the social scene in Scarsdale, New York, in the early 1900s, and he was mentioned in the pages of *New Yorker* magazine. He traveled the world and rubbed elbows with world leaders. The financial legacy that was created by my grandfather Larry has been used by my father, a congressman and career social servant, to improve the world. His legacy was defined by the company he built, the lives of the employees he helped, and the wealth he created.

My grandfather Larry passed the family's wealth and legacy to my father and then to me. On my father's seventieth birthday—

he never thought he would live past 70 since his father died at that age—he called me on the phone and said something like this to me:

> *Randy, as you know, the focus of my life has been to improve the world in any way I could. That has been my life's mission, and it has been extremely gratifying. I have not spent the time or energy to carefully watch after the money your grandfather created. It has not been my passion or interest. I have trusted in professionals to make sure our finances are in good hands. I am not sure they have done a good job. I feel an obligation to our family, to your cousins, your brothers and sisters, to make sure someone in the family continues to watch out for our financial well-being when I am gone. You are the only one in the family who is interested in business, and I would like your help to make sure our investments are in good hands.*

With those words, he started me on my own search for personal significance. I began considering how I might carry out the mission my father described. How would I shepherd our family's wealth while achieving significance for my own life? How do I build a life of meaning and balance doing well and doing good? How do I use my talents, resources, and capabilities to make a difference in the world so that my life has meaning and so that I can leave something of lasting value? How do I raise confident, motivated children and create an environment of openness, trust, and harmony within my family, preserving my family's values now and for future generations? How would I succeed in answering my father's call so that others would benefit?

As I considered these questions in the weeks following our conversation, I decided that my own legacy should include a comprehensive understanding of how the great business leaders and philanthropists around the world have achieved success in these areas. I was seeking, but could not find, a roadmap for best financial, social, and family wealth practices, and felt others would benefit from one as well. In the course of writing this book between 2003 and 2006, I not only learned about the legacy practices of the affluent, but also learned more about myself, my family, and our relationship with money than I ever thought possible.

My research was guided by these few basic questions about the nature of leaving a social, emotional, and financial legacy. These questions drove me to begin the journey of this book and guided me in the interviews, the research, and the writing of these pages. They helped me to find my own answers. My hope is that the lessons I have learned will help you to find answers for your own life.

RANDALL J. OTTINGER

ACKNOWLEDGMENTS

An essential lesson I learned from writing this book is how important it is to share your knowledge, and to lend a hand when there is an opportunity to help. The first to lend me a hand was Howard Stevenson at Harvard Business School. He got the ball rolling, found me a partner in Christine Letts at Harvard's Kennedy School, and identified my agent. The most important person to shape my thinking related to the book was Christine Letts. She is direct and insightful, and helped support me with the design of the questionnaire and the high-level framework for the book. My agent, Jim Levine, took a risk on me as a new author and connected me with McGraw Hill, and I am very appreciative. This book, from the first draft to the final product, would not have happened without the support of Herb Schaffner at McGraw Hill. He took this on not only as the publisher, but as the initial editor as well, sending comments from home and work.

This book could not have happened without the support and openness of some incredibly talented advisers and legacy leaders who were willing to take the time out of their extremely busy lives to share their knowledge. Thanks to Bill Gates Sr., Sandy Weill, Anita Roddick, Bob Buford, Jeff Brotman, John Whitehead, Les Wexner, Mario Morino, Mark Leslie, Paul Brainerd, Peter Karoff, Scott Oki, Mark Schwartz, Bill Zabel, Charles Collier, Doug Mellinger, Ginny Esposito, Kelin Gersick, Peter Karoff, Lee Hausner, Joe Breiteneicher, Steve Johnson, Curtis Meadows, Jackie Novogratz, Page Snow, Phil Cubeta, Peter Hero, Rorrie Gregorio, Phil Strassler, Paul Shoemaker,

Younghee Wait, Michele Lord, Paul Schervish, Alan Pratt, Peter Joers, Peter Evans, Leslie Michelson, William Neukom, Charles Raymond, Phil Cubeta, Mark Davis, Jarett Wait, and many others who provided insight.

A special thanks goes to my wife, Lea Anne, and my children for supporting me while I follow my passion.

BEYOND SUCCESS

INTRODUCTION
Building a Personal Legacy Out
of a $100 Trillion Megatrend

In 2003 I left my position as a senior executive at a public company in Seattle, Washington. I didn't want to go to work anymore, and I had felt this way for several years. There was little meaning for me in that world, and I felt that there was another path for me than the day-to-day rigors of my high-tech job.

Many would say that leaving was a highly risky move, but, like so many things in life, when I made the decision to leave, I found that I was not alone. There were many others feeling the same way and considering the same option. Others, who by all external accounts were successful, having risen to top positions in business or real estate or investment management or who had helped to grow a family business, were not satisfied. Like me, they wanted more.

In my case, growing up in a political family where the topic around our dinner table was how to improve the world, I knew that it was important for me to do something with my time and talents that was not just about making money. What I was seeking was meaning in my life, to go beyond success in order for me to achieve my own personal significance.

What I came to realize was that there is no integrated road map for guiding individuals in the diverse areas of financial, social, and family wealth. The expertise related to these areas is highly fragmented. It exists in silos. If someone is trained as a financial expert or trust and estate lawyer, he or she may not know anything about philanthropy. If someone is trained as a philanthropist or as a social servant, there is no reason to expect that this same person knows anything about investing, family businesses, or preparing heirs for what lies ahead of them.

Over the last several years I became immersed in the study of the broad topic of wealth. During this time I interviewed many of the top advisers to the wealthy, advisers who support successful leaders with their estate plans, investing, philanthropy, family businesses, and heirs. In addition, I spoke to some of the most successful legacy leaders of today, leaders who had gone beyond personal success to leave their mark on the world in a significant and positive way. These individuals have transformed the lives of their employees, families, and those in society who are in need.

Through interviews with legacy leaders such as Bill Gates Sr. (father of Microsoft founder and cofounder of the Bill and Melinda Gates Foundation), Les Wexner (founder of The Limited and of the Wexner Institute for Jewish Leadership), John C. Whitehead (former CEO of Goldman Sachs and founder of Harvard Business School's Social Enterprise Initiative), Sandy Weill (former chairman and CEO of Citigroup and philanthropist), Anita Roddick (founder of The Body Shop, a leading retail company and for-profit social enterprise), Steve Kirsch (founder of Infoseek and Outstanding Philanthropist of the Year in Silicon Valley), Mark Leslie (founder of Veritas), Paul Brainerd (founder of Aldus and of Social Venture partner), Jeff Brotman (CEO of Costco, and Philanthropist of the Year in Seattle), and many,

many others who have turned their focus and attention to the creation of not just a better bank account but a better world, a picture of excellence emerged.

With the support of Chris Letts, of Harvard's Kennedy School, we developed a questionnaire that probed the key milestones in the lives of legacy leaders where they made personal decisions related to their time and money. We were interested in how they uncovered their personal calling in life and achieved a measure of success and personal fulfillment, and how they identified an area of passion with their philanthropy. We also probed similar questions related to how they were preparing their children to be successful and motivated with their wealth. We wanted to know how families who had stayed together for generations created family harmony. We wanted to know what went right as well as what went wrong.

In the end we were searching for patterns from the interviews, the knowledge leaders we spoke to, the literature, and from personal experience. Our objective has been to bring together a diverse body of information in a more holistic way that is digestible and accessible for individuals, and to create a road map of best practices that can assist others as they go through their own life's journey and attempt to leave their own legacies.

In total, between direct interviews with legacy leaders and time spent with advisers to the wealthy, the aggregate knowledge that the individuals who were interviewed represent includes experiences with thousands of successful leaders. We have poured through vast amounts of research and literature that represent a base of current knowledge, and we have attempted to create a framework for thinking about this topic. It is the stories that emerge from this study of wealth leaders that provide clues to help guide others toward achieving successful and fulfilling legacies.

What we learned is that these successful business people and legacy leaders are nothing like us *and everything like us!* They have a talent, a Midas touch, if you will, for making money and building global enterprises. Most of us do not have the same skill set. However, they are exactly like us in that they are all striving for meaning in their lives. They want their lives to matter. They worry about their children. They want to improve the lives of others. They don't want to squander their money. They want to balance their time between work and family and personal and community activities.

They are not alone as they grapple with their wealth and significance. Over the next several decades, a multi-trillion-dollar wealth transfer will take place in this country. This fact reflects the reality that the baby boomers, an unwavering and driving force in Western society, are in fact mortal beings. They have built their businesses, raised their children, affected society in ways never before seen, and will ultimately reach the end of their journeys over the next half century. As they make the transition to a new stage in their lives, with the first of the baby boomers turning 60 in 2006, an unprecedented amount of wealth will transfer to new investments, to philanthropy, and to their heirs.

Paul Schervish and John Havens from Boston College estimate that over the next 50 years an estimated $40 trillion to $136 trillion is expected to transfer to the next generation. Of this amount of money, between $6 trillion and $24 trillion will likely go to charity, while between $24 trillion and $65 trillion will likely go to heirs. The vast majority of the dollars going to charity will come from individuals with $5 million or more in assets.[1]

As they have done throughout their lives, the boomers are having a ripple effect through the global economy. According to Gary Onks, author of *Sold on Seniors*,[2] boomers and seniors:

- Account for over 40 percent of total consumer demand.
- Control over 48 percent of all discretionary purchases that are made.
- Hold over 80 percent of all money in savings accounts.
- Own 79 percent of financial assets in the United States.
- Spend almost $2 trillion on goods and services each year.
- Own 62 percent of all large Wall Street investment accounts.

An estimated $40 trillion to $136 trillion of baby boomers' assets is expected to transfer to the next generation over the next 50 years. Baby boomers own over 79 percent of the financial assets in the United States.

Although these statistics are often mentioned in the abstract, in truth they do not reflect one pot of money or the collective actions of a cohesive whole. They reflect the galaxy of individual choices made for a variety of reasons. The sum of their choices will, in part, determine whether these dollars grow or shrink, whether individual legacies make a lasting impact on society or provide temporary relief, and whether future generations are prepared for the responsibility of wealth.

Most wealthy individuals and families are unprepared for this wealth transfer. They go through a learning curve that is similar with respect to their wealth, philanthropy, and family practices. They wrestle with common issues and ask similar questions. They seek unbiased and trusted advisers who can assist them when they need help. They sort through myriad products and services that are sold to them by a wide variety of providers who are being asked to offer more services for less money.

Few achieve the results they desire or their true potential. Charged with the responsibility of leaving a legacy that will enrich future generations, they inevitably disappoint both themselves and those who anticipated their greatness. The net result is that most family wealth transfers fail, and well-intentioned philanthropy is often not as impactful as donors or charities would like.

The statistics are sobering:

70 percent of wealth transfers fail.[3]

Few providers are perceived as capable of offering truly integrated wealth management services.[4]

There is no family, no couple, and no wealth holder who has done it completely right in all three [areas] *[wealth, family, philanthropy].[5]*

We have gotten an explosion of nonprofit organizations and an explosion of funders . . . and are we really getting at the root causes of homelessness and other causes or is it just keeping this not-for-profit sector alive?[6]

In part, the dismal failure rate reflects a failure of leadership, a failure to prepare others for the task ahead, and a failure to build institutions that will last. This common theme of generational failure is not a new one; historians refer to it as the "shirtsleeves to shirtsleeves" phenomenon, and even the most casual students of history will find it repeated throughout multiple cultures and time periods.

In part the failure reflects the difficulty of navigating the wealth and philanthropy industries where expertise is contained in silos that are rarely brought together in an integrated or holistic way for individuals or families. The silos relate to financial wealth, social wealth, and family wealth. Other than the government, wealth will inevitably flow into these three areas. It will be invested or consumed (financial wealth), given away to society through philanthropy (social wealth), or passed along to heirs (family wealth).

Not surprisingly, whole industries have grown up around these silos. The realm of financial wealth is the domain of bankers and investment bankers, of insurance providers and financial behemoths, of specialized estate planners and accountants. It is in these firms where one finds a brain trust of graduates from the top business and law schools who are charged with shepherding the wealth from one generation to the next. Advisers in this area help preserve and grow financial wealth, and they are paid handsomely to do so.

The second aspect of legacy-leaving is philanthropy. There is a separate and equally vibrant industry around nonprofits and philanthropy. The nonprofit sector represents almost 10 percent of the U.S. gross domestic product (GDP).[7] There are over 1.5 million nonprofits, over 68,000 foundations, and millions of people involved in this industry.[8] Far from losing ground to the more capitalistic financial planning firms, this industry is expected to more than double in size over the next several decades. Unlike the individuals supporting the financial sector, whose passion rises or falls in proportion to their clients' portfolios, individuals with social passion dominate the nonprofit world.

The relationship among philanthropic advisers, nonprofit leaders, and the country's wealthy elite is complex and changing. Historically, wealth builders have been less businesslike in their philanthropic investing than in their financial investing. They have given from the heart rather than with the discipline of a business leader. They have also given to causes and nonprofits that rely on their grants for survival.

Today, we are witnessing the transformation of philanthropy and of the nonprofit sector. This is being driven by new philanthropists who are not satisfied with setting up foundations to give away 5 percent of their wealth a year. These new philanthropists are for the most part younger than their counterparts from history. They come from firms such as eBay, Microsoft, and Google. They are creative. They are social entrepreneurs who are establishing social enterprises that combine a business model of doing well with the potential to do a great deal of good in the world. Many will be giving their wealth away during their lifetimes rather than leaving it to their heirs. The *Economist* (February 25, 2006) termed this trend *philanthrocapitalism*. I prefer the term *social entrepreneurism*.

A third aspect of legacy-leaving, which is more specialized, relates to wealth in families. This sector is less well defined than the areas of financial wealth and philanthropy. Core to the mission of family wealth advisers is to guide the transition of family values, wealth, philanthropy, and family businesses from one generation to the next. Advisers to these families range from estate planners and accountants to succession planning specialists. Their work supports families financially and psychologically through the maze of wealth among generations of family members. They deal with succession issues related to businesses and family foundations. They work to prepare heirs to handle wealth responsibly. They talk about the human, intellectual, social, and financial capital of families. They are professionals and intellectuals. Their focus is to preserve family wealth, values, and enterprises across generations.

The business of legacy-leaving is built on these three legs of an often wobbly stool: financial wealth, social wealth, and family wealth. Often the stool collapses as a result of the sheer complexity that wealth creates and as the needs of wealthy families outstrip the capabilities, incentives, and offerings of advisers. This is the dilemma that wealthy individuals and the industry face today.

Never in history has there been so much wealth created by individuals at such a young age, who therefore have the opportunity to participate actively and personally in the application of their wealth toward the achievement of a positive, multigenerational impact. This trend has resulted in a level of sophistication and focus related to wealth that has exciting implications for civic society and for generations of families.

Beyond Success reveals the best practices and lessons learned from individuals who have successfully charted the legacy journey and who have made effective decisions about their social investing, their financial legacy, and their family's long-term interests. It identifies the practices employed by legacy leaders to translate their highest goals into measurable actions. It also highlights the gaps and misalignments that are created and explains the role advisers play in assisting individuals and families along the way. Finally, it creates a framework for exploring financial, family, and social wealth in an integrated manner with an objective of helping not only the wealthy but others as well to discover their own route to success, fulfillment, and significance.

The insights that are contained herein are divided into three parts: Part I is about the legacy journey. It describes the junctions that people come to after they have achieved success ("Crossing the Wealth Divide"), where things go wrong ("Navigating the Valleys"), and how people learn to be successful with wealth personally, in society, and with their families ("Climbing the Mountains").

Part II is about the best practices of legacy leaders that were learned from the research. There are eight practices of legacy leaders that are highlighted for personal fulfillment ("Self-Actu-alization Practices"), social impact ("Social Impact Practices"), and generational families with wealth ("Generational Family Practices"). At the end of each of these three sections we offer some tools that come from experts in the field to support individuals who desire concrete suggestions on actions they can take toward fulfilling their own potential in these areas.

Part III of *Beyond Success* identifies the two major trends that are likely to result from the trillions of dollars of generational wealth that is expected to transfer as a result of the baby boomers coming of age. They include the transformation of philanthropy due to the innovation of new philanthropists, as well as the transformation of the wealth advisory industry in response to the expanding demands of its wealthiest clients.

For those who have accumulated wealth or who just want to find their own way to make an impact with their lives, *Beyond Success* holds insights into the challenges they will likely face as they attempt to pass along their values and wealth to future generations. For those who work with or touch successful individuals or families or where successful individuals are essential for your success, there are insights that will assist you in your roles. Most of all, it is for those who are on their own path toward success, are striving for personal meaning and fulfillment with their lives, and are hoping to achieve something more, something beyond success.

PART I

THE JOURNEY BEYOND SUCCESS— TO SIGNIFICANCE

I felt as if I were walking with destiny, and that all my past life had been but a preparation for this hour and this trial.

WINSTON CHURCHILL

CROSSING THE WEALTH DIVIDE

Your life is the sum result of all the choices you make, both consciously and unconsciously. If you can control the process of choosing, you can take control of all aspects of your life. You can find the freedom that comes from being in charge of yourself.

ROBERT F. BENNETT

They were born at the same time; two men whose passion and productivity would rival that of the country's greatest wealth builders. Often they would mirror each other in their ruthlessness and ambition, but their legacies would be as different as night and day.

One was the son of a weaver. His father's trade was made obsolete by advancing technology. He grew up in poverty in Scotland. When he was 12, his family moved to the United States full of idealism for political democracy and social justice. Early on in his life he worked as a bobbin boy in a cotton mill and then as a telegrapher for the Pennsylvania Railroad.

When the Civil War broke out in 1861, he went to the front. There he met George Pullman, inventor of the sleeping car, which he introduced to the railroad industry. This became the source of one of his first fortunes. Over time he went on to found an empire in the steel business. He was a shrewd businessman, and during his lifetime became the second wealthiest man in America.

The other was born on a farm in New York. At the age of 16 he went to work for his father in the hardware business. After a brief stint in the lumber and tanning businesses, he went to a Wall Street brokerage house. His career led him to invest in and eventually own railroads. During his lifetime he was in control of 10,000 miles of railway, about one-ninth of the length of rail in the United States at the time.[1] When he died, he was a very wealthy man.

The first son was Andrew Carnegie.

The second was Jay Gould.

Both were strong, aggressive businessmen who took advantage of the opportunities that were presented to them by the times in which they lived, by the growth of the railroad, and by the incentives of the government. Both were shrewd in their own way. Admittedly, Jay Gould was unscrupulous, but the same could be said about others during their day as well.

Both men could attribute a significant amount of their fortunes to the growth in railroads—the emerging technology that would not only bring the country together but drag it into the Industrial Revolution. The story of their legacies, however, is the chronicle of what they did *after* they made their money.

Andrew Carnegie went on to build 3,000 libraries across the United States, as well as in Great Britain, Ireland, Canada, Australia, New Zealand, the West Indies, and Fiji. He started the

Carnegie Institute of Technology at Pittsburgh in 1901 with a $2 million grant and founded Carnegie Hall in New York City as well as establishing or contributing to many other charities. When he died, he gave away his last $30 million to foundations, charities, and pensioners.

What of the archetypal "robber baron," Jay Gould? While Carnegie used his wealth to leave a legacy that enriches thousands of people to this day, Gould, on the other hand, left his entire fortune to his six children, with little recognizable or lasting to show for it.

Gould's fate demonstrates that significant legacies are forged not from the deeds that create success and wealth but from the leadership that success and wealth help to create for families and in society. The choices individuals make when they move beyond success define them and their legacies.

When author and financial adviser Stuart E. Lucas sat down to consider the ramifications of his family's sale of their highly successful Carnation Company to Nestlé for $83 a share—or about $3 billion in cash—back in 1985, he commented in his book, *Wealth: Grow It, Protect It, Spend It and Share It*, "Our family's money represented more than just cash. It represented hard work, history, love, and legacy—a tangible gift from past generations of Stuarts to my own. It was meant to last a long time and to be used in ways that would benefit not just my family and me, but also society and generations of Stuarts yet unborn."[2]

Stuart Lucas was describing the legacy journey he was facing—to figure out how to make his family's history and wealth meaningful for future generations and for society, and to do it in a way that was personally fulfilling. The sale of his family's business was a defining moment because no longer was there a company that defined Lucas's identity.

These defining moments, or junctions in life, and how people handle them are in part what the legacy journey is all about. From our research we have categorized these junctions into three areas:

1. The *success junction* is the point at which decisions are made based on what success means for an individual and family. It is also the point at which individuals determine how much is enough for themselves and their heirs.
2. The *significance junction* is the point at which decisions are made concerning one's purpose in life and how this influences how one spends his or her time.
3. The *generational junction* is the point at which decisions are made with regard to what individuals want to last within their families, including family values, family history, and family businesses.

It is at these junctions that key decisions are made that define an individual and often help clarify his or her values. As individuals decide what they want from their lives, they are often traveling a psychological journey as well. Their identity—the way they think of themselves in this world—can also change.

Many of the individuals we interviewed started from modest means. In the early part of their lives they were striving to establish their careers. Like many of us during the early years, they were attempting to find their place in the world and to achieve personal success. They saw themselves as wealth builders or career builders. As they then became successful financially, they were faced with the great challenge of achieving personal satisfaction along with their success. It is only when people are satisfied with their financial success that they can begin to shift their personal identity beyond that of a wealth builder. Most individuals do not achieve satisfaction with their success. This is their challenge, and what we term the *wealth divide*.

The individuals we interviewed have crossed to the other side of the wealth divide. As a result, they have shifted how they view themselves from that of a wealth builder to that of a legacy builder. They have expanded their definition of success and their goals for themselves. They have wrestled with the questions they encountered at the success, significance, and generational junctions, which get at the heart of a person's values. In the process they have become strategic and thoughtful about the impact they want to achieve with their families and on society. They can then begin as well to climb the wealth mountains, learning how to be a good investor; the philanthropy mountains, learning how to make a social impact; and the family mountains, learning how to support their families across the generations (see Figure 1). This is the journey beyond success—to significance.

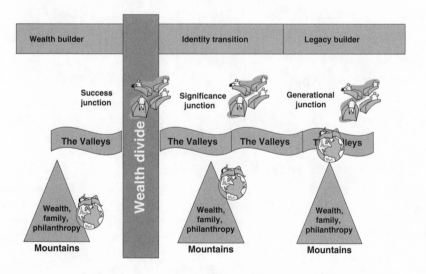

FIGURE 1: *The Legacy Journey Terrain Map*

CHAPTER 1

THE SUCCESS JUNCTION

*Success is the doing, not the getting; in the trying,
not the triumph. Success is a personal standard, reaching
for the highest that is in us, becoming all that we can be.*

ZIG ZIGLAR

It was graduation day, and the students waited with anticipation for one of the icons of entrepreneurism, creativity, and business success to take the podium. In most venues around the country the commencement speech would have been something to endure rather to anticipate. Yet at Stanford in 2005, the students eagerly awaited the words of wisdom from the co-founder of Apple Computer and of Pixar Animation Studios, Steve Jobs.

The personal story of Steve Jobs is a rags-to-riches tale. Jobs was born to a young, single, college graduate student who could not handle having a child. He was therefore put up for adoption. During his youth he dropped out of Reed College after only six months. He could not bear to have his parents pay the cost of college tuition for classes that seemed meaningless to him. At that point Steve Jobs did not know what he wanted to do with his life.

Jobs describes sleeping on the floor of a friend's room, returning Coke bottles to pay for food, and walking seven miles to get a good meal at Hare Krishna temple during these years. Rather than reflect on this period with loathing or as a time of desperation, Jobs saw this time as a period of discovery. He took classes he found interesting, a calligraphy class being one of them, and he found that what he learned and was interested in at that time helped him later when he started Apple Computer.

Jobs's lessons of that day to the graduating class at Stanford were about taking risk, following your instincts, finding what you love to do, having the courage of your own convictions, and keeping things in perspective. These are the qualities of the wealth builder, and these are the qualities that can ultimately lead to personal and financial success. With financial success come the inevitable decisions about what to do with that wealth. These decisions are personal choices that are found at the success junction.

The first leg of life's journey begins with career. It is a time when individuals must prove to themselves, although often it is proving it to others, their capabilities to compete and survive in the world. During the wealth-building years, people are often focused on attaining financial rewards that represent personal success. Wealth builders are achievement-oriented with a willingness to take risk. They often sacrifice now for the rewards that they believe will come later. Families, peer relationships, and even health can sometimes suffer as a result of their overriding passion and commitment to achievement.

Sometimes their focus is so intense that it can shut out some or all other priorities. Since wealth builders often act with blinders on, completely focused on the task at hand, they often are forced to make sacrifices of personal time or family relationships or hobbies that are satisfying to them. It is rare to find a wealth builder who does not sacrifice something for the pursuit of a goal, whether it is to grow a company, develop real estate properties, or invest for financial gain.

Where inherited wealth is concerned, individuals often must cast off the image of success of their heritage in order to build their own vision of success for themselves. In her book, *Navigating the Dark Side of Wealth: A Life Guide for Inheritors*, Thayer Cheatham Willis reflects on wealth-building and self-esteem for the second generation of wealth, "Not motivated by the need for earned income, they don't have enough hunger and self-discipline to begin or sustain a career. They lack the tenacity to see their endeavors through, never achieving the sense of fulfillment from which they yearn. It is as if they are trapped by a shadow: the dark side of wealth."[1]

There is a self-confidence that comes from being self-sufficient and competing successfully in the world, and from the personal sacrifice required during the wealth and career building period in a person's life. It is rare for a wealth builder to lift his or her head up during this time to ask, "How much is enough?" or, "What next?" Yet, invariably these questions occur—for some earlier than others.

How Much Is Enough?

Joe Breiteneicher of The Philanthropic Initiative (TPI) works in spartan offices in Boston, Massachusetts. He has long given up the pursuit of wealth, having built one of the most successful real estate companies in the Boston area. Instead, Joe now heads up a consulting group that works with individuals and families on their philanthropic giving. He is more than a philanthropic coach, however, and works with individuals and families to help them achieve fulfillment with their wealth.

Joe's insights as to why people come to TPI, and what starts them on the wealth planning process, are as follows: "There is a quantitative and qualitative reason why people seek us out. The quantitative side may relate to a liquidity event. Someone sold their business for instance and now has $800 million dollars, which is more than they ever dreamed. As a result they have not thought through what to do with that money or the impact it could have. Or they come to us because of a timing event: They have been too damn busy making money and now have a chance to step back and consider, 'What the hell do I really want to do with my life?' 'What's this about for me?' Those are things that drive folks here."

Often it is events such as these—a liquidity event, a certain age, or a life event or experience, that drive individuals to begin a planned approach to their wealth. This junction in life, which we term the *success junction*, is often the first time individuals begin to consider whether they have satisfied their own personal wealth-building and career goals. The essential question to be answered at this junction is, "How much is enough?"

More and more individuals and families will face the question of how much is enough over the next several decades because of the vast amount of wealth that has been amassed in recent years. The statistics related to global wealth today and the expected wealth transfer in the future in the United States are staggering. According to the *Economist* (February 25, 2006), worldwide, wealth holders include 691 billionaires, over 77,500 families with over $30 million in assets, and 8.3 million people with $1 million or more in assets. Over the next 50 years Paul Schervish and his colleagues at Boston College estimate that the great wealth transfer in the United States alone will run to over 13 million estates in excess of $1 million in assets, over 2 million estates with at least $5 million in assets, and an estimated 800,000 estates with over $10 million in assets.

Worldwide, wealth holders include 691 billionaires and over 8.3 million people with $1 million or more in assets. Over the next 50 years in the United States alone over 13 million estates with in excess of $1 million in assets will transfer their assets.

Most wealth builders are faced with the question of "how much is enough" during the estate planning process, often for the first time. To preserve their wealth and to keep it from going to the government in the form of taxes, they are forced to make certain decisions. The questions come from estate planners like a knife aimed at the heart of one's own values. How much money do you want to go to your children? Do you know that during this year when you have a big tax burden it is the best time to set up a foundation? With how much would you like to initially fund your foundation? How much do you need to maintain your lifestyle, and what return do you expect to receive from your investments? Did you know that there are myriad estate planning techniques (all with varying degrees of complexity and industry jargon) that will allow you to pass increasing amounts of wealth to your children or grandchildren or other family members without having it go to the government?

For many, it is while sitting in the offices of their estate planning attorney that they first begin to make decisions that reflect their own values, values that are expressed by what they want to do with the money they have accumulated. Charles Collier of Harvard University works with individuals and families around the country on issues related to wealth. During our recent interview, he discussed how individuals make decisions concerning how much is enough: "Well, the question of how much is enough," says Collier, "is the defining estate planning question, period. I think at its essence this question is about one's principles and values. There are important subquestions as well: One is how much to give to children. How much is enough for my children, how much is good for my children, how much is appropriate for my children? Another is how much one needs to support one's lifestyle during his or her lifetime."

Collier goes on to say that while minimizing the tax burden drives early decisions, it leaves many other important questions on the table, not the least of which is what someone wants to accomplish with his or her life and wealth. Unfortunately, the traditional wealth advisory industry isn't much help when it comes to providing people with answers to these questions.

Wealth advisers and lawyers are not trained to help individuals develop a plan based on their values. It is not part of the law school curriculum or training classes in financial firms. Advisers aren't trained either to deal with the psychology of wealth in families or the family issues that an estate plan can create. It is only after these values-based decisions are made, however, that there can be acceptance that one has enough.

Howard Stevenson and Laura Nash of Harvard University describe this acceptance of "enough" in their book, *Just Enough*. "Enough is an expression of acceptance, a positive experience of satisfaction, to make or do enough. In really feeling 'this is enough' and knowing why, you find some partial fulfillment of that impossible ideal that you seek from success, which some call the Good Life."[2]

It is only after a person accepts that they have enough money and that wealth accumulation is no longer a singular goal that one is fully free to consider opportunities for achievement or fulfillment. The acceptance for many never happens, however, and represents a large divide to be crossed. Whereas the success junction represents the decision-making process concerning how much is enough for someone to feel satisfied with the wealth they have, the wealth divide is the psychology of wealth builders that leads to the answer that it is never enough.

The Wealth Divide

At some point in time, wealth builders come to the rim of a large canyon. The canyon is vast. The sides of the canyon walls are tall, and the valleys are deep. Sometimes the walls are erected quickly as a liquidity event changes someone's financial circumstances in the blink of an eye. For others, the wealth divide is reached over time as wealth is accumulated in a more methodical and measured way.

On the other side of the wealth divide are financial and psychological freedom for which the wealth builder has been busily striving throughout this first, crucial phase. As individuals create wealth, that freedom seems closer, almost within reach. Then individuals raise their standard of living and their expectations for themselves, and they seem to slip back to the other side of the divide. This phenomenon is true for the ultrawealthy as well as the millions of individuals who are considered affluent, with a million or more in investable assets.

In order for individuals to cross the wealth divide permanently, they must cross it psychologically by accepting the fact that they have wealth beyond what is needed for their lifetime. Many come to the rim of the wealth divide. Few make it across permanently.

The wealth divide separates those who must work to live from those who structure their lives in such a way as to live off their existing means. Very few individuals cross this threshold, most often because of their own intransigence. Many more could make the transition from intransigence to psychological freedom if they were to merely adjust their lifestyles.

Instead, even the ultrawealthy find their expenditures growing to such an extent that they worry about having enough money to live. As a result, most wealthy individuals never leave the wealth-building stage, but instead continue to raise the bar for themselves. As Collier revealed to me in an interview, "It's a common phenomenon for wealthy individuals, which is whatever they have achieved financially they will need '2X.' If you've got $3 million, you'd be satisfied with $6 [million]. If you've got $60 million, you'd be happy with $120 [million]. There is this bizarre psychology based on unrealistic fear that there is never enough, whatever enough means."

A study conducted by HNW WealthPulse and Paul Schervish of Boston College found that, "The higher the net worth, the greater the amount of wealth respondents say they need to feel financially secure. Only 36 percent of pentamillionaires [with at least $5 million in assets] feel completely financially secure."[3]

The logical question is why people just don't plan better. Why don't people just budget what it takes to live comfortably and save the rest? Why don't they just take a look at their bills and determine what a generous annual budget one would need to live and then live within that budget? Few step off of the success track to be more mindful of the planning process. As a result, few achieve psychological peace of mind or control over their wealth.

To illustrate this point, I was invited to a most unusual seminar by a person who is a financial planner. His brother is an accountant. Their parents were the case study for this seminar. The seminar attracted enough people to fill a small conference room in a local Seattle hotel. The brothers were there as were the parents. To break the ice, the brothers walked the attendees through their parents' lives: when they met, what they did for business, how they saved and grew their nest egg, their child-raising years, their empty-nester years, and now, their golden years.

The father worked at the same company for most of his career, watching his pennies, saving every step of the way, and living within his means. Over time he amassed $20 million in net worth. The brothers then laid out the decision-making process that formed the basis of their financial plan. There was this back-and-forth exchange of questions from the brothers and answers from the parents on what their values were and why they made certain decisions with their estate.

The first question that was posed to each and every person attending the seminar was, "In an ideal world, when you are on your deathbed, how much money would you like to go to the government, how much to your heirs, and how much to society through philanthropy?" It led to a lively discussion, to say the least. Dutifully, the brothers wrote the results that came from each attendee on a whiteboard.

Predictably, one common theme was that people wanted nothing to go directly to the government. This is less a comment on government and more a desire to retain control over money that was often hard earned and is now considered personal assets.

They want to retain control of these assets to distribute them where, when, and to whom they so desire. As far as how much might go to philanthropy and how much might go to family, the range was all over the map, reflecting differences in values among the seminar participants.

The brothers then asked if people knew today where their money would go if they died. Most did not. The reality is that, without planning, upwards of 30 percent or more would go to the government.

After the seminar I asked the brothers what percentage of people come back to begin the planning process after the seminar has ended. The answer was a small percentage. It is just not human nature to plan, even when the numbers are right in front of you, unless an extraordinary event happens. It is even more difficult for individuals to step back and to ask the tough questions about what life would look like if they accepted the idea that they had enough and began the process of designing a life of fulfillment, "the good life." Those who do step back find themselves on the doorstep of the significance junction.

Success
Junction Questions

The questions that arise at the success junction and wealth divide include:

- How much wealth is enough to support my life's objectives?

- What lifestyle do I want for my family and myself?

- How much is enough to support my children as they go through life, but not so much that it ruins their motivation?

- How much can I afford to give away to society and to charitable organizations I care about?

- How do I maintain control of my assets and minimize taxes?

- If my spouse and I were to die today, how much money would go to my family, to charity, and to the government?

- If my spouse and I were to die today, how much money would I like to go to my family, to charity, and to the government?

CHAPTER 2

THE SIGNIFICANCE JUNCTION

Destiny is not a matter of chance, it is a matter of choice.
It is not a thing to be waited for, it is a thing to be achieved.

WILLIAM JENNINGS BRYAN

When you pull into the U-shaped entrance of Boston College, you find an unassuming building on the left. On the second floor, there is a small, cluttered office belonging to Paul Schervish, one of the great thinkers in the area of wealth and philanthropy. It is his work, along with that of his colleagues at Boston College, which led to the sizing of the multi-trillion-dollar wealth transfer of the baby boomers discussed earlier. Schervish began his research in 1984 and has published a range of studies along the way.

In the late 1980s Schervish directed the groundbreaking "Study on Wealth and Philanthropy," an examination of the personal and philanthropic strategies of the wealthy. He has also worked with major financial institutions to understand their clients' charitable giving and volunteering habits, attitudes about social issues, socially responsible investing, trust and estate planning, and the transfer of values to heirs. In addition, he has studied the new high-tech wealth to understand the so-called new philanthropy.

One of Schervish's findings is that individuals go through an identity transition that in part is caused by the freedom that wealth brings. With financial freedom individuals no longer need to focus on wealth-building. Rather they move to a higher level of personal introspection, which relates to their life's purpose and calling. This is the essential challenge at the significance junction—to determine one's calling and purpose.

Schervish provides some insights into this identity transition: "There are major transitions that take place in life. The ultimate one of course is the transition to death, but these are the doorways of life. People are motivated when they confront doorways to find new identities because old identities fade away. When you stop working, you not only are putting something behind; there is a motivation to put something ahead of yourself as well. So there's this search for a new moral compass, for new directions, and this really gets to the root of identity." Schervish describes identity as an external way of acting and an internal way of being and suggests that one's identity can shift with age and wealth.

At the significance junction individuals must decide for themselves what they value, where they want to spend their most limited resource—their time—and what impact they would like to have on others. It is during this phase that life often throws curve balls. For some, that means a loss of a job, a divorce, aging and ailing parents, or a health crisis.

Take for example a friend from Seattle, Steve, who in his late 40s learned that he had cancer. Steve is a self-made man. He earns enough money from his office furniture business and through his savvy investing that he does not need to worry about making a living. He, like many others in the United States, is a small-business owner, and he is good at it. Steve knows everyone and everything that is happening in town. He has worked hard to build his business, cover his overhead costs, generate a good living, and grow his net worth. When Steve got married, his priorities began to shift to his wife and two young children. He went through that often difficult transition from personal freedom to the obligations of family responsibility. Over time his business had not only to support him, but his family as well, which it does. His children will receive enough money to help them get a good start in life.

In his late 40s Steve developed prostate cancer, and this was to change his life. As Steve was wheeled into the operating room for his medical procedure, I waited with his other friends and family. When Steve emerged again from his surgery and the anesthesia wore off, Steve was strangely energized. He had been thinking a great deal about turning his negative health issue into a positive. He wanted to become a role model as a cancer survivor, and to help others on a large scale.

Steve's first thought was to sponsor a prostate cancer breakfast in Seattle and to have the table captains all be cancer survivors. The same networking zeal that Steve applied to his business he applied tenfold to his prostate cancer breakfast. He was a one-man networking machine, and through his personal charisma he filled a ballroom with 700 people and raised over $1 million in donations for prostate cancer. The next year he convinced Lance Armstrong to be the keynote speaker for his breakfast, and he raised even more money.

Steve began to receive calls from all over the country, mostly from men who had contracted prostate cancer and were at a personal loss as to what to do. They wanted to speak with someone who had been through the process. They were scared or wanted to cry or just to talk. Steve became something of a counselor to these people. He began to devote more of his personal time to being there for others with this disease. Over time, Steve appeared on the radar screen of a number of companies that were developing treatments for prostate cancer. He received a call from a drug manufacturer asking him to tell his story at a congressional hearing for the approval of a new prostate cancer treatment. This was a dream come true for Steve, and at the hearing he left his audience in tears. Congress approved the next step for this cancer treatment.

Steve is now on a personal crusade to speak about prostate cancer and to raise money for research from around the world. He came to a place in his own life that shook him to the core and made him focus on what was really important. For Steve, his priorities came down to his family and a cause that had personally affected him. He did not succumb to the disease, but took it as a wake-up call to use his talents to make a difference. In this awakening process Steve found a passion that feeds his sense of self worth, and makes him feel alive. It has given him a purpose. It has become part of his identity transition from an unmarried entrepreneur, to a married father with kids, to a health crusader.

Steve is one example of a person who moved from success to significance because of a personal health issue. A more publicized identity transition is that of Bill Gates. It was not long after my interview with Bill Gates Sr., father of the technology billionaire, that Gates Jr. announced he would step down from active duty at Microsoft, the global behemoth he founded during the early days of the personal computer revolution, to spend more time at his foundation. For Gates it was not a health crisis that motivated his decision. He had reached a time in his life when he evaluated what significance meant for him and how he could use his talents to make a difference in the world.

As I waited in the lobby at the Bill & Melinda Gates Foundation near Lake Union in Seattle to speak with Bill Gates Sr., I pondered: What does significance mean to a person who has created so much in business? What caused Bill Gates Jr. to give so much to charity? And, more recently, why has he made the transition from business to spending so much of his time on philanthropy? At the same time, I wondered why Warren Buffett decided not to spend his energy on philanthropy, but to remain focused on wealth-building, and to remain faithful to his shareholders.

Bill Gates Sr. described how Bill Gates Jr. and Melinda Gates became focused on world health issues, and how important it was for Bill and Melinda to experience personally the plight of humanity in the developing world. Their experiences with the suffering and tragedy in the developing world captured their hearts. Bill Gates Sr. describes, "The Bill & Melinda Gates Foundation started really without a particularly big fund. We were just doing pretty traditional good citizen kind of activities, participating in capital fund campaigns for one thing or another. Part of what happened then to get us to where we are today is that there were needs that stopped Bill and Melinda—hit them very hard."

Mr. Gates continued, "They began to see the inequity in health care in the world, and that just struck them as something egregious and deserving of some attention. This at a time when it was pretty unrealistic actually to think in terms of doing something about it at the level in which we were giving money in those days. The truth of the matter is that this one decision, to move into the area of basic health and immunization, was a defining moment in the foundation's history. It had a huge impact on their decision to build the resources of the foundation to what they are today."

Although Melinda Gates had already made an emotional connection to the plight of the developing world, Bill Jr. made this connection over time. He had to free up enough space in his mind for something other than Microsoft. After visiting Africa and experiencing firsthand the poverty and disease, it became a priority for him and now his primary focus. Bill Gates Jr. came to this point in his life as a relatively young person with a great deal of time left to personally be involved with his philanthropy. More and more people are coming to this point at an earlier age, and they are living longer. As a result they can participate actively in their pursuit of significance, whereas years ago this was not the case.

Although some people discover their purpose as a result of an event or illness, like Steve, others come to a certain point in life where they are asking larger-scale questions. Many more either do not actively seek their purpose, or, when they do, they determine that their self worth comes from wealth-building. They, like Warren Buffett, come to the significance junction and decide to stay the same course they were on that brought them great wealth. Warren Buffett is the famous leader of Berkshire Hathaway. His significance, personal satisfaction, skill set, and passion are extremely well suited to his current job. His thought process about what to do with his wealth was very analytical and unemotional. He had always said that he was not going to spend his personal time on philanthropy while he was alive, but instead was going to leave it for others to accomplish after his death. His decision to leave the majority of his wealth to the Bill &

Melinda Gates Foundation reflected a change in timing, but not in what he would do with his life or what he felt was fulfilling or "significant."

In an interview with *Fortune* magazine, Warren Buffett described that he was not going to leave a great fortune to his kids. He feels that it is counterproductive and, as he is famously quoted as saying, "A very rich person should leave his kids enough to do anything but not enough to do nothing." His goal has always been to return his wealth in great measure to society. His most significant decision, however, was not to focus his own time on this pursuit, or to build his own foundation, but instead, as has been publicly revealed, to give it through the Bill & Melinda Gates Foundation, and for the most part to give it away while he is alive.

"I'm getting two people enormously successful at something, where I've had a chance to see what they've done," says Buffett, "where I know they will keep doing it—where they've done it with their own money, so they're not living in some fantasy world—and where in general I agree with their reasoning. If I've found the right vehicle for my goal, there's no reason to wait. . . . And frankly, I have some small hopes that what I'm doing might encourage other very rich people thinking about philanthropy to decide they didn't necessarily have to set up their own foundations but could look around for the best of those that were up and running and available to handle their money."[1]

Warren Buffett moved up his timetable for his philanthropy because he found someone who had the passion and expertise and whom he trusted, to give money away with the same potential for results as he achieved for his shareholders in building their financial assets. Philanthropy has not been his passion or expertise, and so he found someone who had that passion and expertise. He made his decision publicly, not that there was any real way to do this quietly, because he wanted to provide an example for others to follow.

People typically come to the significance junction for any number of reasons. Steve had a personal health crisis. Gates was touched by his experience with the dire health conditions in the developing world, knowing that inexpensive treatments already existed to solve many of their illnesses. Warren Buffett determined that his significance comes from his business, but he wanted to show leadership during his lifetime. He found it greatly appealing to work with his friend in taking a professional approach to philanthropy. Whatever the decision an individual makes about what to do with his or her life, this junction is about finding one's purpose. For some this leads to an identity transition as people start to connect with their core values.

Bob Buford, in his book, *Halftime*, provides insights into this identity transition from a wealth builder to building a life of significance. He calls this transition "halftime" because in many ways it is like playing the second half of a sports game.

Up until my thirty-fifth year, I was in the first half. Then, circumstances intervened that sent me into halftime. Now I am playing the second half, and it's turning into a great game. Along the way, I have come to the conclusion that the second half of our lives should be the best half—that it can be, in fact, a personal renaissance.

During the first half of your life, if you are like me, you probably did not have time to think about how you would spend the rest of your life. You probably rushed through college, fell in love, married, embarked on a career, climbed upward, and acquired many things to help make the journey comfortable.

You played a hard-fought first half. You may have even been winning. But sooner or later you begin to wonder if this really is as good as it gets. Somehow, keeping score does not offer the thrill it once did.

You may have taken some vicious hits. A good share of men and women never make it to halftime without pain. Serious pain. Divorce. Too much alcohol. Not enough time for your kids. Guilt. Loneliness. Like many good players, you started the half with good intentions but got blindsided along the way.

Even if your pain was slight, you are smart enough to see that you cannot play the second half as you did the first. For one thing, you do not have the energy you once had. Fresh out of college, you had no problem with the fourteen-hour days and going in the office on weekends. It was part of your first-half game plan, something almost inevitable if you hoped to succeed. But now you yearn for something more than success.

Then there is the reality of the game itself: The clock is running. What once looked like an eternity ahead of you is now within reach. And while you do not fear the end of the game, you do want to make sure that you finish well, that you leave something behind no one can take away from you. If the first half was a quest for success, the second half is a journey to significance.[2]

Navigating through the significance junction is difficult. There is a personal identity transition that takes place during this time. It means shedding the expectations that one has grown up with to achieve a certain type of wealth and success, and defining one's own path. For some, significance means choosing the road to additional wealth-building, like Warren Buffett did—doing more of the same thing that they did before the wealth divide.

For others, it is about living the wealthy life with all of the trappings of luxury that it entails.

This may be the most common result of crossing the wealth divide. The acquisition of things—of expensive cars, yachts, a private aircraft, a second home in the Hamptons—is very common, but does not yield long-term happiness. For still others their values lead down the road beyond wealth. They, like Bill and Melinda Gates, turn their attention toward investing in their family and/or community with their time and money.

There are few epiphanies or lightning bolts at the significance junction. Individuals stand in front of a mirror naked. They come to see themselves as they are, without the facade they display at work or outside the comfort and privacy of their homes. They must shed the baggage they acquired during their youth, and from the expectations and desires of their parents. They must shed the baggage they acquired from their business life and in their community. They must come to grips with their own calling. And, as they come to see themselves as they truly are, they can then begin to follow a dream, to connect with a passion, and to start to live life fully with the excitement and vitality they had only once dreamed of. That is the challenge and the goal of the significance junction.

Significance Junction Questions

Questions that occur during the significance junction often include:

- What do I do now that I have achieved financial success?

- What do I want to accomplish with my wealth and life?

- What is my calling?

- What am I passionate about, and what will bring me fulfillment?

- What is my moral biography?

- What kind of person do I want to be with my spouse, children, friends, and community?

- Where should I spend my time?

- How do I balance work, family, and community priorities?

- What does having wealth mean for me and my children?

- For what do I want to be known?

CHAPTER 3

THE GENERATIONAL JUNCTION

At some point in life it isn't just about being happy,
it's about having a sense that your life made some difference,
that you are only mortal, and you're not going to get out of this
world alive, and you're not going to get out of this world with
your wealth, and you're not going to get out of this world
with your medals, and your honors and stuff. So what is life
all about to you?

CURTIS MEADOWS, THE MEADOWS FOUNDATION

Over two centuries ago, Henry Ruhle came to Baltimore from Germany and opened a flour mill. George R. Ruhl & Son was established in 1789. There was nothing extraordinary about Henry Ruhle's voyage to America or the company that he founded back then. In truth, Ruhle was one of many millers and grain handlers who started a business in Baltimore. Flour and grain were the city's largest exports back then. Over the years the firm survived the Baltimore fire of 1904 and the

Great Depression. It moved from making grain to distributing bakery supplies.

There was nothing extraordinary about George R. Ruhl & Son except for the fact that it continues to operate today as a small business and after 200 years is still owned by the same Ruhl family (they dropped the "e" somewhere along the line). Over the years the company has been passed down from Henry to Conrad Sr. to Conrad Jr. and then to three generations of George Ruhls. The members of the seventh generation of the Ruhl family are now at the point where they could possibly take over the family legacy, although they claim that there is no pressure for them to do so.

The Ruhl family is an extraordinary example of how to make a family institution last from generation to generation. This is the central issue at the generational junction—how to preserve family businesses, values, and relationships.

Family businesses are the backbone of not only U.S. business but of international enterprise today, and hundreds of thousands of families are facing the issues of succession within family businesses. The statistics on the proliferation of family businesses and wealth is staggering. According to statistics reported by the University of Southern Maine's Institute for Family-Owned Business, William T. O'Hara of Bryant College's Institute for Family Enterprise, as well as by Ronald Anderson and David Reeb in the *Journal of Finance*:

- It is estimated that 75 to 90 percent of business commerce worldwide is conducted by family businesses (outside of socialist countries).
- There are an estimated 20 million family businesses worldwide, up from roughly 10 to 12 million a decade and a half ago.

- Some 35 percent of Fortune 500 companies are family controlled.
- Family businesses account for 50 percent of U.S. gross domestic product.
- Family businesses generate 60 percent of U.S. employment.
- Family businesses are responsible for 78 percent of all new job creation.
- Founding families have substantial stakes in roughly one-third of the largest U.S. companies, including, for example, Ford Motor, Anheuser-Busch, Wal-Mart, and many others.

There are over 20 million family businesses worldwide, and they account for 75 to 90 percent of business commerce worldwide.

Over the last decade, the issues of generational family wealth and succession within family businesses have surfaced as major topics in the United States and around the world. Not only are family businesses such a dominant force in business worldwide, but families are facing similar issues. They need to determine whether to pass along their businesses to family members and how to prepare children to handle a life with wealth even if the children decide not to be involved in the family business. Generational issues are also about making families and family enterprises work more broadly across the generations.

Family enterprises are structures or organizations that are recognized as being "owned" by the family versus by any individual family member. These include the family itself as a system, family businesses (or joint family investments if the family business is sold), and family foundations. These structures require family collaboration, communication, and planning to survive. For these structures to exist, there has to be a desire for families to want them to exist and for families to collaborate to nurture these enterprises over time. For many this is a real challenge.

Consider a family that is in the business of distributing office supplies. It was founded by the patriarch who is now deceased. The business is owned by a brother and two sisters. None of the family members is actively involved in the business, except the brother who is the nonexecutive chairman. The business is run by professional management who operates the company day to day.

The company continues to generate a healthy cash flow which funds the lifestyle of all the family members. If anything should happen to the brother, however, the sisters and the brother's wife probably would not see eye to eye. Preparation has begun to determine how to deal with all eventualities so that there is a plan of action should an unforeseen event occur.

Take another example of a family in the retail business. The father, son, and son-in-law are in the business. Another brother is an artist who lives off the dividends of the company. Should the father die, there is no clear path to a successor. One son would like to run the company. The other son would like to sell the company and receive his inheritance. Again, the lawyers and accountants have been brought in to help shape a plan for the future.

Many members of Young President's Organization (YPO), an organization of company presidents under the age of 42, come from family businesses. Over time many of them worry about succession in their businesses. They worry that money might ruin the motivation of their children. They may have been absentee parents during the wealth-building phase. Their children live

a privileged life; however, they may not be prepared to live a productive life.

Many individuals would like their wealth to be a force for good
within their families and within society. This has been true
throughout history. In the past there have been great prepara-
tions by families to ensure that the businesses and institutions
they have built will endure from generation to generation.

Continental Europe has family companies in their seventh or
eighth generation. In the eighteenth and nineteenth centuries in
Europe, marriage was one answer for keeping wealth within the
family. The Rothschilds, for instance regularly married their
cousins to keep the wealth in the family. Louis XVI, a French
Bourbon prince, married Marie Antoinette, an Austrian Habs-
burg princess, to secure their wealth. Farmers would marry for
additional land. British companies were usually left to the oldest
son in an exact analogy of the way an aristocrat passed on his
title. Over time, as public markets were developed, family businesses were taken public, and individual family members were
free to sell their shares. As old traditions have waned, however,
the issue of how to transfer wealth between the generations
has grown.[1]

Part of transferring wealth and making things last throughout
the generations is about preparing children for wealth and life so
that money does not ruin their motivation. For others it is about
making family businesses or foundations last for generations. For
still others it is about how to leave a better world supported by
the money that was created or inherited.

Roy Williams of The Williams Group has spent over 40
years coaching successful families on issues related to wealth
and transitions. He has conducted research on 3,250 families
who have had wealth transition issues. In his book, *Preparing*

Heirs, he identifies the two largest issues related to wealth transfer failures. One issue is the failure to prepare heirs for wealth and life. The larger issue is the failure of wealth transfers resulting from the breakdown of communication and trust within the family.

Roy Williams and Vic Preisser point out three primary differences between families who have achieved successful transitions and families who have not. Successful family wealth transitions include the following:

1. *Total family involvement (both spouses and bloodline).*
2. *A process that integrates what the family members learn together.*
3. *The learning and practicing (in family situations) of skills in the areas of:*
   a. *Communication*
   b. *Openness*
   c. *Trust*
   d. *Accountability*
   e. *Team consensus-building*
   f. *Articulating and sharing values*
   g. *Unifying behind a common mission*[2]

Many individuals we spoke with are the first generation of wealth and seem less aware or concerned about the impact their wealth will have on their families than families who have had wealth for several generations. However, when asked what they have told their children about what they might inherit, many of these individuals lie or avoid the conversation with their children completely. Others broach the subject on the margin. Most do not want to discuss the subject openly with their family.

Many families find conversations about wealth and how it will be passed on to be uncomfortable, even taboo. Behind the scenes of any family, including multigenerational families with wealth, there are concerns. Families are made up of individuals who have their own constitutions and desires. Family transition issues are often the most difficult to manage. The relatively tiny group of consultants that tackles this challenge is delving deep into family history and dynamics. It requires a business degree, communications degree, and psychology degree to be successful. Sadly, this area is often where legacy breaks down and why the result often leads back to "shirtsleeves," that is, the loss of control of family assets, values, and trust.

Successful generational families find ways to support individual family members and then transcend them to create the identity and power of a family enterprise. They are able to institutionalize the history and values of the family, and to implement structures and systems to support family members from generation to generation. They are leaders with clarity about how they want to support their family, and what they want to leave for future generations.

There is no formula or process to help individuals determine what they want to last and how to make things last. Once the success and significance junctions have been traversed, however, the issue of generational permanence surfaces. Whereas the significance junction is about defining one's self, and connecting with one's values and passions, the generational junction is about educating and empowering others. It is also about institutionalizing values and processes so that family institutions last from generation to generation.

The great wealth transfer that is occurring is not only about the Rockefellers or Carnegies. It is not only about the newly wealthy either. There is a groundswell of activity within middle-American families as they educate their children and determine whether and how they will pass along their family assets. As they wrestle with these issues, and the others mentioned earlier, they often find that living with wealth and financial freedom is not what they expected. It can lead to unintended and unfulfilling outcomes. It can lead to the valleys.

GENERATIONAL PERMANENCE JUNCTION QUESTIONS

Questions and issues raised during the permanence junction often include:

- What do I wish to endure after I am gone?

- What should I do with my time, wealth, and leadership while I am alive?

- How do I make family transitions successful, and what do I want to preserve for my family?

- How do I make my children successful and prepare them for life?

- How can I ensure the values I care about continue to prosper into the future?

- Should I give my money away while I am alive, or let my family do so after I am gone?

- How much control and incentive should I tie to my wealth?

- Whom do I trust to ensure that what I desire happens after I am gone?

KEY SECTION OBSERVATIONS

CROSSING THE WEALTH DIVIDE

- Everyone leaves a legacy. The legacy individuals leave is a result of the decisions they make at key junctions in life. The questions that arise at these junctions cause individuals to be introspective and to come to grips with what is important to them in life.
- The first junction people usually come to, the success junction, concerns issues surrounding how much is enough. These decisions are based on one's values and are the essential components of estate planning.
- When a person can accept that he or she has "enough" and no longer needs to work for financial gain, it brings financial and psychological freedom. This acceptance, and the resulting freedom, is what we term crossing the wealth divide. Most people never accept that they have enough and as a consequence never cross the wealth divide.
- Those who do cross the wealth divide are often faced with decisions about their calling in life and how to achieve personal fulfillment. These are the questions at the significance junction.
- The third set of decisions people must address is what they want to last for themselves and their families. At the generational junction individuals must determine how to preserve family values and institutions across the generations.
- As individuals make life decisions, they move forward down one road or another. The roads they choose lead to their legacies. Their legacies in turn affect the legacies of their children and of the communities and causes they care about.

NAVIGATING THE VALLEYS WHERE THINGS GO WRONG

There is a period of luminality, a threshold, because it is the period of transition where individuals of wealth have the potential to shift an identity from one of acquisition to one of allocation. That's a major turning point in people's lives because it changes what their work life is, their sense of financial security, their relationship to their family. . . . They sometimes don't know just what to do.

PAUL SCHERVISH, BOSTON COLLEGE

M uch has been written about success, wealth, and happiness. In an article that paradoxically appeared at approximately the same time as the second richest man in the world, Warren Buffett, announced that he would donate $37 billion to the Bill & Melinda Gates Foundation and other foundations, Daniel Kahneman and colleagues at Princeton University published in *Science* the results of their study of wealth and subjective well-being.

The results indicate that there is little correlation between wealth and happiness. Other than for the very poor who live on $12,000 annually in the United States, increasing wealth has little affect at all on happiness.[1] In fact, for many wealthy families, their wealth is a negative force. For them, they have hit the valleys. The statistics are daunting:

People with higher incomes spend more time in activities that are associated with negative feelings, such as tension and stress[2]

Seventy percent of wealth transfers fail, with wealth leaving families by the third or fourth generation.[3]

"For the First Time, Nuclear Families Drop Below 25% of Households."[4]

Divorce causes a decrease in wealth that is larger than just splitting a couple's assets in half.[5]

Accomplished leaders in business and the private sector are often shocked to discover how their business skills and leadership talents do not translate to the challenges in the second act. The dream of living the wealthy life with few financial cares is often just that, an unfulfilled dream. The reality is usually very different. The psychological affects on individuals after they have achieved great wealth can be dramatic, leading to confusion rather than fulfillment and happiness. Rather than applying their skills and leadership talents to new pursuits, individuals often find that their newfound freedom has left them rudderless, searching for a new area of passion. Individuals who displayed leadership in their businesses often do not display the same leadership in their personal lives.

There are three valleys where things go wrong for individuals who have achieved success, including the leadership, family, and adviser valleys:

1. The *leadership valleys* are the leadership issues that develop around money that lead to destructive outcomes. Many people who work purposefully and lead vigorous lives to achieve success often find that once financial success is achieved, they are left feeling empty, bored, or apathetic. The leadership qualities that brought them as far as they got on their journeys retreat in this newfound, unfamiliar territory. Some individuals become consumers when they have amassed wealth and begin to purchase all the trappings of wealth. Some wander, seeking a new personal goal beyond wealth accumulation, but they never reconnect. Some are just reactive, letting others determine how to invest their money or set the agenda for their philanthropy. They are not bringing the same leadership they had in business to the achievement of their calling. These are their leadership valleys.

2. The *family valleys* are the issues that arise in families resulting from the lack of preparation of children with wealth, or the breakdown of trust within families. Most family heads worry about the impact of wealth on their children, yet they have difficulty communicating effectively when it comes to the topic of money. In addition, at the heart of many families is a family business that supports the family members financially. As many of these businesses begin to transition, either to the next generation or through a sale, over the decades, emotions run high concerning issues of succession and inheritance.

Tied to money and family business decisions are feelings of love, betrayal, and other emotions. It is in this area where misalignments among family members over family assets and businesses often result.

3. The *adviser valleys* represent the issues surrounding working with many narrowly focused wealth advisers to develop a plan for oneself and for one's family. The wealth advisory industry is highly fragmented with different types of legal, financial, and family advisers all having very specific knowledge and skill sets. The industry is also riddled with conflicts of interest because of the financial interests of wealth advisory firms. This often leads to great difficulties in finding and developing trusted advisers, as well as developing an integrated personal, financial, and family plan.

The basis for the categorization of these three valleys comes from various research studies in the areas of wealth and generational families, as well as from interviews with advisers. Although this information can be found by looking hard into the research archives of multiple disciplines, it is rarely brought together to paint a complete picture of what lies ahead for those who have achieved a certain measure of success. These are the areas where the journey can go wrong, and where certain human dynamics are at work that lead to unintended and unwelcome consequences.

CHAPTER 4

LEADERSHIP VALLEYS

It is not the mountain we conquer, but ourselves.

SIR EDMUND HILLARY

While in his teens, he inherited a fortune from his father, who had patented an invention for oil drilling in previously inaccessible places. When his father and mother died, the company, Hughes Tool Company, passed in great majority to Howard Hughes. As a result, Howard Hughes had inherited great wealth as a young man.

With this newfound wealth, Howard Hughes dropped out of Rice University, got married to his first wife, Ella Rice, and moved to Hollywood. Howard Hughes then embraced the wealth he was given to dream big. He produced Hollywood films, many of them quite successful. He built Hughes Aircraft, which developed new planes and technology for air travel, and in 1939 Howard Hughes bought majority control of Trans World Airlines.

Howard Hughes was also philanthropic. In 1925, at the age of 19, he created the Howard Hughes Medical Institute, and he bequeathed all his stock in the Hughes Aircraft Company to the institute. Today, the Howard Hughes Medical Institute is the largest of its kind devoted to biological and medical research, with an endowment of $16.3 billion as of the end of the fiscal year 2006.[1]

Although Howard Hughes was quite prolific as a businessman and inventor, his personal life was a mess. He was married and divorced twice, and his obsessive-compulsive tendencies spiraled out of control. Hughes eventually became a recluse, locking himself away in darkened rooms and abusing medications. He did not know whom to trust.

At the end of his life, Hughes left his estate in a state of confusion. Although he died in 1976 at the age of 70, the legal battles raged on for almost 10 years. Ultimately, a majority of his estate was left to 22 cousins, while Hughes Aircraft was deemed by the Supreme Court to be owned by Hughes Medical Center.[2]

Howard Hughes did not lack for skills as a businessperson or inventor. His accomplishments have inspired countless books and films, and in the end he he became a legend. Stepping back from how he is portrayed in the media, however, Hughes provides a telling example of an achiever who was outwardly successful but who ultimately lost his way. He left many loose ends related to the deployment of the wealth he had created, and he did not transfer his leadership skills well to his personal life.

Howard Hughes displayed some of the characteristics of the leadership valleys. In these valleys individuals can be *wanderers*, not connecting with a new passion after they have made their money; *consumers*, spending freely as a demonstration of their wealth; *reactors*, not taking responsibility for the wealth they created; or *inheritors*, those who received wealth not through the result of their own hard work but as a gift from others. Our findings are that while individuals don't always fall neatly into one of these identities, these descriptors help highlight certain leadership and personal identity transition issues concerning wealth.

Wanderers

Wanderers in many ways reflect an identity crisis that comes with the freedom that wealth brings. They do not connect to a new career or passion. They wander through life filling up their time with a variety of activities, but not feeling a sense of purpose. Wanderers can be the first generation of wealth that has crossed the wealth divide or inheritors born without a need to work.

Wanderers are in transition to a new personal focus in life; however, they have not figured out what that new focus will be. As a member of the Young Presidents Organization (YPO), I have known many entrepreneurs who have sold their businesses and investors who have hit the jackpot, especially during the dot-com days. Some continue to press on with their lives, unfazed by their newfound wealth. Others decide to explore their newfound financial freedom. They disconnect from their business and start to do the things they were not able to do before because of lack of time or money. Still others take the time to consider what a life of meaning might be. They are introspective and thoughtful about their next steps.

Wanderers are often stuck in a state of limbo where the answers are slow to come, and they are not successful in finding their purpose or a new passion. Take for example the story of an acquaintance who in his early 40s during the dot-com fervor developed a new technology out of his traditional printing business. For the public company that acquired his business, the purchase price was relatively low, but for this young man it was a small fortune. Without a financial care he began to fill his days pursuing his passion for travel and investing on the side. He has an office but rarely uses it. He at some point will connect again with another area of passion, but for now he is filling his days without a particular focus for his life.

Although there are different issues that come with newly created wealth and with multigenerational wealth, one symptom of a leadership valley is an identity crisis that leads to a period of wandering, which is a lack of connection with or passion for any one area of focus. These are the characteristics of the wanderer.

Consumers

Another leadership valley is that of the *consumer*. Consumers have a vision of the life of the wealthy, and they believe that through living the wealthy life they can achieve happiness and fulfillment. This is almost never the case. In truth, *everything you own, owns a piece of you.* The more people have and own, the more obligations and responsibilities they have. Time is filled up with owning and doing, but, for many, not connecting with core values. Curtis Meadows, who heads the Meadows Foundation and advises wealthy clients about their estates and philanthropy, described the consumer mindset in an interview with me:

I think what goes on is that years and years of discipline in your life, of being on a diet, of not spending money on yourself or on personal things, translates into a feeling that you've won the lottery. All of a sudden you've got more money than you need so you indulge yourself. You go and you sit down at that big table, and you eat everything you can put your hands on. You get bigger cars, bigger places. You go to places you want to go, you buy a second home, you do a lot of things that are what I call creature comfort kinds of activities. If that brings you happiness and satisfaction, it's mostly temporary. You may like this life for awhile. You may enjoy it, but it will begin to separate you from your friends. It will begin to change your life. It will begin to change the anchors in your life and the discipline in your life. So I think after you've bought all the toys and cars and planes and stuff and you see that's not really bringing you happiness, there is a rethinking of some of that. It may feel good for a while, but when the experience is over, there may be nothing there that has enriched you or made you feel productive or useful if you don't get back in the so-called game.

Consumers often define success in monetary terms. Their net worth and self worth are very connected. Later in life consumers can face questions of their own significance, and many, as Curtis Meadows describes, lose their passion for monetary things. Often as consumers leave the wealth accumulation race, they are left with the question of defining meaning for themselves. It is rare that meaning comes from owning things. Instead, individuals must look inside themselves to determine their life's purpose. This in turn requires that they complete the hard work of exploring their values, which in turn leads to an understanding of their calling in life.

Reactors

A third leadership valley is that of the reactor. *Reactors* don't approach their wealth with the leadership, diligence, or focus they used in their business. They may leave the management of their financial wealth to the professionals or dabble in it themselves for fun as angel investors or stock pickers. In philanthropy, they may react to those in need who ask them for money. They often are not involved at the level they are capable of bringing to the matter. As a result, many reactors wind up on community boards feeding someone else's passion, rather than their own. Still others pass their wealth on to heirs without a great deal of thought about the consequences. They let others manage them, and are not masters of their wealth or legacy.

Reactors who have inherited wealth often feel guilty about receiving wealth without having done anything to earn it. Some just give their wealth away, and what took decades to create is gone in the blink of an eye. Many have a noble purpose, to improve the lives of others, but the gift of money alone without a thoughtful or strategic approach rarely leads to the outcomes they desire. Often money that they may retain for themselves is placed with wealth advisers, but reactors do not manage their advisers closely or provide leadership over the management of their money. It may be a new area that is not familiar or of interest, and as a result it is not important enough for them to carefully watch.

Take for example the person who has had a liquidity event and then gives his money over to a money manager but does not hold that wealth adviser accountable, and does not really know how his investments are performing. Maybe the managing of wealth holds little interest for this person when compared to building a business, and therefore he does not deploy the business leadership skills he possesses. The results, however, can be devastating as many found out when the technology stock market bubble burst and the stock market crashed.

Many people are not the CEOs of their wealth. Through countless interviews with advisers and in research studies, it is clear that individuals often do not take the time to make a plan for their wealth, much less their legacy. According to Lawyers.com, 55 percent of individuals do not have wills; 59 percent have no living will or medical directive.[3] Individuals by nature do not plan because in some ways planning requires them to face the reality of their own mortality. Reactors go beyond lack of planning, however, to avoid the responsibility of wealth altogether.

Inheritors

Inheritors are often referred to with terms such as "trust-fund babies." They have been handed a gift and a curse. They may have some or all of the characteristics of wanderers, reactors, or consumers, but they are their own separate breed. They must learn wealth and life skills to feel confident that they can make their way in the world on their own. They did not hear the conversations around the dinner table about the struggles with money. They did not have to work to eke out a living. Instead, they were handed "success" on a silver platter. That silver platter, however, often leads to feelings of inadequacy, guilt, or insecurity, which can be quite debilitating.

Inheritors are born on the other side of the wealth divide. They aren't sure they can make it on their own. They often feel guilty about the wealth they have been given. They are often missing wealth and life skills that leave them feeling insecure.

It is hard to imagine that life could be so tough for people who have no need to worry about money, yet worries abound. They worry whether others care about them for their money or for themselves. They worry whether they can make it on their own, or whether they will always have to lean on their parents for help. They wonder whether they should work for the family business, and whether that means they are not following their own path. They are constantly striving to live up to the success of their father or mother or the expectations of their family. What if they fail? Their net worth is often tied to their self worth in complex yet meaningful ways. These are the challenges of the inheritor who was born on the other side of the wealth divide and did not have to strive for his or her own identity and achievement.

The leadership valleys provide insights into the motivations and rationales for why individuals of wealth make decisions or, in certain cases, do not make decisions. Through understanding and addressing issues that come up in the leadership valleys, individuals can move through this transitional stage in their lives to address the substantive issues of their significance and legacy.

CHAPTER 5

FAMILY VALLEYS

They come to me because they hurt. They hurt because their family is falling apart. They hurt because they're estranged from their children. They hurt because they've got kids who are nonproductive, and are a bitter disappointment, and an embarrassment. They come because they're not speaking to brothers and sisters. They come because if they don't do something they're going to end up in court with a lawsuit. Those are the people that come because there is actual real pain and discomfort.

LEE HAUSNER, FAMILY WEALTH ADVISER

In the late 1980s and early 1990s, the Haft family made regular headlines. This family ran one of the most successful companies in the Washington, DC, area, which included Dart Drug and Crown Books. They warred publicly, father against son, and then the family fell apart.

Herbert Haft started with a single drugstore that he built into one of the largest drug chains in the United States, Dart Drug. His innovation was to sell drugs at a discount, and the idea took off. Over time the company expanded to include auto parts, groceries, and commercial real estate.

Then in 1993 things began to unravel.

Haft fired his eldest son, Robert, from the company and started an all-out family feud. Haft's wife and Robert's siblings sided with Robert against his father. Haft and his wife Gloria wound up divorced. Herbert Haft at various times took his wife and kids to court. "The attorneys rushed in like ants to a dropped ice-cream cone, crawling over everything and everyone and quietly, incrementally carrying off so much of their clients' wealth that the contest no longer had much of a point," said the *New York Times*.[1]

This is not an unusual story. At one time or another success can cause a person to fall out of alignment with his or her family. Whether out of power or greed or changing priorities, the results can be devastating for a family. The misalignment between wealth holders and family members represents the second of the valleys.

Consider some of the more public family wars that have erupted over money. Although they make the papers because the names are recognizable and the fortunes they hold are substantial, these same dynamics are playing out in the heart of the United States with family businesses. The following headlines and quotes from the financial pages of various respected publications are examples of the types of issues that arise regularly in families:

Family Feuds: The Oldest Son of Media Tycoon Rupert Murdoch Quit Last Week in an Apparent Tussle with His Father. (Forbes, *August 2, 2005.)*

Mukesh and Anil Ambani Fought Publicly and Bitterly for Months over Control of Reliance Group, One of the Nation's Largest Companies. (Forbes, *August 2, 2005.)*

*Denied by His Late Father, Alvaro Noboa Finally Won Control
of the Family's Banana Business in Ecuador. The Cost: Embit-
tered Siblings and $20 Million Legal Fees. (Forbes, March 17,
2003.)*

*Questions Linger Whether the Pritzker Clan Agreement Will
Remain Intact over the Long Haul. . . .When two young Pritzker
heirs filed suit alleging that some family members had looted their
trust funds of $1 billion, the family shuddered. (Susan Chandler
and Kathy Bergen,* Chicago Tribune, *June 12, 2005.)*

*The Trouble with Harry Winston. . . . When he died in 1978,
Harry Winston left his two sons the most prestigious diamond
emporium in the world. Now their decade-long battle has gotten
so nasty that neither one may get the company. (Nina Burleigh,*
New York Magazine, *January 28, 1999.)*

What could possibly drive individuals or families to behave
this way with the obvious consequences that are sure to result?
Although these are extreme examples, they provide clues into the
large wealth transfer failure rate. Making wealth transfers successful is at the heart of generational families. A majority of families, however, are not successful in this pursuit because there is
often a breakdown of trust and communication within their families, and the children often are not prepared to deal with wealth.

Trust and Communications Breakdowns

In their book, *Preparing Heirs: Five Steps to a Successful Transition
of Family Wealth and Values*, Roy Williams and Vic Preisser point
to three issues that underlie the difficulty of wealth transfers.

Their study of over 3,000 families identified that the largest cause of wealth transfer failures within families is a result of trust and communication breakdowns (60 percent). The second largest issue relates to the failure to prepare heirs (25 percent). Only a relatively small percentage of the time does wealth dissipate within a family because of the lack of a trust and estate plan or other similar issues (15 percent).[2]

> *The largest cause of wealth transfer failures within families is a result of trust and communication breakdowns (60 percent). The second largest issue relates to the failure to prepare heirs (25 percent).*

In part, the breakdown of trust within a family can be attributed to the breakdown of the nuclear family in general, which increases the complexity of communications within a family. Today studies indicate that a majority of households are not nuclear. In other words the biological parents and children are not all under one roof. For any number of reasons, a divorce, lower marriage rate, death, whatever, the United States is not "Mayberry USA" anymore. The distribution of wealth is difficult enough without this added complexity, but when there is a second wife or husband, stepchildren, and other associations, it brings a new level of complexity.

Another reason for the breakdown of trust and communications within families is the fact that the priorities and circumstances of individuals change over time, and as a result it may appear to their loved ones that their values and love for them are changing as well. It is hard to separate financial assets from love when a new spouse receives the family inheritance, or when one sibling and not another takes over the family business. There is meaning assigned to the transfer of assets whether that meaning is intended or not. There are psychological relationships that are assigned to wealth, and often money is used as a way for wealth holders to control their loved ones in one way or another. As a result, legal structures have been created to protect wealth within families, and relationship and communication issues in families are made more complicated because of changing circumstances related to wealth.

Kelin Gersick, a partner at Lansberg, Gersick & Associates, advises families on generational issues. In our interview he highlighted the difference between using wealth to control family members and allowing wealth to provide the opportunity to mentor family members and strengthen communication within families. "The key distinction at this point is between those who decide they want to solve family dilemmas by anticipating and controlling the future, ruling from the grave, versus those who approach the dilemma by trying to strengthen the capacity of the system to thrive in their absence. And those are two totally fundamentally different ways to respond to the awareness of mortality," says Gersick.

More common are the families that desire to do right by their children but don't achieve the goals they desire. In part, these well-meaning individuals are uncomfortable discussing money with their children. It is often off limits. Adults don't want their children to know how much money they have socked away in trusts for fear it will destroy their motivation. Children don't want to bring up the subject of money with their parents for fear it will be misconstrued as wanting more. As a result money matters are the elephant in the room, and as the studies indicate, lack of communication in this area can cause a breakdown of family trust and harmony.

Failure to Prepare Heirs

The second largest issue related to family transitions is the failure to prepare heirs. Jamie Johnson is heir to the Johnson & Johnson fortune, and as such was born rich. *Born Rich* also happens to be the title of a documentary that he produced in 2003, exploring the lives of 10 contemporaries who were born into wealth. They include S.I. Newhouse IV, heir to the Conde Nast publishing empire, Ivanka Trump, daughter of real estate developer Donald Trump, and Georgina Bloomberg, daughter of New York Mayor Michael Bloomberg, among others. These heirs spoke about what it was like to grow up in a wealthy family. They talked about the "voodoo of inherited wealth" and how it colors their world, their dating lives, and their motivation to work.

Not all children of wealth are freeloaders. Some are on a productive track. Jamie Johnson, however, highlights some of the pitfalls of wealth, the drinking and drugs that fill a void, and the excesses that often result. Many families not only don't discuss money, but they don't prepare their children for it either. As a result, for many, their children are adrift.

Often parents don't realize the impact of wealth on their children until their children are more or less grown. If the discussion of values beyond money has not been a part of the dialogue between parents and children at a young age, then money will often become the perceived goal for personal success. If discussions about the value of hard work required to create wealth are not part of the discussion either, if children do not see the trade-offs required when money is a finite commodity, then for children money, and the effort to acquire it, has little meaning. If parenting around wealth and values has not been a priority early on, then trying to control children with wealth, trusts, and other means when they are grown often becomes monumentally more difficult.

There is a growing area of family planning that concerns preparing heirs for wealth and life, succession planning for family businesses and foundations, and generational issues. Lee Hausner, a child psychologist and author of *Children of Paradise, Successful Parenting for Prosperous Families*, identifies a number of key parenting steps to invest in and prepare heirs.[3] She suggests that parents develop their children's self-esteem by helping them learn to master their life, rather than doing it for them. She suggests that individuals make each moment count by being a role model and mentor and by making each interaction a teaching opportunity. To raise a self-motivated child, she suggests shifting priorities from solely being focused on results to also having a focus on effort and allowing a child to handle a variety of independent tasks, even if he or she does not succeed in all of them.[4]

Some of the techniques that Hausner recommends in this area are to, "Learn to listen to your child, and value what your child has to say by making time to listen"; "Be interested, and respect your child"; "Learn how to talk to your child, and to communicate in ways that show interest, avoid negative expectations, give clear and full messages, and avoid conversation stoppers that shut down communications"; "Brat-proof your child by watching what you talk about and do, avoiding unhealthy indulgence, and focusing your child on the bigger issues that include the needs of other people." Finally, Hausner suggests teaching your child the value of a dollar by "learning to discuss issues related to money, creating opportunities to learn about and budget with money, and making the connection between work and money."[5]

Hausner's recommendations almost always relate to effective communications and to modeling the behavior individuals would like to see in their children. She suggests creating teaching opportunities with children that lead to self-esteem and independence. Hausner points out that other common concerns such as lack of an estate or financial plan pales in importance compared to the mentoring relationship between parents and children that leads to self-confidence and preparation for success in life.

CHAPTER 6

ADVISER VALLEYS

There is nothing which we receive with so much reluctance as advice.

JOSEPH ADDISON

Many receive advice, only the wise profit from it.

PUBLIUS SYRUS

George Foreman was born into poverty on January 10, 1949, in Marshall, Texas. In many ways he was saved from a life of crime and destitution by Charles "Doc" Broadus, who saw potential in him as a boxer. Doc helped George Foreman realize his unique capabilities as a boxer. One accomplishment led to another for Foreman in boxing. He accomplished what most can only dream of by winning an Olympic gold medal in boxing for the United States in Mexico City in 1968. In 1973 George Foreman won the greatest fight of his life by defeating Joe Frazier for the heavyweight title of the world. In his boxing career George Foreman won 76 out of 81 fights, 68 by knockouts.

George Foreman lived the American dream. Along with his success came great riches. When he first retired in 1977, he was a multimillionaire. He came out of retirement, however, several times for seemingly no reason and when he was well past his prime. Later he revealed that he was forced out of retirement because of poor financial management that left him afraid that he would not be able to support his wife and children.

George was a victim of the adviser valleys.

When George Foreman was at the top of his game, and a financial success, people came out of the woodwork to offer him the investment opportunities of a lifetime. "Oil wells, gas wells, banks, flop, flop, flop," says George.[1] There are no shortages of opportunities for investment for those with money, or shortage of individuals selling great investment ideas. In truth, George did not surround himself with people he trusted who could have helped him preserve his wealth.

George Foreman is not alone. There are many individuals who squander their money and who could benefit from the advice of professionals who have developed their insights through experience, but people in Foreman's situation don't know whom to trust.

Individuals of wealth collide with the free market system with great force. It is rare that a liquidity event goes unnoticed. A wide cadre of service providers are at the ready to present seemingly attractive financial opportunities to the often unsuspecting, and unprepared, wealthy. The calls come from all corners of the advisory world when a wealth event is known. They come from insurance providers, estate planners, accountants, family consultants, nonprofits, philanthropy firms, and many others. There is no shortage of advisers to choose from. Today there are over 570,000 registered investment advisers and brokers, up to

300,000 general financial advisers offering fee-based financial planning, over 38,000 certified financial planners, and over 80,000 specialized insurance advisers.[2]

Today there are over 570,000 registered investment advisers and brokers, up to 300,000 general finacial advisers offering fee-based financial planning, over 38,000 certified financial planners, and over 80,000 specialized insurance advisers.

These statistics do not include all the private bankers at large financial institutions, specialized accountants, lawyers, philanthropic advisers, trust officers, family office professionals, and estate planners. Although there is a plethora of suppliers and advisers, they are not integrated into a cohesive process or plan. Instead, individuals are faced with an often confusing landscape, and must be the architects of their own wealth plan.

The adviser valleys result from a number of factors. The fragmentation of the advisory industry and specialization of skills often mean that there are few advisers with a broad set of skills to support their clients in multiple areas of wealth (skills gap). The needs of individuals and families often change over time because of their financial circumstances and personal desires, which often means that the types of advisers they require also change (changing needs). In addition, the incentive structure of advisers, which is often based on assets under management or financial transactions completed, is often not aligned with the objectives of the clients (misaligned incentives). These factors often lead to a lack of trust and misalignments between the wealthy and their advisers.

Skills Gap

Most wealth advisers are specialists. They do not have the capabilities or training required to service needs beyond their area of specialization. Even in large firms such as Bank of America, Goldman Sachs, or Citigroup, where the skills exist in one place, their services must be stitched together in order to meet the needs of their wealthy clients. This skills gap makes it difficult for advisers to connect with their customers in a deep and meaningful way.

To fulfill the multifunctional needs of wealthy families one truly needs a law degree, accounting degree, finance degree, and psychology degree. Charles Collier of Harvard University in our interview highlighted that, "More people who serve the wealthy in the investment and private banking areas should be exposed to the idea of cross training in the other circles of family, philanthropy, and wealth psychology. They should know something about philanthropy and something about how families function that would provide them a better window on how the family can make better and more thoughtful decisions with regard to their money, with regard to their philanthropy, with regard to their children."

Advisers who know the investment business, for instance, may not know estate or tax planning. Often neither investment professionals nor estate planners know much about philanthropy, and philanthropists are typically not schooled in investments. In addition, the difficult subject of wealth in families is another highly specialized area that is often not connected to the other areas.

The process wealth advisers follow to meet the needs of their clients is disjointed and not coordinated with the practices of other advisers. It is common as well for a family member to be in the wealth advisory business, which creates additional complexity. For instance an uncle might be in the life insurance business and may be giving advice that is not connected to the overall picture. At the end of the day, most people have to sit down and piecemeal their own financial plan together because there is no overarching process or firm that does it all.

Most individuals identify and cling to a professional they can trust, often an estate planning lawyer or a tax accountant, to guide them through the sea of products and services. However, these trusted individuals often have skills gaps outside their area of specialization. They are often experts with a narrow band of knowledge and are not necessarily the guru trained in the broad area of wealth that leads to happiness and fulfillment. In fact, it often takes a team of trusted advisers to achieve such a goal.

Phil Cubeta, an adviser to the wealthy at The Nautilus Group of New York Life Insurance, states that there is not only a skills gap among advisers, but also with wealth holders who don't necessarily know the questions to ask or have a comfort level with outsiders to discuss the broader topic of wealth. According to Cubeta in our interview, "I think the biggest mistake is the difficulty really of talking about what you most cherish, believe, and love to people you have hired, or are in the process of working with, around money. They're not empowered, or paid, or trained to have these more significant conversations about what kind of world you want to leave and what kind of impact you want to have. Those are not really questions you would normally ask a tax attorney. They are not normally questions you ask an insurance agent or a stock broker, and it's not quite clear whom you would ask."

Just as in the medical profession there are specialists for almost every limb and organ, the same is true in the wealth profession.

In the medical profession, however, there is the family doctor who has a broad knowledge of all of the specialties. The family doctor is the analyst who helps direct individuals to the appropriate specialist. The same opportunity exists in the wealth advisory business, but it is rarely filled.

There is the opportunity for a family wealth doctor, with a broad knowledge of wealth, philanthropy, and family issues, to direct individuals to the right specialists to help guide the family. These family wealth doctors need the training so that they can help fill the skills gap that exists today.

Changing Needs of Individuals and Families

A second advisory industry valley relates to the naturally changing needs of individuals and families. Early in a wealth builder's career the primary service provider is the company employer. It is the employer who typically provides the 401(k) retirement plan, life insurance, an education savings plan, a health and dental plan, and other benefits. Individuals often rely on these employers during the early, wealth-building years.

As individuals create wealth and achieve liquidity, often resulting from a liquidity event such as going public or a private sale, they need other specialty services. Tax issues become more pressing. Trusts and estates become more important. The money that was tied up in a company, real estate, or other areas often require the services of an investment professional. In addition, as individuals become more experienced and thoughtful about the legacy they would like to leave, there is yet another set of professionals required. Legacy involves issues of succession, philanthropy, and family. It is these changing needs that lead to new and different advisers during one's life journey. As a result, it usually takes a team of advisers to support a family of wealth throughout time. (See Figure 2.)

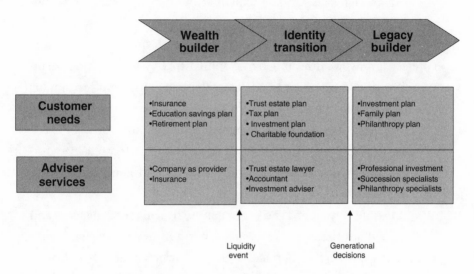

FIGURE 2: *Changing Wealth and Primary Advisers*

Misaligned Incentives

A third reason for adviser misalignments relates to a lack of trust. In a study by The Spectrum Group, a financial industry advisory firm, a key finding is that, "Ultra-high-net-worth investors have learned—often the hard way—the reality of conflicts of interest. . . . Trust and objectivity have become key selection criteria in choosing advisors."[3] The needs and objectives of wealthy families and those of service providers are often in conflict. Wealthy individuals are demanding more services. Wealth advisory firms are responding by expanding their practices. However, this expansion comes at a cost in many situations. The cost is usually to the bottom line of wealth advisory firms, which are often public companies with short-term priorities.

Again, Charles Collier expands on this dilemma, "The big investment firms, due to their quarterly profit figures, are very short-term-oriented. Contrast this fact with the reality that families, family wealth, and family philanthropy are all long term. Some of the investment advisory firms get this, and are in for the long haul, that this is not a 10- or 20-year prospect, or family, or development of the money and the philanthropy. This is a 50- to a 100-year situation. So I think the time frame is way too short for wealth advisers to do powerful and compelling work with families."[4]

In some ways it is a zero-sum game. To win more business and differentiate their offerings, advisers often need to expand their services. Expanding services leads to lower profitability. Lower profitability leads to firms wanting to move back to specialization. The bottom line is that the profit motive of advisers often puts them on the opposite side of the table from the families they advise.

KEY SECTION OBSERVATIONS

NAVIGATING THE VALLEYS—
WHERE THINGS GO WRONG

- There are a number of reasons for failure relating to wealth. They fall into three categories: (1) lack of legacy leadership, (2) misalignment with family members, and (3) fragmentation of the advisory industry.
- The leadership valleys are defined by a shift in identity that comes about through the acquisition of wealth. It can lead to personal freedom but also to apathy, immobilization, or destructive behaviors.
- The family valleys result when wealth is combined with poor communications and lack of preparation of heirs which lead to a breakdown of trust within the family. The breakup of the nuclear family and changing desires of wealth holders with their family members concerning money make the issue of trust within families especially complex.
- The advisory industry valleys represent the misalignments between wealth holders and their advisers. This is caused by the fragmentation of the wealth advisory industry, the lack of broad training of professional advisers in legacy areas, and the profit motive of the advisory industry.
- It is rare to find an integrated, iterative, and effective approach to wealth that guides individuals through all areas of legacy. As a result, each individual must stitch together his or her own wealth and legacy plan and identify specialists to fulfill different aspects of the plan.

CLIMBING THE MOUNTAINS TO LEGACY EXCELLENCE

Wisdom is not a product of schooling but of the lifelong attempt to acquire it.

ALBERT EINSTEIN

It happened at 11:30 on the morning of May 29, 1953. All but two climbers were forced to turn back because of sheer exhaustion. Between 1920 and 1952, seven major expeditions had failed to reach the summit, yet Sir Edmund Hillary, who was considered then the greatest climber of all time and was subsequently knighted, and Tenzing Norgay, the famous Sherpa, stood at the summit of the highest mountain in the world, Mount Everest. In 1953 reaching the top of Mount Everest was one of the great accomplishments of all time. It was one of the last places on earth yet to be conquered, and Sir Edmund Hillary and Tenzing Norgay became heroes within their respective countries.

The climb of Everest by Sir Edmund Hillary and the climb that individuals face with respect to to their wealth, philanthropy, and family are quite similar. As with advanced mountain climbing, building a financial and social legacy requires a concerted amount of learning and experience to reach the summit—and requires a guide who knows the terrain as well. Similarly, individuals rarely reach their full potential without a guide to support them on their way. Just as there are few natural talents in wealth accumulation, rarely is someone immediately a great investor, philanthropist, or parent. There is a learning curve. It takes knowledge, experience, desire, and leadership skills to be successful in creating a legacy.

Through our study of wealth and legacy, we discovered something unique—that individuals move through similar stages of learning whether they are dealing with financial investing, philanthropy, or wealth in families. Being effective with wealth is a learned skill rather than a natural extension of wealth accumulation. Through our interviews we uncovered similarities in human psychology and the ways individuals accumulate knowledge about financial, social, and family legacy practices. Those stages of learning we term *base camp practices*, *planning practices*, *investment practices*, and *portfolio practices* (see Figure 3).

Base Camp Practices

At the bottom of the mountain is base camp. Base camp is the beginning of the climb where for the most part there has been little experience or learning related to wealth. It is here where human nature leads to the least impactful and often most wasteful decisions related to wealth. Individuals at base camp often seek to enjoy their wealth rather than to take a thoughtful or

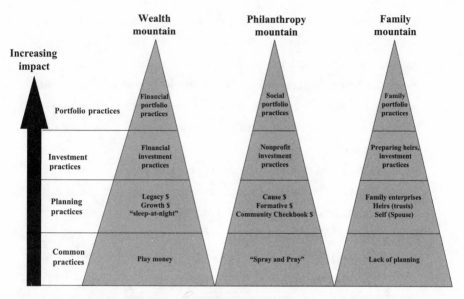

Increasing
impact

	Wealth mountain	Philanthropy mountain	Family mountain
Portfolio practices	Financial portfolio practices	Social portfolio practices	Family portfolio practices
Investment practices	Financial investment practices	Nonprofit investment practices	Preparing heirs, investment practices
Planning practices	Legacy $ Growth $ "sleep-at-night"	Cause $ Formative $ Community Checkbook $	Family enterprises Heirs (trusts) Self (Spouse)
Common practices	Play money	"Spray and Pray"	Lack of planning

FIGURE 3: *The Wealth/Philanthropy/Family Mountains*

planned approach to their assets. At base camp individuals often consider some of their wealth "play money" with which they are willing to take risks for the sake of fun. Some of their philanthropy is done from the heart rather than to make a significant impact. And they may not take a considered approach to wealth in their family, preferring instead to enjoy the newfound wealth they have earned.

It is not surprising that people who are newly wealthy often either spend or gamble away a portion of their money with little understanding of the forces driving their behavior. As is described in the "valleys," individuals often find themselves succumbing to enticing investment opportunities because they lack leadership, discipline, or the involvement of appropriate advisers. It can be very satisfying to play the role of an "angel investor," for instance, investing in emerging companies as so many wealthy individuals do. Others invest some of their wealth in the stock market, believing they can outperform the investment experts. Studies show, however, that over 70 percent of professional money managers in the U.S. equity markets do not beat their benchmark indexes over the long term.[1] While individuals believe they can beat the experts, or transfer the skills that led them to wealth accumulation in business, they are often mistaken.

As with financial investing, a similar psychology is at work at base camp with respect to philanthropy. As Charles Collier described in our interview, "The most common mistake perhaps is an approach to philanthropy, which is 'spray and pray.' They push out money everywhere because now they've got money, they're being approached, they are asked to chair a table at a charity dinner, or they're asked to go on a board, or some friend wants them to give to their philanthropy. They are spreading their money and time too thin, and at some point that becomes unattractive and unsatisfying to them." Just as in financial investing where individuals seek joy from investing without an overarching concern for the most impactful return, a similar practice is at work in philanthropy.

When it comes to wealth in families, there is an analogous psychology of wealth at work in base camp that leads to less than ideal outcomes. That psychology is reflected in an ill-defined plan for wealth in families. Many people are so busy building and spending and living that they do not take the time to sit down and make a plan for what they want to do with their wealth. For those who do have a plan, it is rarely developed with a thoughtful approach that is based on a well-defined process or a clear set of personal guiding principals. More typically an event drives the planning process. Maybe it is a liquidity event, a sale of a family business or of real estate, or the death of a spouse or parent. Whatever the reason, a plan is developed within the offices of the local trust and estate attorney rather than proactively integrating one's values, desires, and dreams. As a result, these plans are rarely satisfying or comprehensive for the long term.

Base camp is the starting point for individuals who have crossed the wealth divide. They must cast off their natural instincts and prepare to address a common learning curve if they are to achieve the goals they hope to achieve with their success. The first skill they must learn is planning.

Planning Practices (Camp 1)

Being effective with wealth requires a plan that is connected with personal values and that fits with one's lifestyle. Planning is important with financial investing, philanthropy, and with wealth in families.

In the area of wealth, individuals often divide their money into categories that fit the way they live their lives, which we term *lifestyle categories*. For instance, for many individuals some of their money is invested for security (sleep-at-night money), some to support future needs for retirement or major purchases (growth money), and some to pass along to children or charity (legacy money). As time marches on, it is often the case that an increasing amount of money is placed in legacy investments for charity and heirs. This money is often invested in a professional way with the guidance of money managers and advisers.

The philanthropy planning process also involves dividing one's assets into lifestyle categories. For instance, individuals often give some of their assets to support friends or perceived noble causes within the community (community checkbook philanthropy). They allocate another portion to institutions that supported them along the way during their formative years, be it a secondary school or university, a religious establishment, or a community organization (formative philanthropy). A third part they allocate to a cause that has real meaning for them (cause philanthropy). The focus on a cause can result from having experienced an illness in the family, a personal connection with a cause, or other reasons that tug at a person's heart. Over time individuals often gain greater personal satisfaction through a focused effort of time and energy on a particular charity or cause, which in turn is where they allocate their greatest amount of time and wealth. As a result of this focused effort, they also achieve their greatest social impact.

The lifestyle categories that individuals identify for their families start with their own personal goals and those of their spouse, if applicable, (self/spouse). Next they identify goals for their children and other family members (heirs). Finally, individuals with family businesses, foundations, or enterprises must determine separate goals for those entities (family enterprises). It is these three categories for which individuals must develop priorities and a plan within their families.

Individuals naturally think about their lives and assets in lifestyle categories. By being clear about how they define these categories and explicitly allocating their resources to these categories, they can develop a plan for success within each category. With a broad plan in place, they can then determine how best to invest within each category.

Investment Practices (Camp 2)

If the first part of the climb is about planning practices, the next phase relates to the development of investment practices. In the wealth mountains, investment practices are about being a responsible and capable financial investor. In the philanthropy mountains, they relate to investing in nonprofits, and in the family mountains, they are about preparing heirs and family enterprises for long-term success. There are some clear analogies among the investment practices in all three areas.

Investment practices in general are about due diligence, or doing one's homework. Great investors diligently investigate an investment before they invest their money. They want to understand all they can about a company or real estate investment or investment fund and management team. They will study an industry and the competition, management team, and anything about the operation of a company that identifies financial value before investing. Investment practices are about investing with discipline and tracking results with respect to a plan.

In the nonprofit sector, investing has not been treated with the same professional rigor as it has been in the financial arena. Many still question whether this is feasible. There is no question, however, that a more diligent and professional approach to philanthropy will yield results over time in social investing as it does in financial investing.

Chris Letts in her paper, "Virtuous Capital: What Foundations Can Learn from Venture Capitalists," published in the *Harvard Business Review* (1997), encapsulated a direct analogy between financial and philanthropic investing, which is referred to as "venture philanthropy." Venture philanthropy takes concepts from venture capital investing and applies them to the nonprofit world. Venture philanthropy is also about conducting due diligence related to a nonprofit organization prior to investing, helping to craft the strategy for the nonprofit, building capacity in the organization by strengthening the board and key management, and determining how best to exit the organization once it is on solid footing.

Investing in families is about preparing future generations. Family leaders build confidence and self-esteem in their children. They help their children develop a plan for their lives. They mentor their children, teaching them how to support themselves on their own. They work to ensure that money does not ruin their motivation. The investment practices they deploy are intended to build capacity in their children so that children can exit the household and live on their own with success, similar to the investment goals related to nonprofit organizations.

Whether it is financial or nonprofit investments or investments in family members, individuals must learn how to build capacity within all these investments and to help these investments succeed and grow. Once they have learned these skills, they can then move on to the most impactful stage of wealth and legacy, that of developing investment portfolios.

Portfolio Practices (Camp 3)

The last phase of the climb is where individuals learn how to make multiple investments work together. They look to strengthen the overall portfolio of financial, social, or family investments rather than any single investment. For instance, rather than focus on a single financial investment, there is a shift to the overall portfolio of financial investments. Rather than a focus on individual nonprofit grants, individuals determine how to support the overall portfolio of stakeholders within an issue area. Rather than a singular effort to make individual family members successful, the overall strength of the family becomes paramount. We term this focus on multiple investments and the systems that support them *portfolio prac-*

tices, and they are an essential part of learning to be effective with wealth, philanthrophy, and families.

Harry Markowitz won a Nobel Prize for the concept of modern portfolio theory with his paper "Portfolio Selection," which appeared in a 1952 issue of the *Journal of Finance*. In his paper, he proposed that two investments together could have more attractive risk-reward characteristics than either investment on its own. In other words, he identified that the construction of a portfolio of multiple investments has much greater impact in predicting returns than does the focus on individual investments. At its simplest level, modern portfolio theory is about putting investments together in a thoughtful and scientific way. It is the notion that the characteristics of the whole portfolio are more important than any one investment alone.

The science of modern portfolio theory has been refined and applied to finance by an increasing number of large institutions and wealthy individuals alike with notable results. Recent studies have shown that over 90 percent of the variation of return in investment portfolios has to do with the asset allocation decisions, that is, the construction of the portfolio of investments.[2] Today, the cornerstone of financial investing is asset allocation, which is the science of deciding how much money to put into each major category of investment (such as U.S. equities, foreign equities, real estate, private equity, etc.), rather than the individual investments themselves. This has been determined to have the greatest impact on returns and is far and away more important than the individual investment decisions, although both are critically important. Today, it is virtually a certainty that any pitch from a brokerage firm, private bank, trust company, or other financial service providers will include asset allocation, an essential component of modern portfolio theory.

Recent studies have shown that over 90 percent of the variation of return in investment portfolios has to do with the asset allocation decisions, that is, the construction of the portfolio of investments.

Philanthropy today is still focused on individual nonprofit investments rather than on the portfolio of nonprofits that form a system of support for a cause or an issue area. There is a real analogy between investing in an area of social concern from multiple angles including government, nonprofits, for-profits and donors, and portfolio investments in finance. The science of placing money into a social cause through multiple grants should be viewed with as much rigor as making individual nonprofit investments work. Just as building a well-constructed portfolio of financial investments can have a long-term, positive impact, a similar impact can result from an analogous process in the social arena. In particular, the energy and creativity of new philanthropists are bringing a businesslike approach to philanthropy. They are pooling donors in creative ways and convening industry and government players with NGOs and nonprofits to create new synergies that did not exist before. They are convening stakeholders in ways that create synergy and collaboration that are yielding results through a portfolio approach as we discuss further in the section on philanthropy summiting practices.

Families can also be viewed as portfolios of family members and the skills and resources they collectively bring to the family. Jay Hughes, an esteemed estate planner and author, originally categorized family assets into financial, human, intellectual, and social capital. Multigenerational families take a portfolio approach to these assets within their families. Just as with investing and philanthropy, there is a learning curve around enriching these family assets and making them work together as a family system.

Successful generational families that stay together communicate as a family, bring skills back to the family, celebrate individual successes within the context of the family, and work toward strengthening the family identity. When there is a family business or enterprise involved, they learn how to support that enterprise so that it continues to nourish the family. The result for families who desire to preserve their family identity and enterprises is a strong foundation to support the family for generations. These portfolio practices in families can have the same long-term, positive impact on generational families as they do for financial or social portfolios.

Summiting Practices

Most individuals are not naturally great climbers. They must learn the basics. Then through experience they can reach the summit. Climbing the mountains is about the stages of learning they go through to reach greater and greater heights. First, they learn to plan and are explicit about their own lifestyle categories. Next, they learn the skills needed to be a good investor with the discipline and leadership that is required to grow assets over time. Finally, they learn how to make multiple investments work together within a portfolio.

The top financial, philanthropic, and family investors, those who have summited the mountains, are adept at all three disciplines. They put these practices together with an integrated and businesslike approach. In the following chapters, we identify examples of financial, social, and family excellence, or summiting practices, as well as how some of the most successful legacy leaders integrate their planning, investing, and portfolio practices to achieve extraordinary results. These examples of excellence provide clues as to how individuals can integrate these practices to maximize the long-term return from their investment, philanthropy, and family wealth practices.

7

SUMMITING THE WEALTH MOUNTAINS

*Speculation is an effort, probably unsuccessful, to turn a little
money into a lot. Investment is an effort, which should
be successful, to prevent a lot of money from becoming a little.*

FRED SCHWED, JR., IN *WHERE ARE THE CUSTOMER'S YACHTS?*

*Wall Street is the only place that people ride to in a
Rolls Royce to get advice from those who take the subway.*

WARREN BUFFETT

D avid Swensen has been the chief investment officer of the Yale Endowment for the last 20 years. He is recognized by his peers and Wall Street as one of the top institutional investors in the world, and is often quoted in various financial publications. A $10,000 gift to Yale made in 1985, when Swenson first joined the Yale Endowment, would have grown to $158,328 over that 20-year period. [1] During the 10 years ending in 2004, the Yale

Endowment grew from $4 billion to $15.2 billion, and its annual net returns were 17.4 percent, which far exceeded the benchmark indexes for other institutional investors.[2]

David Swensen describes his investment approach in his book *Pioneering Portfolio Management: An Unconventional Approach to Institutional Investment.*[3] Here he identifies how he and Yale think about their planning, investing and portfolio practices.

Yale's Planning Practices

Yale's process starts with a strategic focus on investment goals. Not unlike the goals of individuals, institutions have requirements for cash to fund the current needs of the university as well as for growth to fund future needs.

In order to meet these goals, Yale goes through a very thorough planning process designed to construct the best possible portfolio of investments that complement each other. The core of this planning process is termed *asset allocation*, which is a scientific approach to the allocation of investment dollars into discrete categories. Yale has six broad asset categories including absolute return investments, domestic equities, foreign equities, fixed income, private equity, and real assets, in addition to cash. As you can see from Table 1, Yale's asset allocation is quite different from those of its peer group. It is this difference in asset allocation that is the primary driver for the difference in returns between Yale and its peers.

Yale memorializes its investment goals, target asset allocation, and investment policies in what is termed a *policy portfolio*. This written planning document helps guide the trustees of Yale University and helps the institution stay on track as it responds to

	Yale educational (percent)	University institution mean (percent)
Absolute return	23.3	18.6
Domestic equity	11.6	29.1
Fixed income	3.8	14.3
Foreign equity	14.6	20.0
Private equity	16.4	6.4
Real assets	27.8	8.4
Cash	2.5	3.3
Data from *The Yale Endowment, 2006 report*, as of June 30, 2006		

TABLE 1

often dramatic changes in the economic climate. In truth, the trustees of Yale University face the same psychological challenges all individuals face when it comes to investing. When the stock market goes down, they become scared and want to sell. When it goes up, they get overly exuberant and want to buy. This is just a further manifestation of the wayward instincts that come with investing and are described as base camp psychology.

The policy portfolio drives the trustees of Yale to do the opposite of base camp behavior. When one asset class has outperformed its traditional return pattern, say in private equity, this asset class grows beyond the allocation percentage outlined in the policy portfolio. The policy portfolio drives the trustees to sell some of its private equity holdings to get back to the target private equity percentage allocation. Human instincts drive individuals to move in the wrong direction, while the policy portfolio brings them back to rationality by taking the emotion out of the investment decisions. The joint, up-front planning process between the board of trustees and the investment committee of the Yale Endowment leads to an agreed-upon policy portfolio, which in turn supports a rational decision process that in the long term has proven to yield the best returns.

Yale's Investment Practices

Once the planning process is completed, Yale must select the best possible investments to fill the allocations defined in its policy portfolio. Through its scale and networks, Yale has access to some of the top-performing investment managers and funds. David Swensen and the investment group at the Yale Endowment have the expertise and discipline to research the field, identify the top managers, and conduct due diligence on those managers to understand them in detail as well as to ensure that they fill targeted gaps in the policy portfolio.

When it comes to investing, Yale does extensive research on a broad array of investments that range from stocks and bonds to timber, real estate, commodities, and hedge funds in markets around the world. Diversification of investments is important, but selection of investment managers is just as important. For many of its investments Yale relies on outside money managers. It is difficult for Yale to hire experts in all the different investment types in which it is interested. As a result Yale finds the best possible external investment managers who, "Have high integrity, sound investment philosophies, strong track records, superior organizations, and sustainable competitive advantages," as stated in the report on the Yale Endowment.[4]

Individuals can learn from the investment practices of the Yale Endowment. Rather than succumb to a "hot stock tip" or irresistible investment opportunity, individuals are best served by taking their time to do their research before investing, or better still, to identify the best possible investment managers who are ethical, who have a track record, and who spend all their time every day in the pursuit of the best possible investment opportunities.

Yale's Portfolio Practices

Portfolio investment practices involve the construction of a portfolio of diverse investments that will perform well over the long term in various economic climates. This construction process involves the pooling of assets for scale and the science of asset allocation.

In order to achieve scale diversification, and to simplify its investment process, Yale pools its money. In fact Yale is not just one fund, but includes thousands of individual funds resulting from charitable donations to individual schools, departments, or university initiatives. Yale commingles these funds for investment management purposes, using a system similar to that of a mutual fund. By pooling assets, Yale simplifies its investment process and provides scale for access to top investment managers. This pooling of assets allows individual schools at Yale with fewer assets to act more strategically.

As part of Yale's institutional investment process, the university determines how much money to put into each asset class. Asset allocation has become more scientific as institutional investors seek to determine investments that work well together (called *correlation*) and as they attempt to hedge out risk from the overall portfolio (*risk management*). The objective is to achieve steady growth over time in all types of economic markets and cycles. The lessons of financial investing are that steady growth and compounding over the long term are key to a long-term increase in value.

Wealthy individuals can gain some of the same advantages of pooling, asset allocation, and manager selection as Yale by working with investment management firms that follow a similar investment approach. Today, the science of asset allocation is being practiced for the benefit of individuals by a large number of financial consultants, private banks, multifamily offices, and wealth advisers from Goldman Sachs to Bank of America, from Citigroup to a host of trust companies, independent wealth advisers, and smaller financial institutions. Whether it is the investor's favorite private banker at a large investment bank or a more specialized multifamily office, financial institutions today are set up to support individuals with their own personal asset allocation model and to identify best-in-class managers in almost all asset classes.

This consulting approach to investing by large financial institutions on behalf of their wealthy clients has happened over time. The institutions have moved from pushing only their own products to becoming more open to identifying the best investment managers, even if they are not employed by their own institution. They are also pooling assets in order to gain access to the best investment managers and, as a result, providing the same type of scale as Yale.

With that said, the major financial houses, multifamily offices, and private banks all have a profit motive. They are in business to make money. As a result, there can be excessive fees and misaligned incentives, as described in "the valleys." With these caveats, individuals can go a long way toward achieving benefits similar to those of Yale through the careful selection of advisers who follow a similar process.

In summary, Yale University provides clues to how individuals can integrate planning, investment, and portfolio practices to achieve long-term financial results. However, it should be noted that institutions and individuals are different. Many charitable institutions do not pay taxes. Individuals do. Institutions can afford in many cases to put a good chunk of their assets into illiquid investments for the very long term. Individuals often want the flexibility of being able to access their investments whenever they need them. Institutions can negotiate lower fees because of the sheer volume and scale they represent in the market. Individuals often are at the mercy of the investment firms they employ, many of which charge hefty fees for access to institutional quality investments. Although there are few institutions or individuals with the resources of Yale's Endowment, the wealth advisory industry has found a way to offer similar benefits to individuals, and, as a result, individuals are beginning to implement practices similar to those of Yale for long-term results.

CHAPTER 8

SUMMITING THE PHILANTHROPY MOUNTAINS

To give away money . . . is an easy matter and in any man's power, but to decide to whom to give it and how large and when, and for what purpose and how, is neither in every man's power nor an easy matter. Hence, it is that such excellence is rare, praiseworthy and noble.

ARISTOTLE

Michael Milken's story, and the story of the Prostate Cancer Foundation (PCF), is a clear and unambiguous philanthropic success story. His personal journey, however, like that of so many others, was not without its challenges. In the 1970s and 1980s Michael Milken grew to be one of the most influential financiers who ever lived. As part of Drexel Burnham Lambert, Michael Milken almost single-handedly created the junk bond business. During the 1980s, billions of dollars of junk bonds were offered to the market, and they helped provide fuel for growth for many companies. They also made Milken, as well as many of the equity investors he funded, wildly rich.

In 1990, Milken's life was to experience a dramatic twist. He was indicted on charges of market manipulation, required to pay a $600 million fine, and sentenced to two years in prison. After spending time in prison, Milken was released in 1993. His troubles, however, were just beginning because Milken discovered that he had prostate cancer. Rather than succumb to the disease, he used his incredible business skills to attack the problem for himself and the prostate cancer industry in general. What is striking about Milken's story is the way he integrated planning, investing, and portfolio practices to achieve a dramatic social impact in the area of prostate cancer.

Planning Practices of Milken and the PCF

When Milken first established his goal to advance the prostate cancer field, he did not immediately jump in by making large grants without doing his homework. The initial focus of Milken and the PCF was to understand the ecosystem and stakeholders within the prostate cancer issue area. This included understanding the other major donors, government agencies and policies, existing nonprofits in the field and for-profit companies commercializing drugs and treatments, as well as the flow of funds into the prostate cancer issue area.

In doing their research Milken and the PCF determined that the allocation of dollars to prostate cancer in 1993 was skewed to patient care. Of the $100 billion annually that was spent in the United States on cancer, for instance, only about $2 billion was spent on research to find a cure. The rest was on treatment for those who had contracted the disease. Milken asked, "Is there an example, anywhere in private industry, where a company would spend 50 times as much to deal with the consequences of a problem as it would to solve the problem? It doesn't make sense."

Milken and the PCF determined that there was significant leverage in research. Much like the way that Yale's Endowment optimizes the mix of its assets, the PCF determined that a different asset allocation was needed for prostate cancer. More money needed to be allocated to research. Rather than invest broadly in the area of prostate cancer, the PCF's mission became very clearly focused on funneling investment dollars into research by filling gaps in the research where the major institutions were reluctant to fund. The book *A Call to Action* reports on Milken's initial vision and plan for the PCF:

- *Identify the most promising research not being funded by the National Cancer Institute;*
- *Recruit the best scientists and physicians to energize the field;*
- *Limit awards applications to five pages;*
- *Make decisions on applications within 60 days and fund them in no more than 90 days;*
- *Require awardees to share the results of their work with other institutions;*
- *Help build centers of excellence at the nation's leading academic cancer centers and link them digitally;*
- *Get for-profit companies involved.*[1]

This plan outlined by Milken created the marching orders for the PCF and in many ways acted as the policy portfolio for this institution.

Individuals, through their philanthropic planning practices and those of their foundations, can take a strategic approach to a social cause. Joel Fleischman, professor of law and public policy at Duke University, describes in his book, *The Foundation, A Great American Secret*, how the early philanthropists such as Carnegie and Rockefeller were highly strategic: "The early leaders of the Carnegie, Rockefeller, and Commonwealth foundations regarded themselves as applying the scientific method to grant-making. For them, the scientific method involved: (1) getting the facts right by research and/or surveys; (2) identifying the problem clearly and precisely; (3) studying a number of potential options for action; (4) identifying those whose help would be needed or whose opposition must be neutralized in order to achieve the objective; and only then (5) developing a plan of action that included a clearly defined objective, benchmarks of progress, and methods of gathering data to evaluate accomplishment. This, in a nutshell, is strategic thinking."[2]

Milken and the PCF's Investment Practices

The PCF has taken a unique approach to philanthropic investment practices. Within the area of prostate cancer research, the PCF looks across the whole landscape and is able to gain a broad understanding of all the activities that are currently under way. With this broad view, it is able to identify new investment opportunities that complement the existing research and fill gaps in a portfolio of nonprofits. The PCF is willing to fund new research that may not be funded by the National Cancer Institute or the larger research centers.

While it could take years for a researcher to obtain funding from the National Cancer Institute when Milken started in 1993, the PCF could make funding decisions within months. Prior to 1993, researchers could spend anywhere from 30 to 50 percent of their time on raising research dollars, and it could take up to two years to receive funding. As a result, researchers often shied away from prostate cancer research.

In response to this issue, Milken and the PCF designed a new investment process that includes a five-page grant application and an approval cycle of 60 to 90 days. Rather than Milken himself deciding which investment is most worthy, a committee of industry experts makes those decisions to ensure that the philanthropic dollars are put to their best and most productive use. To ensure that PCF grantees share their information with the rest of the industry, it attaches what Leslie Michelson, CEO of the PCF, refers to as a "brilliant string." If an organization wants funding from the PCF, then it is obliged to share its methodology, spending, and results in an annual meeting with all other industry players.

The brilliant string attached to the PCF's investments keeps all parties honest and supports openness and sharing of information among all industry participants. These investment practices help speed up learning and development of new treatments, attract top researchers to work in the area of prostate cancer, and strengthen the prostate cancer sector overall.

Milken's investment practices followed the research he and the PCF conducted up front to understand the stakeholders and flow of funds into prostate cancer. With that knowledge they were then better able to understand where the greatest funding gaps existed. With the help of industry experts they were further able to identify and apply due diligence to the individuals and groups that were conducting research with the greatest potential for impact. Their investment process then ensured that the research results would be shared, thereby enriching the whole issue area. The PCF's investment practices led naturally to the building of a portfolio of investments over the years that filled gaps in the prostate cancer field.

Milken and the PCF's Portfolio Practices

The portfolio practices in the area of philanthropy center around convening practices that encourage the pooling of donor funds and collaboration among many related groups within an issue area.

Just as Yale pools funds from multiple colleges and programs, Milken and the PCF have taken an active role to assemble the donor pool and act with others to increase the size and impact of dollars flowing into prostate cancer research projects. Through a wide variety of public education initiatives, advocacy work, and fund-raising events, Milken and the PCF have raised awareness and dollars for the cause of prostate cancer.

Over a 10-year period the PCF has raised more than $230 million in private donations for prostate cancer research. Total funding from the Department of Defense Prostate Cancer Research Program has grown to $395 million since 1996 in great measure because of the leadership and lobbying efforts of Milken and others. Through its advocacy work, the PCF has helped to increase government research dollars by a factor of 20 to $500 million. The end result is that the PCF, through its public foundation, has been able to exert some control and leverage over the distribution of the dollars into prostate cancer research to fill gaps.

In speaking with Leslie Michelson, CEO of the PCF, it is clear that the PCF tracks the results of its social investments not only on the success of any one research project but on the value that a failed experiment might provide to the industry as well. A well-constructed experiment that fails may provide as much valuable information as a research project that succeeds. The information, however, needs to be quickly disseminated so that the portfolio of other research projects can adjust. The follow-on investments need to adjust to the current information and reality.

Ultimately the measure of success is the reduction in prostate cancer deaths, which is a result of hundreds of researchers and research projects that lead to breakthrough findings. In 1993, when Milken got involved in shaping the industry, prostate cancer was on the rise. Ten years later, the picture had changed dramatically. The quantitative success Milken achieved in reducing prostate cancer deaths through these practices is phenomenal. In 1993 some 34,900 Americans died of prostate cancer. Ten years later prostate cancer deaths had dropped by a dramatic 24 percent per capita.[3]

In a chart published in *Fortune* magazine (November 29, 2004), the success of the PCF is demonstrated numerically compared with the success in other cancer areas (see Figure 4).

Portfolio practices that encourage collaboration and that convene industry stakeholders hold one of the keys to social impact. The PCF determines how the organizations it supports fit within a social portfolio and how it can encourage its grantees to collaborate through meetings that encourage the convening of a broad set of stakeholders in the issue area.

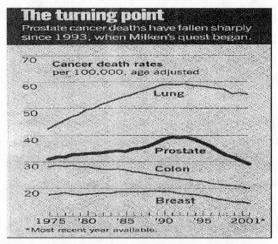

Source: Cora Daniels, "The Man Who Changed Cancer,"
Fortune, November 29, 2004, p. 92.

FIGURE 4: *The Turning Point*

An Integrated Approach to Philanthropy

Many will say, "Well that is Milken, and very few people are like Michael Milken." The truth is that they are right. There are few with the sheer brainpower, the energy, the connections, and the strategic mind of Michael Milken. A rare few individuals reach the summit of the philanthropy mountains for lack of a strategic approach to philanthropy. Social investing today, implemented by individuals and organizations alike, in contrast to financial investing, spends little time on strategic portfolio practices. Instead, the spotlight of much of the nonprofit industry currently is on nonprofit investment practices and management.

One does not need to be Michael Milken, however, to make an impact. In fact, over 75 percent of giving in the United States is from individuals, not wealthy donors with foundations.[4] A number of donors are getting together in donor collaboratives that pool funds and knowledge to make an impact on an issue area. Individuals have the potential to create and strengthen social portfolios whether they sit on a nonprofit board or work in a nonprofit organization, whether they are a donor or work in a charitable foundation, whether they represent the government or a community foundation. In addition, top business schools are now teeming with social entrepreneurs who have the education and skills to make a real difference as philanthropists, nonprofit leaders, and visionaries who can make a true impact.

Making a Milken-like impact is not about individual achievement, but about learning the skills of charitable planning, philanthropic investing, and of portfolio practices that convene stakeholders around a common cause. Putting these practices together within an overall plan and portfolio is how individuals summit the philanthropy mountains and create an impact.

CHAPTER 9

SUMMITING THE
FAMILY MOUNTAINS

*A family is a place where minds come in contact with one another.
If these minds love one another the home will be as beautiful as
a flower garden. But if these minds get out of harmony with one
another it is like a storm that plays havoc with the garden.*

BUDDHA

The Laird Norton family started out in the lumber business
in the Midwest in 1855. The three founders, two brothers
and a cousin, built a thriving lumber business and got really good
at doing things like moving logs down the rivers. Near the end of
their lifetimes, the founders had amassed a small fortune.

Rather than calling it quits, the family's patriarchs liquidated
their business and invested with a man named Weyerhaeuser.
They invested most everything that they had in buying out
900,000 acres of timberland along the railroad and rights-of-way
from the Midwest to Washington State, which was the part of the
initial formation of the Weyerhaeuser Company.

This amazing story is part of the legacy of the Laird Norton family, and it is similar to the stories of wealth creation in many other multigenerational families. Often in families there is a story of a family patriarch or matriarch who took risk to achieve great financial rewards. There is often a family business that was the bedrock for the company. For some families, the business remains intact. For others, the initial business is now a holding company for family investments. What is unusual about the Laird Norton family is that family members have continued to remain together over many generations, which is a feat that is very rare.

The success of the Laird Nortons as a multigenerational family lies in good measure with their planning, investment, and portfolio practices. Just as these practices are critical in building capacity in a nonprofit or venture investment, they are important for multigenerational families who want to build capacity in individual family members.

Laird Norton Planning Practices

Norton Clapp, the third generation patriarch of the Laird Norton family, began the process of convening family members many generations ago. He placed a high value on family and family relationships. "There is a huge archive full of letters, correspondence between him and family members far and wide. He just kept blending people together, he kept calling them together. He had meetings. He drew in the newly married and sons-in-law to come into leadership roles, in some cases creating companies and opportunities for them to work, to be a part of the family. He single-handedly kept it all together. As a result the family started realizing that we had something special," says Peter

Evans, former president of the Laird Norton family enterprise, during my interview with him.

Core to multigenerational families that stay together is a shared set of values and a shared mission. The Laird Norton Family is now a seventh generation family with over 400 members. "We invest together, learn together, conduct philanthropy together, and share our successes in annual family meetings that routinely attract over 300 family members. Our aspiration is to be a fourteenth generation, cohesive family," says Mr. Evans.

The Laird Norton family has a family mission and values statement. It has oversight committees that look after the family wealth and foundations. It has a plan to develop the individual capabilities of each family member as well. Most of all it has a shared vision—to keep the family together as a cohesive group for another seven generations.

These are the planning practices of families that have been successful in staying together through the generations and of family leaders who have established the foundation for keeping the family enterprise together across the generations.

Laird Norton Family Investment Practices

As with nonprofit investing, active involvement and mentoring to build the capacity of individuals in a family are critical. Finding opportunities for family members to grow in their own areas of interest is paramount. Investing in family members for the Laird Norton family is in part about celebrating the individual. It is about helping individuals find their own path and assisting them in achieving their own goals, which enriches the pool of intellectual capital of the family as a whole.

"We pay a lot of attention to inclusion, and to letting people know that they are valued and important even if their thing is underwater basket weaving, because the strength of the family is the breadth and depth of the interests of the family," says Peter Evans. "We celebrate people; we celebrate our history every year. We acknowledge people's achievements. We celebrate every kid who graduates from high school, every kid who graduates from college. We celebrate business successes and business failures. We celebrate achievements in the community. We celebrate the value of each individual in the family."

Mr. Evans continues: "We have a staff person who spends quite a bit of time finding young family members either summer jobs or internships because maybe they don't want to work in a lumberyard. Maybe they are interested in fashion merchandising. So we go tap a friend on the shoulder and say, 'Hey, can our seventh generation kid come over and work in your company? By the way, we'll pay half of their salary.' We try to encourage young people to purse their dreams but also enable them."

These are some of the ways this family has built the capabilities and self-esteem of family members. But it is not only about investing in the value of the individual that makes a family last. It is also about building the strength of the family as a whole that is critically important.

Laird Norton Family Portfolio Practices

Perpetuating the family identity and strengthening the collective whole is the art of family portfolio practices and essential to maintaining a successful, cohesive family.

"I really believe that it's human nature to want to be a part of something bigger than ourselves. Some people find it in their church or in their synagogue. Some people find it in their community organization like a Rotary Club. For many of our family members the family itself is part of their identity. They know they're a part of something that's big," says Mr. Evans.

So how does one create a family identity and strengthen the human, intellectual, and financial capital of families? One answer, similar to philanthropy, is communications and convening activities. Just as convening activities are important for Milken and the PCF to create a common knowledge base and collective learning that expedited new treatments for prostate cancer, convening within a family can create a collective asset base within the family, bring the family closer together and accelerate the personal goals of each individual family member as well.

The Laird Norton family has a retreat each year that brings family members together. Typically the retreat attracts over 300 family members. There are uncles and cousins, in-laws and grandparents all together. They are there to learn together from resources that are brought in from the outside to support the family. They are there to play together. They are there to conduct family business and philanthropy. They hold discussion groups that are a mix of generations and families. It is a way to create a structure around communication and to create similar types of synergies that can be found in the convening activities at the PCF annual conference.

Just as convening is an important portfolio practice in families to create continuity, communication, and harmony, so is the idea of pooling assets for growth across generations. The pooling of financial assets provides some of the same benefits of pooling assets at Yale's Endowment, and in many ways it provides the leverage and scale so that families can act more like an institution.

Just as Yale pools its financial assets, wealthy multigenerational families often pool their financial assets. This allows families to access those top investments that an institution can access and the scale to afford to hire top investment talent. It also can provide a common center of excellence that other family members can tap into to grow their financial assets in a professional manner.

The Laird Norton family took this idea of institutionalizing the management of its money to a logical conclusion by creating its own internal trust company to manage the family's assets first, and then other people's money as well.

"Lots of family members were trying to figure out how to manage their money on their own. Some people, of course, pissed away a lot of money, and some people did really well. So they gathered some very smart people together and formed a trust company. All of a sudden everybody was starting to do well with their investments. The family realized that this was not only good for the family members, but it was a business they could run at a profit for outside investors as well," said Mr. Evans.

An Integrated Approach to Family Enterprises

The Laird Norton family bucks the overwhelming statistics of the failure of wealth transfers in families. Summiting the family mountain is complex. More and more families will face the question as to whether they want their "family enterprises" to survive the generations in a cohesive manner or not. They will decide what they want to preserve of the family history and institutions.

Should wealth be preserved? Should family businesses and/or foundations continue, and if so, for how long? Not every wealthy family wants to be a dynasty. Some want to give away their wealth while they are alive. Others don't want to ruin the motivation of their children and so decide to restrict how much they pass along.

Those who value the family as a multigenerational institution over time must act more like institutions, implementing the investment and portfolio practices that help institutions survive. This does not mean that family dynasties that survive through the generations are without blemish. Families are collections of individuals who in the end live their own journeys. Each individual will take his or her own path.

However, the family can be a bedrock for individuals when they are seeking their place in life. The skills they learn over time can be brought back to the family to enrich the intellectual capital of the family as a whole for generations.

Of all the areas of legacy, family legacies may be the most difficult to master. There is no book that describes the nuances of families; the motivation of parents, brothers and sisters; the individual dreams that drive the personal decisions of each family member. Unlike financial investing, or estate planning where there is a firm foundation of financial theory or of law, family investing is grounded more in art than in science. It is in this area more than any other that wealth can dissipate.

Although the issue of making generational transfers successful is critically important and a growing issue, this area turns out to have the least amount of understanding and the least number of trained professionals to support families. While there is an explosion of programs to assist individuals to become philanthropists or investors, it is rare to find a knowledgeable family wealth expert.

It takes an integrated approach in order for families to stay together across the generations and for them to prosper. In many ways this integrated approach has similar planning, investing, and portfolio elements as the other legacy areas.

As individuals summit the mountains, they are learning to apply their leadership skills to achieve preservation of wealth, social impact, and generational family harmony. The best practices of legacy leaders in support of these goals are revealed in following sections. We attempt to organize these best practices into an integrated framework for aspiring legacy leaders and to provide tools that can help individuals achieve their own personal significance.

KEY SECTION OBSERVATIONS

CLIMBING THE MOUNTAINS
TO LEGACY EXCELLENCE

- The psychology of money and the instinct of investors, philanthropists, and family leaders lead them to take actions that, although satisfying in the short term, are less impactful and fulfilling over the long term.
- There is a learning curve that all individuals go through to become good investors, philanthropists, or family leaders. Successful investors, philanthropists, and family leaders start with a plan that guides their activities and leads to success.
- Individuals must learn financial, social, and family investment practices. These practices include how to identify and apply due diligence to a good financial investment, invest in nonprofits in a productive way, and prepare heirs for wealth.
- To establish long-term financial, social, and family legacies, individuals must learn not only to strengthen individual investments, but also to strengthen financial, social, and family portfolios.

Many of the concepts identified in this chapter apply to people without great wealth as well as to the exceptionally wealthy. All individuals should understand what a portfolio of investments can achieve, how to fit within an ecosystem of nonprofits and community services, how to prepare their children for life, and how to strengthen the family across the generations.

PART II

ROAD MAP FOR LEGACY LEADERS

I look forward to the greatest change which has ever occurred in the material environment of life for human beings. There will be ever larger and larger classes and groups of people from whom problems of economic necessity have been practically removed. For the first time since his creation, man will be faced with his real, his permanent problem—how to use his freedom from pressing economic cares, how to occupy the leisure, which science and compound interest will have won for him, to live wisely and agreeably and well. . . . When the accumulation of wealth is no longer of high social importance, there will be great changes in the code of morals. Central to this change in the code of morals will be a change in the nature of one's duty to one's neighbor.

JOHN MAYNARD KEYNES

It was asked innocently enough, "Who is your hero?" The question was posed as part of a school project and is one of the most asked questions ever. It is also one of the most difficult to answer. In answering this simple question, people must reach deep into the heart of their own value system and pull out the traits that they hold most dear.

In preparing to answer this question, one could contemplate global leaders and Nobel Peace Prize winners throughout history such as Martin Luther King, Jr., Mother Teresa, Mohamed Anwar al-Sadat and Menachem Begin, Lech Walesa, Nelson Mandela, the 14th Dalai Lama, Mikhail Gorbachev, Desmond Tutu, Kofi Annan, or Muhammad Yunus (founder of Grameen Bank). Others might consider the great philanthropists such as Andrew Carnegie, John D. Rockefeller, or George Soros. Then there are the spiritual leaders such as Abraham, Confucius, Buddha, Moses, Jesus, Mohammad and Mahatma Gandhi.

What becomes clear in this contemplation of heroes and role models is that they all have certain characteristics in common: They are great leaders with clarity of vision, strong personal character, a moral compass, and the conviction of their own beliefs. They follow their own path and enlist others to share in their vision. They have left lasting legacies that survive the generations precisely because they are role models that others choose to follow.

The legacy leaders who are the subjects of this book similarly have strong value systems. They are forging their own paths on this earth which are fulfilling to them. They are in the process of leaving legacies for society and for future generations that will have great impact. They have cracked the code for developing a set of skills that supports them as legacy leaders.

In almost all of the cases in this book, the legacy leaders have leadership skills that led to great wealth in business. They then translated those skills to other areas of their lives. If they were in technology for instance, they brought a venture investing approach to their philanthropy. If they were in retail, they often had a framework of testing, say, a nonprofit concept before rolling it out. Their stories reveal extreme examples of leadership traits and practices that can be successfully leveraged to create lasting legacies.

Great wealth, however, is not a necessary requirement for legacy leadership. The potential exists within all individuals to take the skills they possess and apply them in their own lives, learning from the practices of others. The wealthy may have more financial resources and broader networks, but leadership turns out to be the key ingredient for legacy, as is evidenced by the likes of Martin Luther King, Jr., Mahatma Gandhi, and others who came from modest means.

The definition of *legacy leadership* for the purpose of this exploration is leaders who are making use of their skills and assets in a thoughtful, strategic, and leveraged way to make a positive, multigenerational impact. The focus could be on growing charitable financial assets, passing along values that will last within the family, or making a positive impact in society through one's own leadership skills.

It is rare to find an integrated legacy road map that addresses the concerns of personal fulfillment and self-actualization, lasting social impact, and generational family harmony. After all, the complexities of the human psyche, family systems, and social structures are not easily reconciled. Few have proposed a planning process or best practice that integrates these three areas; however, it is in these three areas that successful legacies are forged.

1. *Self-actualization practices.* These practices concern aligning one's time and other resources in order to obtain balance and fulfillment in life. They attempt to answer the questions raised during the legacy journey about one's calling in life and about personal fulfillment.

2. *Social impact practices.* These practices concern how to be effective in maximizing one's impact on society. They attempt to provide insight into how one might apply his or her innate and learned leadership talents to philanthropy, leverage one's broad set of assets for the good of society, and work with others to make a social impact.

3. *Generational family practices.* These practices are about creating and sustaining family harmony harnessing the unique values and assets of families and making them last for generations. The tools here revolve around preparing heirs, creating a family value system, and building a brain trust of advisers who can support a family for multiple generations.

These leadership practices sit on top of the wealth, philanthropy, and family mountains, where individuals have learned planning, investment, and portfolio skills. Together they create an integrated framework of personal, financial, and philanthropic legacies (see Figure 5).

While Part I, "The Journey Beyond Success—To Significance," provides insights into the complexity of wealth, Part II, "Road Map for Legacy Leaders," provides insights into leadership practices that are yielding results. The following three sections highlight the three areas of legacy leadership: self-actualization, social impact, and generational family harmony. Within each section are examples of the practices that have been effective for legacy leaders in achieving success in those areas.

FIGURE 5: *Multigenerational Legacies*

There are eight best practices in total. They reflect common practices from the leaders and advisers we studied that appear to be effective in achieving results. At the end of each section we identify a number of tools from leading advisers in the field that can help individuals take concrete steps toward achieving their own results as well.

SECTION

SELF-ACTUALIZATION PRACTICES

How do I build a life of meaning, passion, and balance,
with the flexibility to control my own time and achieve
all that I want to achieve in life on my own terms?

THE ESSENTIAL SELF-ACTUALIZATION QUESTION

In the 1930s and 1940s Abraham Maslow set out to study the psychology of human needs and to identify how they change as individuals become more and more successful. Maslow studied exemplary people such as Albert Einstein, Jane Addams, Eleanor Roosevelt, and others to develop this theory. The result of his research culminated with the creation of Maslow's famous hierarchy of needs. Abraham Maslow in 1943 proposed in his paper, "A Theory of Human Motivation," that as humans meet "basic needs" they seek to satisfy successively higher needs that represent a personal hierarchy. Maslow expressed this hierarchy as a pyramid with basic needs at the bottom and self-actualization at the top.

In their book, *Psychology—The Search for Understanding*, Janet Simons, Donald Irwin, and Beverly Drinnien describe Maslow's hierarchy and the meaning of self-actualization: "Per Maslow's theory, when all of the lower level needs are satisfied, then and only then are the needs for self-actualization activated. Maslow describes self-actualization as a person's need to be and do that which the person was 'born to do.' A musician must make music, an artist must paint, and a poet must write." These needs make themselves felt as signs of restlessness. The person feels on edge, tense, lacking something, in short, restless. If a person is hungry, unsafe, not loved or accepted, or lacking in self-esteem, it is very easy to know what the person is restless about. It is not always clear what a person wants when there is a need for self-actualization."[1]

Abraham Maslow's concept of self-actualization parallels our book's analysis of the legacy journey. Just as he studied successful people to understand the growth of human psychological needs, we have studied legacy leaders to understand best practices for leaving a legacy. Our belief is that legacy has a great deal to do with self-actualization. For many, however, achieving self-actualization is often elusive. Many people lose their passion to achieve new objectives and their sense of purpose once they have had a career full of challenges and achievements. The process of self-actualization can help individuals connect with a new set of personal objectives that ignite their creativity and passion.

There are two approaches that set legacy leaders on a course of growth and that can lead to self-actualization:

1. *Pulling off the road and visioning your purpose.* Pulling off the road is about personal reflection. Visioning your purpose is about goal setting. Together these practices help individuals define for themselves what they want from life, the relationships that matter most to them, how to build value into those relationships, as well as how they can gain control of and leverage their time, the most limited of resources, to achieve their personal goals.

2. *Researching the terrain and developing a route map.* Once an individual has visioned a set of personal, philanthropic, and family goals, then that person must determine specifically what options are available to achieve those goals and develop a plan within each area. Researching the terrain is about identifying options to pursue. Developing a route map is about establishing a personal plan of action.

At the end of this section are tools for self-actualization, which are practical approaches that come from experts in the field to help individuals set relevant goals based on their values, prioritize and extend their time, and develop a legacy plan based on their personal guiding principles. These tools provide practical ways of getting started down the road to self-actualization.

CHAPTER 10

PRACTICE 1: PULLING OFF THE ROAD AND VISIONING YOUR PURPOSE

Two roads diverged in a yellow wood,
And sorry I could not travel both
And be one traveler, long I stood
And looked down one as far as I could
To where it bent in the undergrowth;

Then took the other, as just as fair,
And having perhaps the better claim,
Because it was grassy and wanted wear;
Though as for that the passing there
Had worn them really about the same,

And both that morning equally lay
In leaves no step had trodden black.
Oh, I kept the first for another day!
Yet knowing how way leads on to way,
I doubted if I should ever come back.

I shall be telling this with a sigh
Somewhere ages and ages hence:
Two roads diverged in a wood, and I—
I took the one less traveled by,
And that has made all the difference.

ROBERT FROST, "THE ROAD NOT TAKEN" (1920)

In a secluded area in Tucson, Arizona, there is a labyrinth that sits on a hill overlooking the mountains. The labyrinth is outlined by small rocks that demark the path one is to walk. Before entering the labyrinth, a guide suggests that, as people walk, they might want to consider how they want to walk on this earth.

Do you want to walk swiftly like those who built the railroads,
leaving tracks that allow you to travel quickly in a straight line,
but barely able to make out the landscape as the train goes by?
Do you want to travel like the Indians, lightly, with respect for the
spirit in everything and everyone be they plants, rocks or animals?
Do you want to travel like the explorer, taking in everything, as
you uncover the wonders around you?
Or do you want to travel like the conqueror, with purpose, but
leaving death and destruction behind you as you go?

Although one could walk the labyrinth in three minutes, the guide suggests that people take at least 30 minutes to walk it and that they try not to let their minds wander. As the walker begins the walk through the maze, slowing down to a glacial pace, an amazing transformation takes place. The walker begins to hear the sound of the wind, of the animals, a bird taking off from the branch of a tree. The walker begins to see mountains on the horizon that seemingly were not there before. The rocks and beetles take on new interest. The mind settles down. The walker experiences life in a different way, totally present, appreciating what has always been there, at one with the world.

Not many people feel at one with the world nor are they walking on this earth in ways that fulfill their own personal destinies and passions. We walk on this earth starting with the hand that was dealt to us. Some walk on this earth coming from poverty, maybe from an impoverished part of Africa. Others come from privileged backgrounds, born into freedom and possibly into wealth.

For those fortunate enough to have been dealt a favorable hand, success often comes with a feeling that there is a higher calling, that fate has played into it in some way. Paul Schervish of Boston College, in an extensive study of the new, high-tech wealth describes this feeling of fate and the spiritual aspect of money in this way: "Behind the desire to give back is a sense of gratitude and behind that gratitude is the appreciation of blessings, gift, luck, or fortune. There are many dimensions to the spiritual secret of money, but one of the most powerful is the recognition that just as my fortune is not due entirely to my own merit, others' misfortune may not be completely attributable to their own failure." [1]

Wealth, philanthropy, religion, and spirituality are all tied together in intricate ways. In an annual study of giving by the American Association of Fundraising Counsel, it becomes clear that over 76.5 percent of giving in 2005 was by individuals rather than foundations. Of the total amount given, the largest category of giving was to religious institutions (35.5 percent in 2004).[2]

Whether the motivation is religious or secular, most individuals do not waver too far from the path down which they start their walk. Success in school leads to a good job, which leads to a successful career, which leads to greater responsibility, and so on. Yet many people end up trapped in their own success. They have gained stature but lost control of their most precious gift—time.

A successful senior executive of a financial firm in New York City was bemoaning to me that he is scared to step off the treadmill that has led to his successful career because when he does, he feels his career will be over. What does he lose from his gaining? More importantly, what could he gain by walking down a different path?

Rarely do individuals pull off of the road they are on, the path that has led to a certain kind of success, in order to assess another path. They do not contemplate the road not taken. They put one foot in front of the other, continuing down the same path, often realizing they are out of balance or trapped in an endeavor that lacks meaning, but they are unable or unwilling to take a deep internal look to understand what their true path to fulfillment might be. They are not investigating the road not taken.

We found that legacy leaders often do pull off the road to connect with their values and to develop a new vision for what is important in their lives. Pulling off of the road does *not* imply that one has to leave the job in which he or she is engaged, but instead it is about making time to connect with one's values and purpose in life. The vision that results from personal introspection usually drives the activities of legacy leaders as they strive to create a thoughtful legacy. Two examples of legacy leaders who pulled off of the road to create a new vision for their lives are Bob Buford and Scott Oki.

Bob Buford's Halftime Experience

Bob Buford, who was mentioned earlier, chronicles his move from business success to spiritual philanthropist in his book called *Halftime*. In his book he notes that others are taking time out to connect with their core values and beliefs to live a more fulfilling life. The inflection point for Bob was when one of his friends pointed out to him how intense he had become in business. This awakened a desire in Bob to seek out his true calling, as he recalls in our interview:

"It was somebody telling me that my level of focus was kind of frightening, that caused me to ask myself what am I going to lose in all this gaining? In 1991 after several years of talking about this [my calling] Peter Drucker said to me that it's your mission to work on transforming the latent energy in American Christianity into active energy, and everything I do works toward that end."

Through a planned and thoughtful visioning approach, Bob Buford wrote down his goals for his life and went about moving in an expanded and more fulfilling direction. He describes these goals in his book and in our interview. "There were six areas of focus that became the way I allocated all of my time. I just didn't allocate time to much of anything else than those six things. The first area of focus was to serve God by serving others. Next, to be married to the same person I married in the first place, and for that to be a very rich and robust relationship. Third, was for my son to grow with self-esteem, or as Peter Drucker would say, the development of an existential core. Fourth, at age 34, was for my company to grow at 10 percent a year. My fifth area of focus was to grow culturally and intellectually, and I'm a lifelong student to this day with a tutor and personal trainer in literature. My sixth area of focus, which I wrote down for myself, was to redeploy the wealth I created. So I resolved at age 34 to give my money away in my lifetime to the highest cause I could uncover, and that has been to build God's kingdom on earth..."

Bob searched outside of his business for how he might achieve his various goals. He has a tutor, for instance, to help him with his fifth goal of growing culturally and intellectually. He and the tutor sit down together and study regularly various literary works of art. His greatest passion, however, is to serve God by serving others. That is Bob's also calling. To fulfill this calling, Bob determined that he wanted to create and grow Christian ministries. Bob sought out what he termed "innovators," leaders with great leadership potential. Bob also calls them "100X leaders." There are 18 innovators who get together every six months. Along with Bob's support they have started 466 new churches, 266 of which are outside the United States. They have also held 360 conferences, which are individual teaching events that have served about 15,000 organizations.

Through his actions, Bob Buford demonstrates the practice of pulling off the road and visioning his purpose. Although his focus has been spiritual in nature, others like Scott Oki visioned a more secular set of personal goals when he pulled off the road and retired from the senior ranks of Microsoft.

Scott Oki's Philanthropy and Entrepreneurism after Microsoft

Scott was born to a Japanese-American family, and was one of the early executives at Microsoft. He joined Microsoft in 1982 and was responsible for building Microsoft's international operations.

Within five years the company's sales rose from $100 million to $1 billion. When Oki retired 10 years later, he began a new chapter of his life, focused on the Seattle community and philanthropy.

In Scott's case, it required him pulling off of the road to free up his time and energy to pursue a career beyond Microsoft. Scott recalls in our interview, "Working at Microsoft, I had no time to even remotely think about doing anything from a community standpoint. When I did retire, I hit the radar screen of a lot of nonprofits and joined their boards. For the first four months I also hit a lot of golf balls, but I got pretty bored because I wasn't going to be the next Tiger Woods. After a period of time I actually sat myself down and tried to sort through what it was I was going to do with the rest of my life."

Scott continued, "I thought about it, and it just dawned on me that my first passion is entrepreneurship. I've always been attracted by start-ups; I've always been attracted to trying new things. My risk adversity is nil; I love the frenetic pace; I love the risk rewards. So entrepreneurism is something that I'm very passionate about. The other thing that I was getting very passionate about was volunteerism and philanthropy.

"I devised a personal mission statement that afternoon, and it is to marry my passion for things entrepreneurial to things philanthropic in ways that encourage others to do the same. Almost instantly I had some structure in my life as to what I was going to be doing for the next 20-, 30-odd years, and really from that day I have been living my mission statement."

After Microsoft, Oki went on to be cofounder of Social Venture Partners, a national organization of funders. He has been a major force in the Boy Scouts and has taken his entrepreneurial zeal to the nonprofit world, having sat on over 70 nonprofit boards. He has also been given numerous awards for his philanthropic contributions in Seattle and elsewhere. Scott pulled off of the road, evaluated where he wanted to travel, and set a course for that destination.

As both Scott Oki and Bob Buford demonstrate, it is often difficult for individuals to create their higher vision without an active internal search and without setting aside personal time to contemplate goals beyond wealth-building activities. Instead, both had to make time to find the quiet to connect with their souls.

Sometimes pulling off the road is a forced decision as a result of, say, the sale of a business. Sometimes it comes about from the desire to fulfill goals or passions in a part of life that has been neglected, as was the case with Bob Buford and Scott Oki. No matter the circumstance, when individuals pull off the road, they free themselves to think expansively and to create a new vision for themselves. They then begin to research the terrain related to their new vision and to develop a route map for success.

CHAPTER 11

PRACTICE 2: RESEARCHING THE TERRAIN AND DEVELOPING A ROUTE MAP

Before they embark on the planning process, before they involve the attorneys, the CPA, and the financial people, they should pull back and have the conversations that maybe they have postponed between a husband and wife, and maybe with the children; to look at some of these larger issues about what they're trying to accomplish.

PHIL CUBETA, NY LIFE

On June 15, 2006, Bill Gates announced his retirement from Microsoft, effective July 2008. This announcement highlighted one of the most publicized personal transitions in history. Although the story about the endowment of the Bill & Melinda Gates Foundation, and subsequent gargantuan gifts by Warren

Buffett, are well known, it is the personal transition of Bill Gates that reflects his pursuit of significance.

To understand the personal transition of Bill Gates first requires an understanding of his family and the values that were modeled for him as he was growing up. Bill Gates is the product of two Seattle parents, Mary Maxwell Gates and William H. Gates III. Mary Gates is often considered the philanthropic role model for her son. She graduated from the University of Washington and became a school teacher and civic leader in the Seattle area. She was the first woman to chair the national United Way executive committee, and the first woman to be a director of the First Interstate Bank of Washington.[1] She chaired the board of the highly successful Children's Hospital Foundation in 1972, and in 1975 she was appointed to the University of Washington board of regents.

On the eve of Bill and Melinda Gates's wedding day in January 1994, and just prior to her death, Mary Gates is reported to have read them a letter from which she is quoted as saying, "From those who are given great resources, great things are expected."[2] Through her actions and her words, Mary Gates modeled for her son the values in which she believed.

It is no accident that shortly after the death of Mary Gates, Bill Gates endowed a scholarship program at the University of Washington in her name, or that in 1994, he and Melinda Gates established the William H. Gates Foundation. It is also no accident that Bill Gates Jr. selected his father to run his foundation or that Bill Gates's sister, Kristi Blake, served as an accountant for the foundation. Bill Gates Sr. and Mary Gates instilled in their son the values of family and of philanthropy, and they modeled the behavior they thought was important in their own lives. This in return has been reflected in the actions taken by Bill Gates Jr.

The transition of Bill Gates from Microsoft to the Bill & Melinda Gates Foundation is one example of researching the terrain and developing a personal and philanthropic route map.

Bill Gates Develops a Personal Route Map

Bill Gates's personal philanthropic journey to significance, although jump-started in part by the death of his mother, has evolved over time. In the early 1990s there was chirping from outsiders about whether and when Mr. Gates would begin to give back some of his wealth to society. Mr. Gates, however, at that time was running one of the largest companies in the world, and he indicated that he intended to start his philanthropy with a focus many years down the road when he was less engaged in the business of Microsoft.[3] Mr. Gates, like many others during this period in their lives, was fully engaged as a wealth builder, and there was little time for anything else other than Microsoft and his family.

It was Bill Gates Sr.'s willingness to look after the foundation, however, that prompted Bill Gates Jr. to start his philanthropy earlier than he had planned.[4] Gates Sr. was no slacker himself. After graduating from the University of Washington with a law degree in 1950, he joined a firm that was later to become the law firm of Preston, Gates & Ellis, now K&L Gates. Bill Gates Sr., like his wife, also served in many civic leadership positions in Seattle. He was and is one of the people that Bill Gates trusts to carry out his vision. With his father at his side, Bill Gates began to focus more on his philanthropy.

Even so, the William H. Gates Foundation, as it was originally known, started with less focus than many might expect. Some of the first gifts were oriented to the Seattle area such as the YMCA, Seattle Public Library, the Tacoma Art Museum, and various programs at the University of Washington. In 1997, the Gates Library Foundation was endowed with $200 million, supporting the program that had been started by the Microsoft Foundation with the American Library Program. Over the following 18 months, Microsoft donated software and $17 million to some 200 U.S. libraries. The program was coordinated by Patty Stonesifer who was to become the head of the Bill & Melinda Gates Foundation several years later.

The third area of focus for Gates became global health with an initial emphasis on distributing already available vaccines to those in need in developing countries. Bill Gates Sr. described to me in an interview how Bill Gates Jr. and Melinda Gates became focused on world health issues and how difficult it was for them to understand the health-care landscape, taking almost three years to fully come up to speed.

"I would say that from the time that the decision was made that we were going to really do something about enhancing the vaccination effort to the time it really became effective and was really getting to the level of penetration that we wanted was probably three years" said Bill Gates Sr. "We spent the better part of a year getting organized before we spent any real money. Then there was a progression as we learned more and got better organized. It's very, very complicated to think in terms of vaccinating literally millions of people. We would go to a place, and thousands of families would show up with kids to get the polio vaccine. It's awesome to see, but the kind of things that have to occur, the kind of obstacles that have to be overcome, are quite large."

What moved Gates from researching the terrain to developing a route map in the area of global immunization was a 1993 World Bank development report that outlined in a detailed, 329-page document how many millions of people in developing countries were dying from diseases that already had cures. The report also outlined some cost-effective methods for minimizing those deaths. It was in part this detailed report that provided the impetus for a focus in the area of world health. "We could go down the list and see what was killing children around the world," said Melinda Gates. "Very quickly, we came to the point that this was something we wanted to do."[5]

Bill Gates Sr. discussed how important it was to research the terrain before the Bill & Melinda Gates Foundation started making major gifts to the area of global health. "There are experts in this world about everything. There is an array of people who've been in this activity, who understand about vaccines or are scientifically confident. If you're interested in doing something about it, the intelligence will be at your doorstep." Gates continued, "As we began to be somewhat expansive [to support the health needs of the poor], we ran into the vaccine and immunization efforts, which had been conducted by the World Health Organization over some period of time. They had a very significant activity over a period of some years with a goal to immunize something like 75 percent of the kids in the world by 1995. It started very robustly, but it was a program that was diminishing. What we did in that area was to extend the existing resources."

By 1997, the Gates's philanthropic focus had evolved into three primary areas: developing world health care, library and information technologies, and support for the Pacific Northwest and education.[6] On August 22, 1999, the Bill & Melinda Gates

Foundation was formally organized with a total endowment of $17 billion. The new foundation consolidated the existing William H. Gates and Gates Learning Foundations under the direction of Gates Sr. and Pattie Stonesifer.

In 2006, Bill Gates announced a timetable for his transition from founder of one of the most successful companies in the world to active coleader of the Bill & Melinda Gates Foundation, completing a transition that started over a decade before.

In an interview Mr. Gates conducted regarding his retirement from Microsoft, and using almost exactly the same words his mother spoke to him before her death, he is quoted as saying, "I've decided that two years from today, I will reorganize my personal priorities. I have one of the best jobs in the world. . . . I believe with great wealth comes great responsibility—the responsibility to give back to society and make sure those resources are given back in the best possible way to those in need. It's not a retirement, it's a reordering of my priorities."[7]

What does the personal transition of Bill Gates teach us about legacy and self-actualization? Bill Gates, like others we've studied, took the time to reflect on his priorities. He did this with his spouse and partner Melinda Gates. Over time his priorities for his time and resources have changed. Along his personal road, Mr. Gates, with his wife, has made some explicit decisions about what to do with his wealth based on his values and priorities. He determined that he did not want the vast majority of his wealth to go to his children. This was an explicit decision that was reported in a 2005 *Time* magazine article ("From Riches to Rags" by Amanda Ripley with Amanda Bower, p. 85). He also determined that he wanted to be actively involved in the disposition of his money to society while he and his wife are alive. As a result, the Gates Foundation will shut down 50 years after the last of its three current trustees—Bill and Melinda Gates, and Warren Buffett—dies.[8]

Over time he has also set out a road map for himself and his philanthropy. This did not happen all at once. Mr. Gates had to first become clear on his philanthropic priorities as well as his personal priorities. In both areas he researched the terrain, tapping into trusted peers, such as Warren Buffett, for advice on what he should do personally and into various philanthropic possibilities before selecting a focus on world health.

Now, Mr. Gates is drawing a route map for himself and his foundation in the area of world health. It is instructive to see how this route map is reflected in the priorities and guiding principles of the Bill & Melinda Gates Foundation, which are displayed on its Web site.[9] They read as follows:

- *This is a family foundation driven by the interests and passions of the Gates family.*
- *Philanthropy plays an important but limited role.*
- *Science and technology have great potential to improve lives around the world.*
- *We are funders and shapers—we rely on others to act and implement.*
- *Our focus is clear—and limited—and prioritizes some of the most neglected issues.*
- *We identify a specific point of intervention and apply our efforts against a theory of change.*
- *We take risks, make big bets, and move with urgency. We are in it for the long haul.*
- *We advocate—vigorously but responsibly—in our areas of focus.*

- *We must be humble and mindful in our actions and words. We seek and heed the counsel of outside voices.*
- *We treat our grantees as valued partners, and we treat the ultimate beneficiaries of our work with respect.*
- *Delivering results with the resources we have been given is of the utmost importance—and we seek and share information about those results.*
- *We demand ethical behavior of ourselves.*
- *We treat each other as valued colleagues.*
- *Meeting our mission—to increase opportunity and equity for those most in need—requires great stewardship of the money we have available.*
- *We leave room for growth and change.*

Bill Gates provides a clear example of how a person moves from success to significance over time by researching the terrain and developing a route map. Others provide insights as well on this transition in different ways.

Mario Morino Develops a Venture Philanthropy Route Map

When Mario Morino sold his company, Legent Corp., to Computer Associates, he was the recipient of a large payout. With his newfound wealth, Morino set about the goal of figuring out for himself, and for the cause he cares about—youth and poverty in the Washington, DC, area—what he should do with his time and his money.

As I spoke with Mario Morino, he relayed his thought process at the time he decided to leave the company he had started: "In

1991 I simply said it's time for me to step out. What drove me were several things. One, I felt a personal need to do something to give back because I came from a pretty modest and poor family. We had more money than we could have envisioned in our life, and I didn't envision using it all for myself. So putting it to some kind of constructive use was important. Two, I sensed that we as a society, and technology, were going to go through an enormous change, and I felt if I stayed inside the company, I would see it through the blinders of the company. The other huge change was that I got remarried in 1990, and we had our first child. I never had a family before, and I was worried that my competitive nature [in business] would be so great that I would basically ruin my family."

Upon the sale of Legent Corp., Mario Morino became focused on how he could make a positive impact with his skills and resources. In an incredibly focused way, Morino researched the terrain to determine how he could successfully make an impact in the youth and poverty area and, as a result, model the way for others. Over an intense couple of years Morino conducted 700 interviews before deciding to start Venture Philanthropy Partners (VPP), a philanthropic funding collaborative. Morino discussed his process of researching the terrain in our interview.

"Starting in '93 and half of '94 I went out and I met people. I met over 700 individuals with a friend. Personally, I talked to a number of people that I knew who had cashed in to understand what they were doing with their lives. . . . This went on for a period of 18 months. It was really a highly exhilarating process and at the same time a highly frustrating if not demoralizing process. On any given day I was on murderers corner in Hartford, going through projects, being escorted past gang leaders, and then meeting with college presidents two hours later. I walked away with an awful lot of observations and the beginning of a lot of relationships."

This type of peer interview process is not unusual for those who are researching the terrain to uncover their own new area of passion and to understand the lessons of others who have tread before. In fact, most often individuals do seek out peers who they feel are in a similar economic, social, or family position. Witness that peer groups of wealthy individuals are cropping up around the country to sit down on a regular basis to talk about their net worth and self-worth, to talk about wealth in their families, and to discuss their shared experiences with respect to investing and philanthropy.

Once he completed this research process, Morino formed Venture Philanthropy Partners (VPP), with the objective of creating a high-impact funding vehicle for charities. The idea behind VPP was to bring in other funders and together to attack the issue of serving children in poverty in the Washington, DC, area. Similar to the process that Bill and Melinda Gates went through, Morino zeroed in on the cause that fired his imagination and passion. He set about defining for himself a personal route map of what he was going to do and how he was going to do it. That route map had a number of elements that Morino highlighted to me.

"In '91 I wrote a paper to myself, and the paper was what I would do, and why I was leaving. First was for the family. Second, I knew that whatever I ended up doing it would be around youth, learning, and community. I actually had a schematic of what I called the architectural level. We would have a certain amount of money to create a foundation for giving over the years. But I knew that the money was so small relatively speaking that it would have no influence. So to have any kind of impact, we would have to form influence in the sector.

"The conclusion we came away with," said Morino, "was that the nonprofit sector serving kids and families in low-income environments was truly at risk. The fundamental problem affecting its effectiveness was the funding system itself. The funding system basically impedes two things: the flow of capital and the flow of talent into the sector. Until those things change, the sector will not change. So we then launched our program, Venture Philanthropy Partners, which was meant to be a demonstration project."

Morino went on to say, "Ultimately if these issues are to be addressed, we have to have a voice—a national voice in public policy and in philanthropy—and you have to earn that voice. In my view we're in the process of earning that voice today, that seat at the table. . . . Venture Philanthropy Partners is an investment approach that is meant to demonstrate something; it is a means to an end, not an end in and of itself. My thought was to illustrate what it would mean when you put significant capital and significant executive talent in place to the right types of nonprofit organizations and how that would see a societal yield. I think at the end of the day what will be the single biggest contribution will be what we will have learned and experienced."

The net result of Morino's experiment is that VPP has become somewhat of a model of venture philanthropy, where there is a clear investment strategy, and where results are measured. To date, VPP has committed $30 million along with other investment partners to nine high-potential organizations serving children of low-income families.[10]

Once legacy leaders have created their vision and once the research is over, they set a plan in place, as they would in business, as to how they will govern their life. By researching the terrain, they begin to find a new area of passion. Sometimes that passion relates to philanthropy, sometimes to business or family relationships, sometimes to living the good life, and sometimes to more wealth-building. Once legacy leaders have redirected into a new area of focus, then their existing leadership capabilities kick in, and they are back in familiar territory with route map in hand.

CHAPTER 12

BUILDING A PLAN FOR SELF-ACTUALIZATION

Don't limit yourself. Many people limit themselves to what they think they can do. You can go as far as your mind lets you. What you believe, remember, you can achieve.

MARY KAY ASH

To achieve self-actualization, individuals must move from a chaotic and reactive state, responding to random requests for time or money that may not be based on personal values or priorities, to a legacy plan that maximizes one's time, money, and relationships. A legacy plan provides a methodology for visioning your purpose and for researching the terrain and developing a route map to make the greatest headway toward achieving the goals you establish. There are three steps to developing a legacy plan.

The first step for individuals is to *develop their guiding principles* for themselves, their family, and their community. The methodology for defining your principles involves clarifying your values and determining where they come from. It also involves clearly defining the roles you are most vested in that relate to personal achievement, family, and the community, and developing a vision for those roles.

The second step in the legacy planning process is to *develop priorities* for your time, money, and relationships. This is done by identifying the stage of life you are in; assessing your current time, money, and relationship practices; and then developing a desired allocation of these three key resources to achieve the long-term goals and vision you identified in your guiding principles.

The last step is to *develop a measurable plan* that has goals, objectives, and actions that will move you closer to achieving the vision you have established for yourself. This plan is a written document that then can be shared and communicated to those who play critical roles in your life. (See Figure 6.)

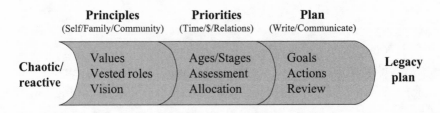

Principles (Self/Family/Community)	**Priorities** (Time/$/Relations)	**Plan** (Write/Communicate)	
Chaotic/ **reactive**	Values Vested roles Vision	Ages/Stages Assessment Allocation	Goals Actions Review	**Legacy** **plan**

FIGURE 6: *Legacy Planning Process*

Developing Your Guiding Principles

Guiding principles are the values, vested roles, and vision individuals establish for themselves over the long term. The clearer individuals are about their guiding principles, the easier it becomes to establish a plan to achieve the vision they wish to achieve. The more aligned one's vision is with one's values, the more a person is able to live with purpose.

Guiding principles contain the values by which individuals live their lives. Those values come from parents, teachers, siblings, spouses, friends, business colleagues, mentors, family members, and personal experiences. Values are reflected in people's personal and family history and the experiences that shape their beliefs and world view. Values are the foundation on which decisions are based whether through instinct or introspection. When people move closer to their core values and embrace activities and choices that support those values, they begin to ignite their passion and to uncover their purpose. Take time to reflect on where your values come from. Who are the key individuals that helped shape your values? What are the key events that shaped your values? What lessons did you learn from those events? Write down your values and where those values come from so that you are able to communicate them to others.

Individuals play various roles in life. They not only live for personal achievement, which reflects self-focused roles, but they take on roles and responsibilities in their family, businesses, and in communities. A vested role is a role or relationship that matters most and that is important enough to invest in and develop. Individuals at the end of their lives are not defined as much by their individual achievements as they are by their success in the roles they define as being important. Here are some of the common roles to consider.

1. *Self-Focused Roles* Self-focused roles most often relate to personal health, growth, achievement, and lifestyle. Personal health and growth activities are essential in order for an indi-

vidual to function at a high level; to grow personally, intellectually, and spiritually; and to enrich one's mind, body, and soul. Bob Buford's goal to grow intellectually and spiritually with a tutor, for instance, is a self-focused goal. Others focus on personal health and exercise to stay sharp. Personal achievement roles are those that are focused on the achievement of personal, career, and avocation goals. Personal achievement goals are about achieving professional or vocational objectives. One's profession or vocation could range from that of an investor, philanthropist, care giver, doctor, lawyer, businessperson, scientist, researcher, golfer, photographer, or something else. Professional and vocational goals are often tied to lifestyle considerations as well. Lifestyle goals relate to how people want to live their life and the financial assets required to achieve that vision. The achievement of one's aspirations for career and lifestyle often can lead to personal recognition and fulfillment. Consider what goals you have for your personal health, growth, achievement, and lifestyle. What would you need to accomplish in this area to feel fulfilled and to have no regrets? Write down the vision you desire for yourself for your personal health, growth, achievement, and lifestyle.

2. *Family Roles* Individuals play a number of different roles in their families. They are sons or daughters, brothers or sisters, cousins, parents, grandparents and/or patriarchs or matriarchs of family enterprises. They may also play a role in a family business, in a foundation, or in family governance. The quality of time one invests in family members serves to enrich one's own life. Some family roles are more vested than others. Often there is a family history and values that have become important for an individual and part of one's own value system

to be carried forward. Individuals need to determine within their families the roles and relationships in which they are most vested. What is the family history and values that are worth preserving? What does it mean to you to be a good father or mother, son or daughter, brother or sister? What are the most important family roles for you and why? What does success look like in your most important family roles, and what would you need to accomplish to have no regrets in this area? Write down the family roles you are most vested in and the vision you hope to achieve in those roles.

3. *Community/Philanthropy Roles* Individuals play a number of different roles within their communities and society. They are a volunteer, board member, philanthropist, civic leader, or friend, or they play some other community role. The network of relationships within the community can enrich one's life and help a person with business opportunities and personal or family issues, as well as enrich the life of the community that supports the family. It is all intertwined. Again, some roles and relationships are more vested than others, and some are more personally fulfilling than others. What are the roles you are most vested in within your community and why? What does it mean to be a good friend or member of your community? What causes are most important to you? What does success look like to you in your most important community roles, and what would you need to accomplish to have no regrets in this area? Write down the community roles you are most vested in and the vision you hope to achieve in those roles.

4. *Business Roles* Finally, individuals often have roles in business or organizations as employees, managers, or company leaders. They often have functional roles as well. Business or organizational roles often involve responsibilities for employees, cus-

tomers, suppliers, and shareholders. Success may be related to company stakeholders, financial performance, or work group outcomes. What roles are you vested in at work, and what does success look like to you in those roles? What would you need to accomplish in your business roles to have no regrets in this area? Write down the business roles you are most vested in and the vision you hope to achieve in those roles.

The practice of "visioning one's purpose" for one's life is about setting and aligning personal goals. For many this means creating an expanded set of goals. Most people can become myopic, focusing on a few discrete personal objectives. They may then be missing out on the richness that an expanded set of life goals would provide for them. The focus on the immediate business deal or the frenzied pace of child rearing can be all-consuming. People need to step back and develop a plan for their lives that takes into account an expanded set of goals.

The visioning process follows a person's assessment of his or her vested roles. Visioning is long term in nature and establishes long-term goals for one's vested roles. Stephen Covey suggests that an effective visioning technique is to, "Begin with the end in mind."[1] In other words, if you were sitting at your own funeral looking at who showed up and listening to what people had to say about you—your accomplishments, your humanity—what would you like them to say? Consider what it would take achieve the outcomes you desire and to be the person who would receive the accolades you would want to receive. As a friend is fond of saying, "There are no luggage racks on a hearse." Have the courage, and it takes courage, to take the actions necessary to make the life changes that will bring you closer to your personal destiny.

Take each vested role that you identified, and set a long-term goal beginning with the end in mind. Do this in each area including self, family, community, and business. For instance, in the family area maybe a vested role is that of a father. A goal might be as follows: "In my role as a father, I would like to help my child find her purpose, and I will actively mentor her to help her achieve her goals for her life. This means being available for my daughter when she needs me and developing a plan with her." A community vision might be: "In my role as community leader I would like to support the leadership in my community to help develop the infrastructure for business and cultural growth. This means I will make time available to support and mentor the local leadership." A philanthropic goal might be: "In my role as philanthropist I would like to help achieve great strides to raise the level of education of minority youth, and I will support the initiatives, individuals, and groups that are committed to this same goal."

While a goal is specific and measurable, one's vision for a vested role is general and personal. Although individuals are often comfortable with the idea of planning in business, they are often less structured about how they construct a life plan. Legacy leaders must develop a vision of success for themselves. Bob Buford created a legacy plan that had six elements. Scott Oki and Mario Morino similarly defined a set of goals for their lives. Many other legacy leaders do the same thing. In fact, they often write down the key things they want to accomplish with their lives so that they can revisit them on a regular basis and make sure that they do not go off course.

Take the time to vision what you want to accomplish with the vested roles in your life. Free yourself from obstacles. If everything worked perfectly, what would you like to accomplish with your life?

Defining Your Priorities

Life is about making choices. Some of those choices support the goals we seek, while others do not. The clearer individuals can be about their guiding principles, personal vision, and long-term goals, as discussed in the previous paragraphs, the better prepared they are to establish their priorities. I propose that there are three key resources: time, money, and relationships, that if optimized will maximize the time value of your life.

What if you were able to spend the majority of your time on activities and relationships that were directly connected with the activities that are associated with your desired vision for yourself, your family, and your community? Wouldn't this be highly valuable time? Conversely, the time you spend on relationships and activities that are not connected with your desired vision is likely to be less valuable. *Life units*, if you will, are not just about where you spend your time, but the quality of the time you spend as well. Thus maximizing the time value of life is in part about spending quality time on the life units that hold the most value because they are connected with the outcomes you desire.

Now, what if you could maximize not only your time but your money and relationships as well? What if all three resources where lined up to directly support the long-term goals you set out for yourself? This in fact is the concept of maximizing the time value of life. If it were a formula, then the time value of life would equal your time allocation plus your money allocation plus your relationship allocation. It is the quality and allocation of your time, money, and relationships that are required to achieve your long-term goals. The time value of money for each individual ultimately comes down to developing priorities for these three resources during your lifetime.

Your priorities for your time, money, and relationships, however are not stagnant. In fact they change primarily based on your stage of life. In an earlier chapter we spoke about wealth builders becoming legacy builders. The *wealth-building* stage is where one is making his or her way in the world, building a career, and establishing one's own priorities. During this stage of life the resource of time is often allocated to career, the resource of money is often being accumulated rather than allocated, and relationships are primarily focused on one's self and career.

The next stage we term *identity transition*. It is also the stage where there are significant others and dependents in the picture. During this stage there are multiple competing priorities for one's time, money, and relationships. It is during this stage that it is most difficult to balance priorities for work, family, community, and self. Time is divided multiple ways to fulfill many different roles. Work roles can change from an employee responsible for one's self to that of a leader or manager. Family roles may begin with the responsibility of being a spouse or parent. Community roles may begin as well. During this time, money is not only still being accumulated, but it is also being allocated to support one's various roles. Relationships during this time are greatly expanded. It is during this time that balancing priorities becomes most difficult.

The final stage we term the *legacy* stage. It is during this stage that roles mature and time, money, and relationships are reprioritized. Time is often spent mentoring rather than being mentored. Family time can shift to supporting aging parents rather than raising children. And more time may be allocated to community and personal activities rather than business. During this time the resource of money is often spent to support social and personal goals that have become clearer with age rather than the goal of wealth accumulation. And relationships are often reprioritized to maximize one's time with those most dear.

Life's stages matter a great deal when setting priorities for time, money, and relationships; however, they are only partially about age. Some achieve the legacy stage earlier than others because of fortunate circumstances. It is important to understand what life stage you are currently in and what that means with respect to the allocation of your time, money, and relationships. It also becomes critically important for you to know when you have shifted to another stage and to reprioritize your key resources when this happens.

Take the time to determine what stage of life you are in and what that means for your priorities of time, money and relationships. Take note of the events that take you to another stage of life. When transitions take place, take the time to reflect on how those changes will affect the three key resources that you can control.

Prioritizing Your Time

There is an exercise that is helpful in prioritizing your time. It goes like this: People are asked to track their time in major categories over a one-month period of time. The categories relate to self, family, community, and business roles defined at the outset.

If any specific activity takes up more than 10 percent of a person's time, the activity should be called out as a discrete category. At the end of a month, individuals are asked to show a pie chart of where they spent their time. In addition, they are asked to show a pie chart that displays where they would like to be spending their time. If there is a disparity between the two charts, then this highlights an opportunity for change.

For example, let's take the categories of (1) self, (2) family, (3) friends, (4) business, and (5) community. Let's say that you tracked your time in these categories and came up with the the time allocations outlined in the second column of Table 2. However, to achieve the guiding principles and vision that you outlined for yourself, you aspire to a division of time shown in the first column of Table 2.

	Goal (%)	Actual (%)
Self	15	5
Family	30	10
Friends	10	5
Business	35	65
Community	10	15

TABLE 2: *Time Allocation*

In this example your actual time allocation and goals for your time allocation are out of balance. Maybe your overall objective is not realistic at this stage of your life given the goals you visioned initially. Clearly, in this example you are not valuing work as highly as the time you are allocating to it. By building a time allocation chart, a clear picture will emerge of the disparity between your time goals and actual time allocation. With this insight you can begin to develop some concrete goals that will move you closer to the time allocation that will fulfill your personal goals.

Take the time to identify where you are currently spending your time and where you would like to be spend time to achieve your life goals. Revisit this exercise when there are material changes in your life that might move you to a different life stage.

Prioritizing Your Roles and Relationships

Given that time is the most limited resource, how does one extend time? The answer is by enlisting and empowering others to take over key roles. Consider the labyrinth. Why do some people appear to walk so easily on this earth, accomplishing so much more than others seemingly without trying? Why do others find it so difficult to get things done and get mired down, often after expending great amounts of energy?

One key to accomplishing monumentally more with one's time is by enlisting and empowering others. This skill is about developing relationships to take over key roles. Bob Buford for instance was incredibly successful at building Christian ministries, running his company, leading the Peter Drucker Foundation, and still having time for lifelong learning. He was able to do all this by enlisting and empowering what he terms "100X leaders." He found talented people with a similar passion, and he supported them. They did the heavy lifting, while Bob put the essential ingredients of ideas and money together. This freed up his time so that he could do other things on his life planning list.

Scott Oki is able to sit on a significant number of boards, build golf courses, and spend time with his family because others are taking care of the day-to-day tasks in each area. Someone is focused on his golf operations, while others are responsible for running the various nonprofit activities of the organizations on whose boards Scott sits.

In almost every case, legacy leaders are effective at identifying the talents and individuals they need to extend their own capabilities and to thereby extend their time. They are successful in moving from an implementer, running the operation and working out all of the details, to an organizer, developing the strategy, identifying funding sources, and hiring the key human resources to support their goals.

Let's refine the time exercise that we outline in Table 2. Within each major category identify the vested roles and relationships that are most important to you. In business, for instance, what is the key relationship that is important to your business's success? If business is taking up too much time, as shown in Table 2, then maybe it is important to redefine this role and key relationship. Maybe you are acting as the implementer rather than the organizer.

Let's take another example. The individual in Table 2 is spending too much time at this stage of life on community-related activities. Maybe he is too actively involved in the community, when his desire in his role as a father is to spend time with the kids before they leave home. The question is whether there is a different role he could play in the community by partnering with his spouse or by hiring someone to direct his community philanthropy. This was the case with Paul Brainerd who decided not to be the implementer of his environmental philanthropy but to empower others as directors to help him extend his reach in this area.

Take the time to review the activities that are taking up most of your time and the key relationships in your vested roles.

Determine whether you are the implementer or organizer of those activities. Where possible, enlist others to support key roles. Spend your time on high-level activities that generate a great deal of value. You cannot always avoid implementation issues, but being explicit about the role you are playing and enlisting others will help leverage your time.

Prioritizing Your Money

The third key resource beyond time and relationships is money. Money falls into two categories: (1) cash flow to support your lifestyle and (2) assets that support your cash flow and are part of your estate. An assessment of both categories needs to start with your values and guiding principles. Cash flow planning for instance needs to start with a clear understanding of your lifestyle goals. What standard of living do you want to achieve for yourself and family? How much cash flow comes from your current business activities and investments to cover your lifestyle needs? Lifestyle needs cover living expenses for your family, as well as your annual community expenditures.

Cash flow planning is about budgeting your annual sources of income against your annual expenditures. Although this budgeting analysis seems straightforward, it is often not completed, or if completed, not revisited on a regular basis. As a result, individuals are often left to wonder whether they really have enough money to cover their current lifestyle much less have anything left over for other uses. In addition, people know that at a certain stage of life, say the legacy stage or retirement, their earning potential will change. They may not have an annual paycheck or business income. As a result, the budgeting process is a bit more complex because individuals need to anticipate the assets they will have when they move to the legacy stage of life. This budgeting complexity is one reason why successful individuals often feel insecure about their wealth.

Now let's turn to estate planning. Estate planning is not the same as cash flow planning. Estate planning is the planning that is conducted for the disposition of your assets. The planning and disposition often start with the creation of trusts and charitable entities such as foundations and donor-advised funds. For some people a majority of the disposition of their assets is done while they are alive. For others, the disposition of their assets happens after they die. There is a balancing act that takes place with estate planning. That balancing act is to ensure that enough assets remain in an individual's estate to pay for current lifestyle needs—what we call sleep-at-night money—while implementing planning techniques to maximize the amount of money after tax that goes to family members and philanthropy—what we term legacy money. Just as with cash flow planning, estate planning is best accomplished when one has clearly defined his or her values.

Scott Fithian in his book, *Values-Based Estate Planning*, describes one of the most thoughtful processes of estate planning out there today. Rather than starting the planning process after an event has occurred, or more typically in the offices of one's local estate planning attorney, a values-based plan starts with your overall guiding principles and values first. To help individuals and couples become clear about their values, the values-based estate planning process usually begins with a series of questions. Scott Fithian suggests that the important questions should cover the following:

- *One's guiding principals*
- *One's values at this point in life*
- *To whom one feels a sense of obligation*
- *One's relative goals for personal financial freedom, to support heirs, to give back to society and to minimize estate taxes*
- *The amount needed to feel financially independent*
- *The amount one would like to leave to immediate heirs and future generations*
- *The worries one has about leaving money to heirs*
- *The amount one would ideally like to leave to society*
- *The amount and involvement in charitable giving one hopes to achieve during one's life as compared to the amount in an estate plan*
- *The areas of charitable giving that are of most importance*
- *Feelings about shared philanthropy and a family foundation[2]*

Take the time to put together your current annual budget. Are you spending your money at the levels you desire for yourself, your family, and your community? Then, attempt to develop a cash flow budget for yourself for when you retire or reach the legacy stage of your life. Are you spending more than you earn, or are you saving at the end of the day? If appropriate, go to an outside adviser who is skilled at legacy and estate planning. Let the adviser ask you and your spouse the questions that will help you document your values and priorities.

The final step in legacy planning is to develop and share your written plan. A written plan outlines your (1) guiding principles and values; (2) a long-term vision for your time, money, and vested roles and relationships; and (3) specific, measurable objectives and actions that you will take in the coming months and years to achieve your vision. This plan creates a common picture of what you want to achieve with your life that can be shared with key family members and advisers. It through this legacy planning process, and the communication of the results of your work, that you will be able to help coordinate your advisers, support your key relationships, and move down the path toward achieving self-actualization.

KEY SECTION OBSERVATIONS

SELF-ACTUALIZATION PRACTICES

- Self-actualization often requires the development of a legacy plan. A legacy plan involves developing one's guiding principals; setting priorities for time, money, and relationships; and designing specific, measurable objectives for key roles and relationships.

- Legacy leaders vision their purpose by gaining clarity about their values and for the key roles and relationships in which they are vested. They often use a technique of "beginning with the end in mind" to achieve this clarity.

- Developing a route map is about setting priorities for the allocation of time, money, and relationships. By aligning these key resources to achieve overall goals, legacy leaders are often able to maximize the time value of their life.

- Legacy leaders gain control of their time by enlisting and empowering others to take over key roles. They become the organizer of key activities and enlist others to take over implementation tasks. This allows them to extend their time and achieve multiple priorities.

- Legacy leaders often utilize a values-based planning process to develop a specific plan for their time, money, and relationships that is measurable. The planning process often results in a written legacy plan that is shared with important people in their lives and their advisers.

SOCIAL IMPACT PRACTICES

How do I use my talents, resources, and capabilities to make a difference in the world so I can leave something of lasting value for society?

THE ESSENTIAL SOCIAL IMPACT QUESTION

A t about 8:00 in the morning of December 26, 2004, an earthquake of immense magnitude erupted in the Indian Ocean, 250 kilometers from the west coast of Sumatra, Indonesia. The quake was much greater than any that had occurred in the world since 1964; the energy it released was equivalent to roughly 23,000 atomic bombs of the size that devastated Nagasaki. The quake caused enormous tsunamis measuring 6 meters and higher which pounded the shoreline.[1] The images of one of the world's largest natural disasters were vividly displayed in newspapers and magazines, and on TV. Bodies were seen draped on the ground, houses were turned to rubble, and thousands were left homeless or went missing.

The outpouring of caring from the world, although slow at first, grew rapidly. At the end of 2005, the amount of relief donated was over $13 billion dollars. Although half of the aid is said to have been related to government actions, the other half was the result of the generosity of individuals. In the United States almost one out of every three individual households contributed to the relief effort.[2]

In response to the Asian tsunami, a vast number of fund-raising events took place all over the world. New funds were created to funnel money to the afflicted areas. Churches and synagogues collected donations. University students and company employees held fund-raising events on their local campuses and in their local businesses. Thousands of children in over 3,000 schools raised over $4.7 million for the thousands of children affected by the tsunami. Bands played free concerts with the proceeds going to help the cause. Sports figures donated money at celebrity events. The actions that were taken by individuals who wanted to help in some tangible way relieve the grief from this terrible tragedy were of an unprecedented number.

The lessons learned from the Asian tsunami are not only about the generosity of the human spirit but are also about legacy leadership. In virtually every town in the United States, and in many other countries, individuals displayed acts of leadership. They used their talents, their connections, their skills, and their money, and they took action. They worked in teams, within their various religious institutions, companies, and universities. They sought out places to give of their time and of their money. They showed that the actions of individuals can wield a tsunami-sized impact when pooled together for a common cause.

At issue is how individuals can achieve a similar result when there is no apparent natural disaster with an emotional tug of monumental scope and size. Social impact practices are about applying leadership to philanthropy in ways that move the needle and yield results. Our observations of legacy leaders are that they must first become clear about what they care about before they are willing to apply their time and money in a meaningful way for the social good. In other words, it must be part of their own definition of personal significance. Some see philanthropy as an obligation. They have been given much, and they feel they owe much in return. Some see it as an opportunity to help make the world a better place. Some see this as spiritual, and they make charitable acts part of their daily routine. No matter what the motivation, the challenge is how best to make an impact with the talents, financial assets, and personal resources available to an individual.

Once individuals determine that philanthropy is important for their personal significance, then the issue quickly moves to what they want to affect and how they can leverage their resources to achieve the greatest results. Through discussions with a large sample of philanthropic advisers who consult with hundreds of wealthy individuals, we identified three legacy leadership practices that lead to a positive, social impact:

1. *Applying your learned and innate skills close to home.* Effective social leaders apply their leadership skills and experiences in business to philanthropy. In addition, they often identify a social cause that is close to home, that has affected them personally, or where they have unique knowledge because the issue area is tangential to their business. In Chapter 13 we identify how legacy leaders are effective in adapting their business skills to the social sector.

2. *Packing more than your wallet and keys.* Legacy leaders who are making a social impact are effective in leveraging their broad assets. For them it is not enough to just give their money or

sit on boards. They pack more than their wallet and keys and bring their broad set of assets, leadership, and networks to bear on their community and philanthropic causes. Chapter 14 provides examples of leveraging.

3. *Acting with others.* When leaders take action in the social sector, they are acting within an existing system of nonprofits, government policies, and donor initiatives. Effective social leaders find ways to help convene these social networks and, whenever possible, pool donor assets. Chapter 15 provides examples of how a number of legacy leaders are achieving results with their portfolio practices.

In this section we devote a chapter to each practice. At the end of this section, we highlight some effective tools for developing a philanthropic plan.

PRACTICE 3: APPLYING YOUR LEARNED AND INNATE SKILLS CLOSE TO HOME

This, then, is held to be the duty of the man of wealth: First, to set an example of modest, unostentatious living, shunning display or extravagance; to provide moderately for the legitimate wants of those dependent upon him; and, after doing so, to consider all surplus revenues which come to him simply as trust funds, which he is called upon to administer, and strictly bound as a matter of duty to administer in the manner which, in his judgment, is best calculated to produce the most beneficial results for the community.

ANDREW CARNEGIE

I t was the largest rock concert for charity ever in history when it took place on July 13, 1985. Seventy-two thousand people piled into Wembley Stadium in London, England, and 90,000 people into JFK Stadium in Philadelphia, Pennsylvania, to hear the greatest assemblage of famous rock bands ever. Over 1.5 billion viewers in over 100 countries watched the live broadcast. At one point it was claimed that 95 percent of the television sets in the world were tuned to the event. Live Aid, as it was known, was one of the most ambitious organizing events for charity ever. The concert lasted for 16 hours with hundreds of performers on two continents. In total the event raised over £150 million (over $250 million) for the plight of the starving people in Ethiopia.

The amazing thing about this event, other than its sheer magnitude, is how its organizer, Bob Geldof, came onto the scene and pulled off this incredible organizing feat. Bob utilized a critical practice of legacy leaders by applying his learned skills in the area of music and his innate talents as an organizer to congeal the music industry around the plight of poverty in Africa. Others have done the same thing, applying their business skills in the areas of technology, retail, and other industries and professions to the field of philanthropy. The question is how?

Bob Geldof's Music to Combat World Poverty

Bob Geldof was born in Dun Laoghaire, Ireland, on October 5, 1951, and raised by his father, a traveling salesman, after his mother died in 1958. From this modest beginning Bob Geldof went on to a career in music, founding a punk rock band called the Boomtown Rats in 1975, before landing his biggest hit, Live Aid.

Bob is not by outward appearances the type of person to lead a global organizing effort. He has a punk rock demeanor and a sense of outrage at the world. Bob, however, has some business experience, having run a television production company and travel company, which provided some underpinning for organizing. And he certainly knows the music business, having spent his whole life in it.

In October 1984, while watching a broadcast by the BBC about the famine in Ethiopia, Bob was moved, and became determined to do something to help. In an interview with the BBC, Bob Geldof talked about his motivation and inspiration for the Live Aid concert: "In 1984, I was watching a news broadcast about a famine that was occurring in Ethiopia. And I felt I had to do something about it. And I got a lot of musician friends together and recorded a song called, "Do They Know It's Christmas?" And we called the group Band-Aid, and we raised money for the famine victims in Ethiopia. But subsequently I realized that that would not be enough to do all we wanted to do. So I organized a concert. And it was called Live Aid."[1]

In total, Band-Aid had raised £8 million for the famine relief program, but Geldof wanted to do more for the cause. Using the enormous success of the Band-Aid single, Geldof went on to organize the Live Aid concert.

Although there are lots of music producers, agents, and financiers who work with famous bands and musicians, Bob Geldof took his knowledge of this industry, and his personal passion for some of the most destitute people in the world, and created a way for rock stars to contribute their talents to support a social cause. Bob Geldof could not have been successful if he were an outsider to the music business. He could not have done this without some fairly persuasive leadership and organizing skills. Bob Geldof through his active leadership represents a prime example of applying his learned and innate talents close to home.

Applying the Lessons of Venture Capitalists to Philanthropy

Another example of how an industry is applying its business framework for the social good is the venture capital industry. In 1994, visionary corporate leaders, many of whom had made their money through venture investing in technology companies in Silicon Valley, brought their venture investing skills to attack the problems of K–12 education in the Bay Area. They designed a venture philanthropy funding organization called Joint Venture: Silicon Valley Network, and created a $25 million education initiative to build the financial and organizational capacity of K–12 public schools. The Center for Venture Philanthropy (CVP), as it is called today, uses the framework of venture investing, called *venture philanthropy*, to identify the initiatives it wants to support and to track results.[2]

Peninsula Community Foundation, serving San Francisco and Silicon Valley areas, was the first community foundation to evolve and practice a specific set of investment practices called venture philanthropy. These venture capitalists applied their venture capital business context to the nonprofit realm by implementing five elements that are used in venture investing. They include:[3]

1. *Investing in long-term (three- to six-year) business plans.* Often philanthropists and foundations provide grants for a year or two, but as a nonprofit begins to show results, they back away feeling that funding will be provided from elsewhere. Since many nonprofits can survive only on grants from foundations, they must spend extraordinary amounts of time to find other

sources of funding. Venture philanthropists, like venture capitalists, create investment milestones, and as their nonprofit
investment organizations meet their stated goals, these venture philanthropists provide increasing funding.

2. *Having a managing partner relationship.* Venture capitalists do not
   run the companies in which they invest. Instead, they help with
   the strategy, identify key management talent, and strengthen
   the board of directors. They have a managing partner relationship, and the same is true with venture philanthropists.

3. *Having an accountability-for-results process.* While early-stage
   companies, which are the beneficiaries of venture investments, are accountable for results, nonprofits have been less
   scrutinized about their results. Today venture philanthropists
   are attempting to measure the results of their social investments in more quantitative ways. This is a much more difficult task than the quantifiable financial returns of businesses,
   but it has become essential to measure the social investment
   results of nonprofit activities.

4. *Providing cash and expertise.* Venture philanthropists, like their
   for-profit counterparts, provide funding as well as management and other expertise to help their investments succeed.
   Many venture philanthropists get actively involved to help
   their social investments with contacts, additional funding,
   accounting, and professional advice.

5. *Developing an exit strategy.* Venture capitalists must sell their
   stakes in the companies in which they invest to the public,
   through a public offering, or to another firm, if they are to
   realize gains on their investments. This is referred to as *exit-
   ing a company.* Venture philanthropists must do the same
   thing, but instead of selling their companies, they must help

the nonprofits they invest in achieve the scale of funding they need to support themselves by bringing in other foundations and sources of funding. In this way venture philanthropists can exit a nonprofit while still leaving it in a strong position to survive.

Today CVP has made a difference in the lives of over 30,000 low-income children and their families. The venture philanthropy model has spread as well around the United States, capturing the imagination of other technology and business executives who are comfortable with applying the framework of business structure to nonprofits. Venture philanthropists provide another example of how leaders apply their business framework, in this case venture investing, to philanthropy to make a social impact.

Sandy Weill's Leadership from Citigroup to the National Academy Foundation

Sandy Weill's story is a personification of the American dream. He came from a modest family in Brooklyn, New York, to lead the world's largest financial institution, Citicorp. Along the way Mr. Weill became involved with Carnegie Hall, the Cornell-Weill Medical Center, and the National Academy Foundation (NAF). In all three nonprofit pursuits Mr. Weill employed his business skills to improve the organizations with which he was involved. Of those three examples, the NAF is the best example of applying his learned and innate talents close to home.

In the late 1970s there was not enough skilled labor to support the growth of the expanding financial institutions headquartered in New York City. In some instances these large investment banks and lending institutions were considering leaving New York City because of this labor shortage. Mr. Weill knew the financial industry well, having grown his first company, which became Shearson/Lehman and then merged with American Express. He was also concerned as he looked at young, primarily minority, kids who were often not engaged in productive pursuits and not able to break into legitimate banking jobs.

Rather than sit back and watch this scenario play out for his company, for minority kids in New York, and for the financial services industry, Mr. Weill took action. Mr. Weill's first call was to the chancellor of the New York City schools about creating a business curriculum in financial services. This led to the first academy of finance in 1982 in a Brooklyn public high school.

Over the years Sandy Weill has helped the NAF grow and apply its curriculum from a single school to 660 schools and 50,000 students, mainly for inner-city youth. The NAF has extended its model beyond a financial services curriculum to hospitality and tourism, as well as to information technology. It has received support from a wide variety of corporations and has helped to fill an education gap so that inner-city youth are prepared for real business employment opportunities.

In his book, *The Real Deal*, Mr. Weill speaks about the analogies he perceives between the leadership requirements of the for-profit and nonprofit worlds: "Marrying my business skills to the philanthropic organizations with which I've chosen to become involved has given me immense satisfaction. I've always been a grinder. I stay at something until I see results. After years of commitment to Carnegie Hall, Weill Cornell Medical College, and the National Academy Foundation, I feel I've made an important impact on each of these institutions. Perhaps one of the things that motivated me was my insight early on that the business and philanthropic worlds offer similar means of leading people and promoting advances in society."[4]

By identifying a gap in the financial services industry and filling it with trained minority students, Sandy Weill was utilizing the practice of applying his skills close to home. By helping the NAF grow and succeed, he was applying his learned and innate leadership talents. As a result, Sandy Weill provides a solid example of this leadership practice.

Jeff Brotman's Leadership from Costco to the United Way of King County

Jeff Brotman grew up in the Pacific Northwest to become the founder of Costco, the renowned warehouse retailer. It was the Seattle community that supported Mr. Brotman's other businesses initially, and it was the Seattle community that he knew well. So when Jeff Brotman determined he wanted to give back, he did it close to home, to strengthen the social safety net of the community he grew up in. In the process, Jeff Brotman brought his business skills as the founder of Costco to accelerate the success of the United Way of King County.

"I've always wanted to be engaged in the community," said Brotman in our interview. "I get two pleasures out of it. One, I get a personal pleasure out of it. Then of course I'm able to do something good. I've tried to do things where I could leverage my time and the experience I had as a business person, and organizer, reader, planner. In my particular case I'm very interested in the social safety net. It's an area people don't want to fund because to do it properly is like buying a mutual fund. The argument about mutual funds is that the returns are reduced, and therefore you just do it differently. My view is that people like Bill Gates will focus on the world, and I'll focus on making a difference in Seattle, which is where my money came from in good measure."

Jeff Brotman was involved first as a donor to and volunteer for the United Way. As his interest in the social safety net for Seattle grew, he took on more responsibility and ultimately restructured the strategy and organization of the United Way in the Pacific Northwest. "I always was supportive of the United Way, made personal contributions, and put United Way programs into our business. But in terms of leadership I didn't take any of the more mundane board roles. Instead, I took on the campaign and in the process completely restructured the United Way organization and campaign apparatus. My feeling was that even if we didn't have a great fund-raising year, the time I spent in reorganizing would benefit the community in the future so it would have an impact."

Mr. Brotman went on to say, "When people like me see an opportunity to reorganize, we seize it. We created a new business plan for United Way, presented it to the board, and got it adopted. We pared the number of agencies down from a 150 to about 90. We completely changed the entitlement process and reorganized the way we thought about delivering social services. We changed the whole nature of the way things were being done here."

In 2004, The United Way of King County passed New York, Chicago, and all other major cities to become the top revenue-generating affiliate in the national network of more than 1,300 agencies.[5] In May 2005, Jeff and Susan Brotman were honored as First Citizens by the Seattle King County Association of Realtors, an award presented to King County residents who have provided outstanding public service and leadership to the region.

Legacy leaders enjoy applying their leadership, creativity, and entrepreneurial zeal to exploit unfulfilled opportunities or niches that others have yet to see. They do this as entrepreneurs, as investors, and as leaders of great enterprises. In philanthropy, they look to do the same thing, to identify and fill unfulfilled needs. Often they bring with them the same construct they utilized in business. If they were in technology, they may have a venture approach to philanthropy. If they were in retail, they may have a test and rollout construct. For legacy leaders philanthropy is often about bringing business discipline and personal leadership to the nonprofit arena to make a difference. They do this by applying their learned and innate skills close to home.

CHAPTER 14

PRACTICE 4: PACKING MORE THAN YOUR WALLET AND KEYS

Successful business entrepreneurs that really get involved in philanthropy don't see constraints. They use friendships, business knowledge, acumen, and all they have learned that can help a nonprofit organization. They're multi-capable machines that offer themselves, their talent, knowledge, and networks, as well as their money, to make a difference in an organization.

CURTIS MEADOWS, THE MEADOWS FOUNDATION

In 1989 Anita Roddick, founder of one of the most famous public social enterprises, The Body Shop, came to meet with me and my wife at her headquarters, located in New Jersey. We had stumbled upon The Body Shop by chance when our trip from China was interrupted by the Tiananmen Square incident.

That night, as we watched the events unfold in China outside our window, we decided it would be best to reroute our planned trip. One thing led to another, and we found ourselves in London, standing on a corner, watching the tourists milling around and doing a bit of shopping ourselves.

We walked into a soap shop called The Body Shop. It had green shelves and a wonderful smell. That is what my wife observed. What I observed was that the shop was packed full of people, and my wife wanted to buy everything in the store. What we did not know at that time was that this chance encounter we had with The Body Shop in London would turn out to be our first encounter with social entrepreneurism, or that my wife and I would become one of the first franchise owners of The Body Shop in the United States. For us Anita Roddick became a living example of how one can leverage her leadership and company strategically for social good.

Legacy leaders such as Anita Roddick often define their assets broadly to include their financial assets, human networks, organizational affiliations, family businesses, foundation assets, and government connections. They believe in the concept of leverage and seek out the opportunity to leverage their broad set of assets whenever they can. When leaders become involved in a social cause, their actions almost always involve more than money.

Anita Roddick, Leveraging Her Company for Social Change

Anita Roddick came from a poor immigrant family in the United Kingdom to become the founder of The Body Shop, a global retail company with thousands of stores in over 50 countries. In the process she transformed her public company into a social change enterprise, leveraging this very public asset to improve the lives of her employees and the cultures of the peoples from whom she sourced her products.

Anita Roddick was an early pioneer of social entrepreneurism that combines "doing well" (and The Body Shop has been a profitable company for its shareholders) and doing good with a positive social mission. In her book, *Body and Soul*, Anita Roddick talks about how she leveraged her company to make a positive impact on her employees, on the communities surrounding the shops, and on the developing world.

"For someone like myself whose thinking was forged in the sixties," said Ms. Roddick, "it was a magical prospect to think of doing something worthwhile with our company. The very notion of using a business as a crusader, of harnessing success to ideals, set my imagination on fire. From that moment The Body Shop ceased to exist, at least in my eyes, as just another trading business. It became a force for social change. It became a lobbying group to campaign on environmental and human rights issues. It became a communicator and an educator."[1]

The concept of creating a social change company underpinned the mission of The Body Shop and matched Anita's world vision. She felt so strongly about this mission that she wrote into the legal articles of association memoranda for The Body Shop that the company stands for human rights advocacy as well as social and environmental change. That was the legal purpose of The Body Shop, and it would take 70 percent of the shareholders to change this mission. "So we made sure that The Body Shop had a different purpose other than just creating products to sell and to generate profits, and that was enormously powerful for us," said Roddick.

It is what Anita Roddick did with the assets of her company, the employees, the suppliers, and the profits that makes her an example of packing more than her wallet and keys. As Anita recalls, "We looked at how we could set up social enterprises in The Body Shop such as setting up Soapworks in Glasgow in the worst housing area in Western Europe. We made sure it was the most state-of-the-art factory, and 25 percent of its profits went back into the community. So we used all the models of the cooperative movement by the Quakers within the company in terms of building and protecting community.

"We also turned the shops into action stations," continued Anita. "We had a highly successful voter registration campaign in the States where we registered voters in the stores. We had all of our franchisees and company stores take on community projects within their local communities. They picked the projects. It could be a homeless shelter, animal rights group or environmental cause. Think of thousands of stores all over the world paying their employees to get involved and improve their own communities. It is very empowering."

Anita also got involved in what she called "trade not aid" projects. Trade not aid is the idea that instead of giving money to charity in the developing world where The Body Shop sources its products, the company would set up small businesses that would supply The Body Shop with products. The Body Shop in this way could set up sustainable aid for poor people, while providing them with self-esteem and a sustainable livelihood.

One example of a trade not aid project developed by The Body Shop relates to the production of wood "footsie rollers" in India. Footsie rollers are grooved cylinders to massage the feet. Anita was traveling in India when she witnessed the poverty there. She was compelled to do something and essentially adopted a village. She bought the villagers a lathe, and she taught them what they needed to know to produce the massagers. Instead of paying the villagers discounted prices for their products, she paid them first-world wages for what they created. She not only bought the footsie rollers from the villagers, but she also encouraged them to sell these footsie rollers to other companies in Europe and the United States. As a result she helped this village create a sustainable source of income.

Anita has created trade not aid projects around the world. She has empowered the employees of The Body shop to become social activists. She has required franchisees to take on community projects. She helped start an organization called Businesses for Social Responsibility to help other business people make a social impact with their companies. In this way and many others she has leveraged her position and her leadership, helping to accelerate the whole field of social entrepreneurship in the process.

Today, corporate social responsibility (CSR), which incorporates societal practices within the strategy and supply chain of companies, is becoming more popular. Mainstream companies such as Starbucks and IBM have developed comprehensive CSR programs. Starbucks, for instance, publishes its CSR practices, and measures the results of its key CSR initiatives in a 75-page report. They have a 20-person organization focused on implementing programs in this area. It is part of their culture, and it is part of the ethos of their stores.

CSR is one example of leveraging, of bringing more than your wallet and keys. It is also good business, helping to create a strong business culture that helps to retain employees and connect with customers and suppliers.

Bono, Leveraging His Celebrity to Fight AIDS in Africa

One of the most visible examples of packing more than his wallet and keys is Bono, who, by leveraging his celebrity, has made a big difference in the fight against AIDS and poverty in Africa.

It seems obvious today that celebrities are able to leverage their notoriety for social good. Barbra Streisand and Jane Fonda have worked effectively for years for the causes and political candidates they care about. Oprah Winfrey has turned her talk show into a crusade for the underprivileged. She has also backed this up with her personal philanthropy and support of specific charities. Few celebrities, however, have been able to mobilize governments or to engage their celebrity network to enlist world leaders to their causes as has Bono, the lead singer of the rock band U2.

The philanthropic feats of Bono in combating AIDS and poverty in Africa are now legendary. Bono appeared on the cover of *Time* magazine in 2005, along with Bill and Melinda Gates, as a man of the year. He has been nominated for a Nobel Peace prize. He has met with the pope and leaders from around the world. He is the founder of DATA (Debt, AIDS, Trade, Africa), an organization that fights poverty and HIV in the developing world. From that organization was spawned the ONE Campaign to eradicate AIDS and poverty around the globe. He is one of the organizers behind the Live 8 concerts in nine cities worldwide. This was the encore to the Live Aid concert that was conceived of many years earlier by Geldof. Through these concerts and Bono's lobbying efforts with the leaders of the G8 summit, he helped to double aid to Africa and cancel many of the debts of the poorest African nations.

Time magazine is quoted as saying about Bono's efforts, "Bono charmed and bullied and morally blackmailed the leaders of the world's richest countries into forgiving $40 billion in debt owed by the poorest." So what business does a rock star have as a champion in world hunger and disease, and what does it teach us about leadership?

The lessons of Bono are clearly not about giving away money. We rarely hear about how much Bono has personally given away. Instead, he is leveraging his broad set of assets and his celebrity. It is striking how Bono not only has taken the cause he cares about to the leaders of the world but to the common people as well. In an interview from a corporate gathering of TNT, a global delivery company like Fedex or DHL, Bono was addressing the crowd of employees. This crowd was about as far away from a rock concert as a New Yorker in Texas! At that meeting Bono spoke about his inspiration for his activism and provided a vision and road map for others.

"The journey that brought me here started in 1985 with Band Aid, when my friend Bob Geldof issued a challenge to feed the world. It changed my life. That summer, my wife and I worked in Ethiopia for a month in an orphanage. On our last day, a man handed me his baby and said: 'Please, take him with you.' He knew in Ireland his son would live, and in Ethiopia he would die. And I turned him down, because those are the rules. It's a feeling I'll never forget. In that moment, I became a rock star with a cause."

Bono continued in the interview by saying, "The fact is, we are the first generation that can look disease and extreme poverty in the eye and say: We don't have to stand for this. Changing the world is an achievable goal; we have the know-how, we have the cash and we have the life-saving drugs. Do we have the will? It's not just about heart, it's about being smart. The global war against terror is bound up in the war against poverty. There are many potential Afghanistans in Africa. Poverty breeds despair; despair breeds violence. Isn't it cheaper and smarter to make friends out of potential enemies than to defend yourself against them later? The problems in the developing world are a chance for us to redefine ourselves. We won't transform lives, we will transform the way these people see us. There are moments in history when civilization redefines itself. When we change the status quo, because we can no longer live with it. The abolition of slavery in America, the end of colonial rule in India, the fall of the Berlin Wall, the end of apartheid. This might be such a moment. 2005 might be the year we decide that the wanton loss of life in Africa through obscene poverty and disease is something we can no longer live with."[2]

Bono, by leveraging his personal network, celebrity and leadership, demonstrates the legacy leadership practice of packing more than his wallet and keys. Leveraging, however, does not require celebrity.

Jeff Skoll, Leveraging His Network to Empower Social Entrepreneurs

Jeff Skoll is the first president of eBay. In 1999 Jeff Skoll created the Skoll Foundation with the belief that he could leverage his money, time, and network to empower social entrepreneurs. Social entrepreneurs are proven leaders whose approaches and solutions to social problems are helping to better the lives of others. Jeff Skoll empowers social entrepreneurs by providing them with grants and then utilizing his network to extend their reach. Jeff Skoll in this way is developing new leaders, which is another way of leveraging.

"Philanthropy is all about making a positive difference in the world by devoting your resources and your time to causes you believe in," says Skoll. "In my case, I like to support causes where 'a lot of good comes from a little bit of good,' or, in other words, where the positive social returns vastly exceed the amount of time and money invested. I also like the idea that philanthropy can be innovative, using the latest advancements to bring results to many people, ideally on a global basis." [3]

"Like most of us," continues Skoll, "I want to live in a world where healthy communities flourish and where individuals are given the opportunity to use their talents and abilities to achieve their full potential. With the fundamental philosophy of empowerment in mind, I led the creation of the eBay Foundation in 1998, followed by my own personal foundation, the Skoll Foundation, a year later."

In a speech Jeff Skoll made at the Skoll World Forum on Social Entrepreneurship in 2006, he expanded on this idea of the social entrepreneur as providing leverage, "Some charities give people food. Some charities teach farmers to grow food. But social entrepreneurs aren't happy with that. They have to teach the farmers to grow food, teach them how to make money, turn it back over to the farm and hire ten more people. They're not satisfied until they have transformed the entire food industry."

Jeff Skoll determined that his significance would involve packing more than his wallet and keys to empower new leaders in their journeys to make a social impact. Anita Roddick leveraged her company, and made it into a social enterprise machine. Bono leveraged his celebrity and his personal network to mobilize governments. All three leaders went well beyond the donation of money to make a social impact by leveraging their broad set of assets, which is a philanthropic best practice.

CHAPTER 15

PRACTICE 5: ACTING WITH OTHERS

We're the biggest foundation in the world, and we couldn't possibly accomplish our objectives on our own. . . . The big objectives just can't be done without multi-parties being involved.

BILL GATES SR.

The trial came to a head in January 2000 when Deborah Lipstadt, professor at Emory University, was accused of libel for describing author and historian David Irving as, "One of the most dangerous spokespersons for Holocaust denial."[1] Irving went on the offensive, claiming his reputation as a historian was defamed by Lipstadt and British publisher Penguin Books. Instead of Irving being on trial, Lipstadt found that she was the one having to defend herself and the history of the Holocaust.

It was Les Wexner's involvement, however, and how he mobilized a network of people to support Deborah Lipstadt that illustrates the practice of acting with others. This legacy leadership practice recognizes that social change does not happen alone. Making a social impact in any nonprofit issue area involves multiple stakeholders. Individuals are acting within a preexisting ecosphere of donors, foundations, nonprofits, government policies, and for-profit businesses. It is the process of strengthening those networks that leads to social impact. Les Wexner and others serve as examples of how this is done.

Les Wexner, Acting with Others to Combat the Denial of the Holocaust

Despite the enormous amount of evidence of the Nazi's murder of approximately 6 million Jews during World War II, shortly after the war a few former Nazis began spreading the lie that the Holocaust never occurred. David Irving, a British historian, declared that there were no gas chambers or a systematic extermination of 6 million Jews. As part of denying the Holocaust, he also denied Hitler's involvement in it.[2]

The suit was filed in London in the Royal High Court of Justice, and the trial began on January 12, 2000. The trial attracted a great deal of attention, as a judgment for Irving might have emboldened the Holocaust deniers who claim that the genocide of European Jews was a hoax. As the trial was being prepared, Dr. Lipstadt was facing increasing legal and financial challenges for mounting a defense. Enter the picture, Les Wexner, founder of The Limited.

Les Wexner came from a modest Jewish background to become the founder of The Limited, and one of the most successful retailers in the history of the United States. The Limited is the parent of retail concepts such as The Limit, Limited Express, Victoria's Secret, and others. Mr. Wexner is an active community leader and philanthropist in Cleveland, Ohio, and founder of The Wexner Foundation and Institute for Jewish leadership.

When Mr. Wexner learned of Deborah Lipstadt and the trial, he very thoughtfully considered the impact he could have in support of her efforts. There is no question that he could write Dr. Lipstadt and her distinguished legal team a check to pay for support of their legal efforts, but this in some ways did not maximize the potential impact that Mr. Wexner could make. After fully considering his options, he made some calls to enlist others who together could show solidarity against the outrage of this trial.

"Under English law the burden of proof was on Dr. Lipstadt, so in a way she had to prove that the Holocaust happened," said Mr. Wexner.[3] "It's a lawsuit that she probably would have won just on the merit, but not a certainty that the verdict would have been more than her favor for a penny. It might have been a simple verdict, and it was called to my attention. I asked Deborah if I could help. She said she needed help, and that she didn't really know how to manage the case."

Mr. Wexner continued, "I met with her English attorneys and just assessed how we could build a case so strong, with walls so wide, so high, that an English court has to not only find in favor of her, but hopefully writes the strongest possible verdict. That means you have to pull scholars together from all over the world, Jews, gentiles, Russians, Americans, Germans, and set up a scholarship base that forever proves that the Holocaust did happen, that Hitler did know about the gas chambers. It needs to repeat the whole story.

"They said, well, to do that would cost several million dollars, and I said go forward and build the case. Don't worry about the money, I'll fund it.

"The part I am proud of is not that when history is told, the notion that one Jewish merchant from Columbus, Ohio, cared enough to defend a Jewish studies professor from Atlanta. That isn't a great story. It's a good story, but it's not a great story. The great story should be that a network of people from all over the world came together, and they said they wanted to be part of it.

"So, I called Steven Spielberg, and he agreed. He said he would take part, I would take part, and we would both find other funders who would quietly fund this. Then I thought since this is happening in an English court, even though it's an American defendant, the Jews of England ought to care too, and we solicited them to be partners.

"If I had to write the whole check, it would have been the best check I ever wrote, but I'm really proud that I thought to stand back and say no, you really want this to be about our people and how they care."

Dr. Lipstadt and Penguin Press won their case resoundingly in a 334-page ruling, which Deborah Lipstadt chronicles in her book, *History on Trial*, recounting the details of the trial. This story is not about the Holocaust, however. It is not about Deborah Lipstadt either. Instead, it illustrates the power of collaboration and of networks, of acting with others.

While Wexner acted with others on a specific project, Paul Brainerd, high-tech founder of Aldus, the developer of Page Maker software, created a collaborative learning and giving organization to, in a sustainable way, pool donors to advance K–12 education and the environment.

Paul Brainerd, Pooling Donors to Improve K–12 Education and the Environment

Paul Brainerd's first career was as a journalist, working at the *Minneapolis Star Tribune*. In 1984 he saw the opportunity to marry his knowledge of publishing with the computer capabilities of the Apple Macintosh. This led to the founding of the Aldus software company, which produced one of the first desktop computer publishing programs, called PageMaker. The product transformed printing and publishing, and, when in 1994 Aldus was sold to Adobe Systems for $525 million, launched Brainerd into the exclusive millionaire's club.

Brainerd knew that his significance involved giving back to his community. He also knew that he was interested in the environment, having grown up in a household in rural Oregon. With a journalist's appetite for information, Brainerd began the process of learning to be a philanthropist. After interviewing 60 people about environmental issues, he began to form a plan for himself. He also realized through his research process the difficulty in truly understanding how to make an impact in philanthropy.

It is precisely because Brainerd understood the difficulty of climbing the philanthropy mountain to learn to be an effective philanthropist that he created a learning and investment organization called Social Venture Partners (SVP). Social Venture Partners was founded with a vision that by pooling philanthropic money from lots of community-minded individuals and then donating that money as a large professional foundation might invest in society, SVP could help others learn professional philanthropic practices. In addition, SVP could make an impact in a targeted philanthropic issue area such as K–12 education.

Brainerd recruited other leaders in the local tech scene to help launch the new organization. The founding members included Scott Oki; Ida Cole, a former Microsoft executive; Doug Walker, the president of WRQ, a Seattle-based software company; and Bill Neukom, Microsoft's senior vice president of law and corporate affairs, and others.

Originally Brainerd recruited 100 other wealthy, mostly high-tech individuals. The initial focus was on K–12 education. Individuals contributed $5,000 (now $5,500) each year to be donated to youth and education organizations. These funds were pooled, and a grants committee of SVP funders was formed to determine which groups would receive the nonprofit grants. Donor partners of SVP then took their business expertise and contributed their time to help actively support the nonprofits that received their grants.

The idea took off, and SVP grew not only in the Seattle area but nationally. The organization recruited leaders in other communities who then brought together other new philanthropists, ultimately reaching 20 communities with over 1,000 members/partners who give $5,500 each to be pooled and donated to charity. They expanded beyond K–12 education to the environment. They developed donor education tools and training. They involved the children of partners in philanthropy. They took donor collaboration to its logical extreme and in the process gave millions of dollars to charity in a thoughtful manner.

Paul Brainerd developed SVP as an organization designed to act with others to achieve philanthropic education and impact. On the other coast, in New York, another legacy leader from the new wealth crowd, Paul Tudor Jones, was doing something similar to Brainerd, but with a focus on fighting poverty in the New York area.

Paul Tudor Jones, Bringing Hedge Fund Managers Together to Fight Poverty in New York

Paul Tudor Jones has the Midas touch, and at the age of 32 had already started his own firm and made a fortune as an investor. Yet Mr. Jones will be better known for the social network he founded, the Robin Hood Foundation, than for his accomplishments as an investor.

Paul Tudor Jones is a hedge fund manager. Not just any hedge fund manager; he is one of the most successful hedge fund managers in the world. Hedge funds are investment funds that use various investment strategies to capture inefficiencies in the financial markets. Hedge funds invest in a wide variety of investment vehicles such as public equities, fixed income, real estate, private equity, commodities, and virtually any other investment that can be monetized. They received their name because these funds are designed not just to bet on the long-term growth of their investments, but also to bet on their decline. By combining bets on growth with bets on the downside, they essentially "hedge" their investments and attempt to reduce risk.

In 1987, when the world of investing was skyrocketing, Paul Tudor Jones was on top of this world. Jones, however, was worried because when everything is rosy in the investment world, the smart money runs for the hills. Jones in fact predicted a major sell-off in the stock market. He became famous because the sell-off happened almost exactly as he predicted. On what has become known as "black Monday," the stock market lost almost 22 percent of its value. When everyone else was losing money, Mr. Jones tripled his investment by betting on the downside of the market.[4] His expertise as an investor led to great fortune, and in 2005 alone he made $500 million in personal compensation.

It was precisely because Mr. Jones felt that the world was falling apart in 1987 that he decided to form a foundation, called the Robin Hood Foundation. Its mission is to take money from the rich in New York and to give it to nonprofits and charter schools that support inner-city youth. Like Brainerd in Seattle, the concept required bringing together a network of wealthy individuals first, and then to find effective ways for them to work with nonprofits and policy makers to make an impact.

So how did Paul Tudor Jones create a social portfolio? How did he move from an idea to creating one of the most powerful public foundations in the country? The following insights relate to the power of networking and of acting with others.

One of the first actions Paul Tudor Jones took when he decided to start the Robin Hood Foundation was to call his friends and fellow hedge fund managers, Glenn Dubin and Peter Borish. They became cofounders and in turn recruited David Saltzman to become the executive director of Robin Hood. Jann Wenner, publisher of *Rolling Stone*, came onboard, and there was an effort as well to recruit other board members from the hedge fund world. The objective was to have the board cover all the administrative costs of running the foundation including its staff of over 66 people so that 100 percent of the donations would go to charity.

Over time the founders recruited a blue chip board with people like Jeffrey Immelt, head of GE, Harvey Weinstein, founder of Miramax, Tom Brokaw, Gwyneth Paltrow, and others. David Saltzman brought in John F. Kennedy, Jr., who was a college friend. John F. Kennedy, Jr. brought in Marie-Josee Kravitz, wife of the famous hedge fund manager Henry Kravitz of Kohlberg, Kravis, Roberts & Company. And the list goes on. Soon it was the cool thing to be associated with the Robin Hood Foundation. Its charity balls were a place to be seen, and it raised millions of dollars for charity. The high-end business and social network from New York found an outlet to work with its peers to fight poverty in New York City.

This network of capable business leaders was then extended to make an impact on the programs that the Robin Hood Foundation funded. For instance, the Robin Hood Foundation supports charter schools. In Bedford-Stuyvesant, one of the poorest parts of Brooklyn, the Robin Hood Foundation pooled its grant money with the New York City Board of Education and Paul Tudor Jones himself to start a charter school. The building in which the charter school is housed was acquired by another grantee of the Robin Hood Foundation. They used their connections to convince a world-class architect to design the school. And this partnership led to a transformation of this low-income neighborhood.

There are hundreds if not thousands of examples of how individuals create philanthropic networks. The growth of community foundations is an example of how communities are bringing together financial resources and people to make an impact. Public-private partnerships, which are collaborative initiatives that combine government organizations and funding with business organizations and funding, are also growing around the country as another trend. Legacy leaders find ways to tap into their networks and to extend them in order to achieve the philanthropic results they desire.

Les Wexner, Paul Brainerd, and Paul Tudor Jones represent examples of legacy leaders who, by acting with others and within a portfolio of needs, have been able to leverage their skills and influence. They do this by convening donors, for-profit and non-profit stakeholders, by pooling their networks and assets, and by employing active leadership. They map the other players that affect the nonprofit landscape. They scope out the gaps in the landscape that they can fill. Sometimes they can even convene an industry around a cause. These are examples of the legacy leadership practice of acting with others.

16

BUILDING A PLAN FOR SOCIAL IMPACT

Philanthropy is all about making a positive difference in the world by devoting your resources and your time to causes you believe in. In my case, I like to support causes where "a lot of good comes from a little bit of good," or, in other words, where the positive social returns vastly exceed the amount of time and money invested.

JEFF SKOLL

Social impact practices are about how to make a difference in the world. Ultimately, impact comes back to leadership: the leadership to apply business skills to philanthropy, the way Bob Geldof, Sandy Weill, and Jeff Brotman have done; the leadership to pack more than one's wallet and keys, leveraging a broad set of assets the way Anita Roddick, Jeff Skoll, and Bono have done; and the leadership to act with others and within a portfolio of needs, the way Les Wexner, Paul Brainerd, and Paul Tudor Jones have done.

Some of the essential tools for social impact involve developing your philanthropic mission and plan, discovering your passionate cause, leveraging your broad set of assets, and convening and pooling stakeholders.

Developing a Philanthropic Mission and Plan

Giving often starts from the heart—and without a plan. As a result, it often takes on a life of its own. Individuals who want to make a significant social impact, however, need to be proactive about their philanthropy and formulate a plan.

When it comes to developing a philanthropic mission and plan, the first thing to realize is that there are three types of philanthropy: individual philanthropy, family philanthropy, and corporate philanthropy, or corporate citizenship. Just as with the

	Individual Philanthropy	Family Philanthropy	Corporate Philanthropy
Principles	Vision for individual philanthropy	Vision for family philanthropy	Vision for corporate philanthropy
Priorities	• Community checkbook • Formative philanthropy • Cause philanthropy	• Family mission (internal) • Social impact (external)	• Employees • Supply chain partners • Customers • Shareholders
Plan	Goals, actions, review	Goals, actions, review	Goals, actions, review

TABLE 3: *Individual, Family, and Corporate Philanthropy*

creation of a plan for self-actualization, a philanthropic plan involves the development of principles, priorities, and a plan for each area of philanthropy. (See Table 3.)

Individual philanthropy involves volunteering and giving to charitable causes out of your cash flow. It is helpful to think through what you want to accomplish with your individual philanthropy, and compare it with the objectives of your spouse if applicable. The priorities for giving in the area of individual philanthropy falls into three categories, as mentioned earlier. The first is giving to the community out of your checkbook, which is the giving to support friends and good works in the community that tug at your heart. The second category is giving to schools, religious establishments, and other institutions that were formative in supporting you along your path to success. The third category of philanthropy is giving to a cause you are passionate about. Any plan related to individual philanthropy involves budgeting time in the form of volunteerism, and money in the form of charitable giving, toward these three categories on an annual basis.

Family philanthropy, especially where there is a family foundation involved, requires a collective family mission statement or guiding principles. Ideally there is a buy-in from family members to a common set of philanthropic objectives that drive the charitable work of the family. In addition, family philanthropy has two missions and sets of priorities: The first is to positively support family education, communications, and trust. A family foundation, when run as a democratic organization, allows parents, children, and professionals to communicate as peers. It allows multiple generations to learn together and to build trust. A family philanthropy mission statement should include objectives for educating children and passing along philanthropic values.

The second mission of a family foundation is to make a social impact by supporting charities and philanthropic strategies in a leveraged and strategic manner. Effective family foundations are clear about the issue area they would like to impact, and the strategies they hope to support within that issue. For example, there could be the desire to support a sustainable environment, and within that issue area to promote alternative energies by investing in new environmental leaders, or in alternative energy education, or in new alternative energy technologies. Any family mission statement should include both internal and external goals, as well as the issue areas and strategies to achieve those goals.

The last philanthropic area relates to corporate philanthropy. Many individuals are leaders of family businesses or companies. They must consider not only their individual and family philanthropy, but their corporate philanthropy as well. Corporate philanthropy has very different objectives than the other two types of philanthropy. The primary mission is to support the company's strategy and stakeholders. For corporate philanthropy, or corporate social responsibility (CSR) as it is called, to be effective it must be sponsored by the company's leadership and incorporated into the company's strategy. It should support the goals of the employees, and bind the employees to the company. In addition, it should help bind the company to its customers and supply chain partners as well. If done thoughtfully, CSR can support both the strategy of the company and the financial goals of the shareholders as well.

The benefits of CSR are being recognized by an increasing number of mainstream companies today. CSR is core to the strategy of Starbucks, for instance, and is a reflection of the values of its founder, Howard Schultz. Starbucks implements its CSR programs with business professionalism. It develops CSR objectives and programs and tracks results. It employs 20 people to implement its programs, and CSR is on the Starbucks organization chart. In addition, every year Starbucks publishes the results of its CSR initiatives in a 75-page CSR report. Other companies such as The Body Shop and Levi Strauss treat CSR as part of their corporate strategy as well. They tie their suppliers to the company with trade not aid projects, and their customers to the company with community volunteer programs. Today, whether it is the green movement in real estate, living wage practices for employees, or sustainable practices with suppliers, companies and their customers are recognizing the need for CSR programs.

As part of developing their individual, family, and corporate philanthropy mission statements, leaders should include other key stakeholders. People should develop an individual philanthropy mission with their spouses if applicable, a family philanthropy mission with family members who are on the board, and a corporate philanthropy mission with the leadership team. The buy-in of stakeholders is important for success. Family members must feel they have a say if the internal goals for the family are to be achieved. Executives in a company, and oftentimes the employees, need to have a say in the development of the mission as well if they are expected to carry out the CSR program objectives in an effective manner.

Any philanthropic mission statement or plan should also have objectives and targets for giving, which outline where and how much to give. Often it is helpful to evaluate one's current giving patterns as part of this process, especially for individual philanthropy. For instance, people should evaluate how much they are currently giving to charities and friends in the community, to schools and other formative charities, and to their cause areas. With a planned approach, they should also determine how much they would like to be giving in each area, and what percentage of their annual cash flow they want to target for individual philanthropy. With their philanthropic mission established, they can revisit their giving and determine whether their philanthropic dollars are going where they want them to go. If there is a gap between their goals for giving and what they are currently giving, then they can take the opportunity to adjust.

Take the time to outline your philanthropic mission in the areas of individual, family, and corporate philanthropy. Identify the key stakeholders in each area and involve them in the process. Develop specific giving objectives and targets, as well as your focus areas. Use an outside facilitator if it makes sense for you, your family, or your company. Use the individual, family, or company philanthropic mission statement to guide your philanthropic activities. Revisit it regularly, especially when new individuals or generations are involved. Identify a few concrete steps that will lead you closer to your ideal philanthropic goals.

Discovering Your Passionate Cause

When it comes to identifying a charitable cause to invest in with your time and money, it is not always easy to select one that ignites your passion. If there is any one thing that came out clearly from speaking with legacy leaders and philanthropic advisers, it is that often philanthropy is a random event that is initiated by others rather than being thoughtfully identified by an individual in a proactive manner. In other words philanthropy is often not close to home.

So how does one develop a plan that connects with some cause or area of passion? The answer is that people need to connect from the heart. If the connection from the heart does not exist, then researching the terrain needs to be part of your philanthropic plan. You need to go visit an orphanage in Africa if global poverty is your issue. You need to make the connection with an AIDS or cancer treatment center if healthcare appears to have an appeal. You need to explore where your business expertise lies and how you might apply it to a cause, adding the value gained from your years of experience. Or, you need to take the hobbies you love and determine how they might be utilized for philanthropic ends. For instance, you may not know that the PGA tour, which is the organization that supports professional golf, has raised over $970 million for charity since 1938. This is just one example of turning a hobby into philanthropy.

For someone to be truly passionate about something philanthropically, it needs to be close to home. Ask yourself this question: Is there *one* cause or organization that I would like to support over a long period of time, knowing that if I made a significant impact on that organization with my time and money, I would feel personally fulfilled? If you answer yes, then you are able to focus your resources for the advancement of that cause or institution. If you answer no, then you have work to do researching the terrain and identifying an organization for which you can have passion.

Page Snow is a consultant at Foundation Source, an organization that provides software for foundations. She advises families on their philanthropy. Ms. Snow relayed a story to me about a person in the boating industry that illustrates how people often connect with an area of passion. "When this particular person made his money," says Ms. Snow, "he started giving to lots of local causes and local nonprofits, his kids' schools, and other similar charities. This person was going to give a big gift to his child's school where there was a naming opportunity, but the donor really did not have a passion around this cause." As Page Snow recounts, she helped to guide him into an area where he had knowledge, which was closer to home in the fishing industry, and where he had passion.

"I said, well, you made your money boating," recalls Ms. Snow. "Are you interested in oceans or anything like that? And the donor's eyes lit up, and he starts talking about his background and what's happened to fishing, boating, and oceans. Well, he is in a position to bring together recreational fishermen with environmentalists, which are two sort of strange bedfellows, who have not necessarily gotten together. Because he transcends both sides of the issue, he is able to act in the role of convener, bringing together groups that he was uniquely suited to do."

Take the time to identify one cause or organization that you feel passionate about as your long-term cause. If you cannot easily identify a passionate cause, take the time to research an issue area you are interested in. Find out who the players are and what creative philanthropic options are currently being pursued. Identify one organization close to home where you can apply your learned and innate skills to make a difference in the world.

Leveraging Practices

Packing more than your wallet and keys is about how individuals leverage their assets for social impact. People can leverage their money, their personal networks, their companies, their foundations, and their celebrity. The idea of leveraging dates back to the early philanthropists, where for them matching grants was a form of leveraging. Today, matching grants are in many ways table stakes for philanthropy. They require that nonprofits raise money from other donors in order to receive an equal (matching) amount promised by the original donor. It is also an incentive for other donors to give, because they know that when they do give, they will be actually providing two dollars for every one dollar committed.

People can leverage their companies in certain circumstances for the good of society and positively affect customers, employees, and suppliers. Anita Roddick did this with her employees who in 50 countries took on community projects, and she paid employees to volunteer in the local community. This allowed the retailer to connect with her customers and with the community in a deeper way, which was good for business. Individuals can leverage their networks and celebrity as well. Bono, for instance, had a large network to begin with, which was made larger by his celebrity. Jeff Skoll is funding new philanthropic leaders and allowing them to access his network, which in turn is helping them to expand their networks. Bob Geldof and Bono tapped their music networks and recruited others to make a significant philanthropic impact.

Take inventory of the assets you have in addition to your financial assets. Determine how those assets might be used to support a cause you care about. What kind of personal or business network do you have, and how might you bring it to bear on a social issue? How might you engage your company's employees, suppliers, customers, and other assets to impact the community in a way that is consistent with your company's strategy? How might you engage your family and their expertise to benefit society and your family as well? These are the questions the answers to which can lead to leveraging your time and resources.

Convening and Pooling Practices

Almost everything in philanthropy exists in some sphere of networks and/or relationships. This is especially true in the nonprofit sector. When people declare an interest in a certain area, there is an expansive network they are tapping into knowingly or unknowingly. Les Wexner reached out to a Jewish network instead of acting on his own when he stood up for Debra Lipstadt. Michael Milken brought together the stakeholders in prostate cancer to maximize his impact. Paul Brainerd focused on pooling donors around philanthropic education with Social Venture Partners.

The top foundations take the time to research the landscape of the issue area they are investing in first so that they understand fully the networks they are affecting. Progressive foundations are proactively convening stakeholders. They are bringing like-minded people together in donor collaboratives to get educated about an issue area and to invest charitable dollars with a strategic approach. They are creating forums to bring government policy makers together with nongovernmental organizations, other foundations, and for-profit companies, in order to attack an issue area from multiple directions with a portfolio approach. They are pooling their financial assets with professional money managers such as The Common Fund, a $56 billion investment fund, to grow their charitable dollars with a professional approach. More than ever there is a need to act with others in a strategic way to truly combat some of society's largest issues.

Any philanthropic plan should take into account pooling and convening. Consider the first dollars you spend in philanthropy to be research dollars so you can fully scope out an issue area and understand the existing stakeholders For instance, as Milken did in the area of prostate cancer, identify the key academic thought leaders, nonprofit leaders, companies that are commercializing technologies, drugs, or treatments, and government stakeholders, as well as other foundations and major donors. This research will be extremely helpful in determining the linkages that exist or could be facilitated within an issue area. You can fund a study in the area you are interested in or join an existing collaborative. You can tap into the knowledge base of your local foundations that provide information on groups within a community. Once you understand the issue area and stakeholders, you are in a better position to identify where you might like to get involved and how your involvement relates to other players in the field. Attempt to identify or create a pooled charitable investment vehicle that will take a long-term strategic approach to grant making. Determine how you can get involved with organizations and initiatives that help convene issue area stakeholders including policy makers, nonprofits, for-profits, donors, and others.

KEY SECTION OBSERVATIONS

SOCIAL IMPACT PRACTICES

- Legacy leaders learn to make an external impact on society with their leadership skills once they become truly focused on the cause they care about. Often the cause relates to something close to home such as an illness in the family or a social issue that affects the industry in which an individual has been involved.
- The external process of creating social impact requires active leadership. Legacy leaders apply their learned and innate business skills to philanthropic endeavors, adapting their leadership to philanthropy.
- Legacy leaders pack more than their wallet and keys by leveraging their broad set of assets. They leverage more than just money. They leverage their companies, their networks, their celebrity, and other assets.
- Acting with others is about understanding the relationship between various stakeholders that affect a social cause and then implementing the practices of convening and pooling to strengthen that network.
- There are three types of philanthropy that individuals may be involved with: individual, family, and corporate philanthropy. A philanthropic mission and plan should be developed in each area in conjunction with the key stakeholders who are involved in those areas.

GENERATIONAL FAMILY PRACTICES

How do I raise confident, motivated children and create an environment of openness, trust, and harmony within my family, preserving family values and enterprises now and for future generations?

THE ESSENTIAL GENERATIONAL FAMILY QUESTION

In 1997, William T. O'Hara, then president emeritus of Bryant College and the founder and executive director of the Institute for Family Enterprise at Bryant, decided to take on a project, to study the oldest family businesses in the world. His search may appear to an outside observer to be something like a modern-day version of the DaVinci code.

His research uncovered two ancient societies in Europe that require members to be from family businesses for at least 200 to 300 years. They were Paris-based Les Henokiens, and U.K.-based Tercentenarians. After stumbling upon these associations, he began to understand their membership, and they began to understand his intentions. Over time a trust developed, and Mr. O'Hara was allowed to interview the descendants of these ancient family businesses, in some ways opening the vaults of deeply private families and their business and family practices. One thing led to another, and what Mr. O'Hara found, among many findings, was one of the oldest, continuous family businesses in the world, Kongo Gumi.

Kongo Gumi was founded when Prince Shotoku, the second son of an emperor commissioned a Buddhist temple called Shitennoji. He selected a Korean builder named Kongo in 578, according to family records. The project took 15 years to complete.[1] With this as the beginning, the family was responsible for building or restoring one imperial project after another, quickly becoming the builders of many of Japan's religious and political structures. Over the centuries, nearly 1,300 years, the family business endured many changes of government, wars, fires, and storms. It contributed to the creation of the historical skyline of Japan with its temples, shrines, and castles.

Kongo Gumi is now in its 39th generation, and it is going through another business transfer to the 40th generation. With such an enduring family business, the guiding principles are quite simple:

- *Always use common sense.*
- *Do not drink too much, use obscene words, or harbor vicious will towards others.*
- *Master reading and calculating with the abacus, and practice [your craft] all the time.*
- *Give each task your full attention.*
- *Don't diversify. Concentrate on your core business.*
- *Be well mannered and humble, and respect status.*

- *Respect others and listen to what they have to say, but don't be overly influenced by their words.*
- *Treat employees with a warm heart and kind words. Make them feel comfortable and work with them heart-to-heart, but create an atmosphere that reinforces your role as the boss.*
- *Once you accept a job, do not fight with other people about it— especially clients.*[2]

Generational family alignment is about preparing others to take the wheel—modeling values and mentoring children so that they are prepared for life and wealth. It is also about building lines of communications and bridges between family members, as well as pulling together a brain trust of advisers to support the family across the generations.

1. *Preparing others to take the wheel.* For family enterprises to be successful through multiple generations and for children to be successful with money, there is a real need to prepare heirs. Even if family enterprises are taken out of the picture, there is still the need to provide children with the values that will help support them throughout their lives. This involves modeling the values you want your children to live by and mentoring them in a number of different areas.

2. *Constructing family communication lines and bridges.* A key to making things last in families through the generations, and for creating family harmony, relates to continuity, communication, and governance systems within families. Communication within families involves the issues of wealth, succession, philanthropy, and values, which are often difficult to discuss. However, families who have survived the generations intact have found formal and informal ways to communicate, to gov-

ern family enterprises, and to ensure continuity. They create a family identity that bonds generations of family members together.

3. *Building a brain trust.* The wishes of parents for children are often carried out by a number of different professionals and family members filling specific roles related to the family. They may be trustees, estate planners, accountants, investment advisers, insurance professionals, or others. They all participate in a piece of the picture related to families, but rarely do they work together to support families. Building a brain trust of advisers that is coordinated to help a family grow its human, financial, intellectual, and social capital across generations is another key success area related to generational family alignment.

In this section we discuss these three best practices, as well as the tools from the industry to make money a positive force within families.

CHAPTER 17

PRACTICE 6: PREPARING OTHERS TO TAKE THE WHEEL

To put the world in order, we must first put the nation in order; to put the nation in order, we must put the family in order; to put the family in order, we must cultivate our personal life; and to cultivate our personal life, we must first set our hearts right.

CONFUCIUS

The stories come freely from great leaders about defining moments in their lives where values were forged from parents. The stories are supercharged with emotion. It is as if the leaders, many of whom are in their sixties and beyond, are reliving memories that happened yesterday and that are core to their existence.

Take for instance this story which Mario Morino described to me about the impact his mother and older brother had on his values.

"My mother cared for other people, and our house was like Grand Central Station. My cousin was out of work in Pittsburgh and moved in with us for two months. You grow up in that very tight ethnic orientation, and I hate to say it, but if someone was building a garage, everybody would just show up. It was work ethic. To me things like volunteering and public service are absolutely ingrained as part of my life.

"In terms of my values, I remember a story about my older brother when I was about 10 years old that I will never forget. We were driving in an area of Cleveland, typical blue-collar world, and it was late at night. A person hit a pedestrian walking across the street from us, a pedestrian that today we would call a street person. In those days others referred to them as bums. I remember my brother doing an immediate U-turn. The driver of the car was getting back in his car and driving off. My brother stopped him, and the guy says he's only a bum, what are you worried about? I remember my brother telling the guy, that the person he hit is a human being, and I will never ever forgot that moment."[1]

A young Les Wexner has similar stories of values learned from parents:

"In terms of shaping my views, my dad did so mostly by just doing the right thing and being honest and being respectful. I remember once we were in a Woolworth; he was having a cup of coffee. Somebody was bitching at the waitress, and I was wide-eyed. I was probably 12 or 13 years old. I'd never heard anybody tear into somebody. My dad didn't say anything, but things quieted down, and he said you know that's really not fair. People ought to pick on somebody their own size. The waitress just had to stand there and take it because she needed the job. Because she was a waitress, somebody felt they could abuse her. It was simply values about being fair and being honest."

Wexner continued, "I also remember one winter, it was Christmas Eve, and my father closed his store late. We were driving home in a hell of a snowstorm. I wasn't old enough to drive. We got about halfway home, and my dad was saying, 'Your mom is going to be worried the roads are so bad.' The next minute I hear him say, 'Oh my God.' 'What happened Dad?' He said, 'I forgot to give the maintenance man his Christmas present.' He said, 'It's his Christmas, and people should get their Christmas presents on time.' So he turned around, drove 30 minutes the other way and went to the guy's house, and gave him an envelope with $5 dollars or something. It was that kind of ethical behavior that made a real impact on me."[2]

Many of the legacy leaders we spoke with discussed the values they learned from their parents and how the stories translated into life lessons for them. In almost all cases their parents modeled the way with their actions and words. There was a consistency between what their parents or relatives said and what they did that was truly genuine for these leaders as children. As they grew up to be legacy leaders themselves, they translated the lessons learned from their families into values that guided their own lives and actions. It is through stories that they communicate their values, and it is through actively and consistently walking the walk that legacy leaders earn credibility and respect.

Great leaders in business are effective at not only making things happen themselves, but they also build the capabilities of others. Over time they move from doers to mentors, changing from the entrepreneurial leader out in front to the mentor of others. So in a real way they pass values down from parent to child to others. This is what defines the legacy leadership practice of preparing others to take the wheel.

When a person moves from a doer to a mentor, preparing others to take the wheel, there is an investment being made in the learning and growth of others. It is no longer just about themselves as leaders and competitors in the marketplace of life. Legacy leaders find ways to facilitate the discovery of goals and objectives of their family members as well as to mentor them to achieve the goals they choose.

People are born with their own individual wiring at birth, say psychologists, and they develop their own set of interests. The objective of parents is to help their children uncover their own purpose in life and to then support their purpose. For no matter how much one wants his or her child to be the next generation doctor or lawyer, or family business head for that matter, it may not be the path for that child. When it comes to children, the preparation is psychological, financial, and philanthropic, writes Charles Collier of Harvard University, the author of *Wealth in Families*.

Psychological Mentoring

Legacy leaders often check their personal agendas for their children at the door. Charles Collier calls this "managing oneself." They help their heirs find an appropriate role, whether in the family business or outside, and assist them with the pursuit of their objectives. There is an understanding in this that the skills and interests of children likely differ from the skills and interests of parents. Psychological parenting is about building an emotional platform for children so that they can confidently pursue their own purpose in life and their own passions.

In 1992, Barbara Blouin, Katherine Gibson, and Margaret Kiersted, heirs who share an interest in the emotional consequences of inherited wealth, started an organization called the Inheritance Project. Their objective was to explore the emotional and social impact of inherited wealth. In their publication, *Coming into Money: Preparing Your Children for an Inheritance*, they recommend that parents consider a number of key activities to support the emotional platform for their children:

- *Learn to recognize, and avoid, enabling your children.*
- *Show your children that you love them by spending plenty of time with them.*
- *Don't try to protect your children from the rawness of life.*
- *Encourage your children to develop the competence and confidence that come from learning how to do things for themselves.*
- *Start teaching the value of work early: Give your children chores.*
- *When teaching your children, always strive for balance.*
- *The best way to teach healthy values is to model them for your children.*
- *Help your children learn how to handle money responsibly.*
- *Speak honestly: Talk about money with your children.*
- *When you talk about money, be positive. Avoid negative messages.*
- *Tell your children about the good things your family's wealth has accomplished.*
- *Teach your children to share their wealth—and start early.*[3]

Psychological parenting is the domain of psychologists, and they teach a number of lessons. First is modeling. We discussed this before, but it is worth repeating. Children will model the values that their parents display more than what their parents say.

Second is to spend time with your children. There is no substitute for time, although making your time as high quality as possible is important. Third is to support your children to develop their own competence, to support themselves in the world, and to learn the lesson of failure and resilience. Last is to communicate in a way that builds self-esteem. These are the lessons of psychological mentoring.

Financial Mentoring

One common concern of all parents of means is that they don't want to ruin the motivation of their children. They don't want to simply give their children an inheritance and destroy the opportunity and joy that comes with personal achievement. Lee Hausner, author of *Children of Paradise*, says that the key here is to make the connection between work and money, and to understand the basics of managing one's financial life.

Financial parenting can begin with children as young as ages 6 to 12 with an allowance and the responsibilities that come with maybe opening a savings account at a bank. In the teen years experts feel it is important for children to work and to receive a paycheck. With that paycheck they need to begin to budget for the payment of certain items. Some recommend teaching investment skills by following a stock so a child can begin to understand how investments work.

In the college years, it becomes more and more important for the now young adults to learn budgeting skills and what it means to live within a certain financial budget. The more a child takes responsibility for budgeting, the more there is a learning opportunity for that child. In some families, financial parenting extends to making a pool of capital available for entrepreneurial ventures that encourage children to pursue their own business interests.

With regards to budgeting, take for example Mark Leslie, the founder of Veritas, a highly successful Silicon Valley software company. Mark grew in the job as founder and CEO of Veritas to develop a unique leadership style that he then applied to his family. Through his leadership, Mark and his wife helped prepare their children to live a life with wealth and philanthropy.

"My wife was a full-time mother, and very devoted, very committed. Both of us were responsible for transferring values related to money. I probably was more strenuous about financial values than she was, and I always insisted that they have a metered allowance that was the same every week. When they were little, I said if you put a dollar in the bank, I'll put a dollar in the bank with you. They always had jobs after school, and they lived in a community where a lot of the peers they had didn't have jobs. We said look, this is how much you're getting, and if you want more, you go to work. If you don't want more that's fine.

"When my first son went to college, I said to him you're about to go to school, and I'd like you to go figure out how much this is going to cost you for this year, tuition, room, board, whatever, all the expenses are your own. I'm going to write you a check on day one for the total amount, and you're going to go manage that money, and I'll see you next year. I knew there might be a little bit of learning along the way, but I had no concern that they would go down to the race track and put it on a horse and that they'd be standing there without tuition. That never entered my mind. I thought it would be a good experience for them. When I would tell our peers, our friends who had children exactly the same age, what we were doing, they would look at us like we'd lost our minds. They had their children on little credit cards. They were sending them money every month. They'd pay the tuition themselves, and they were controlling everything and making sure that the children didn't err.

"My second son, during his first year away at college, came to me about three or four months before the end of the year and said, 'I need about $500 more.' I said, 'Well, that's fine; I have no problem with doing that. What I need you to do is to figure out what you're original budget was, what's over, by how much, what you did not consider, and you need to come back and show me all that stuff, and show me why you're $500 short.'

"He was just furious at me. He wouldn't even speak to me for three weeks. 'Like, what do you mean; don't you trust me?' I said, 'No, no, that's what you've got to do.' So he did it very reluctantly, with anger, and he came in and showed me all this stuff, and I wrote him a check. Six months later he's sitting there telling me, 'Dad you wouldn't believe it. These kids, they have no idea what the fees are in this place, what tuition is, nobody knows. It's like they're clueless, they have no idea what anything costs.' I said, 'Well, that's the way it is sometimes.'

"I was very strong on creating financial values in the children, and they were very comfortable. They never felt deprived, they never felt like we held anything back, they never felt unloved, they never felt that we were doing something bad to them; they just thought it was fine. They just thought it was normal." [4]

Financial mentoring is about preparing children with the skills needed to support themselves financially. These skills include budgeting, saving, investing, managing credit in all its forms, and other similar skills. Financial proficiency helps to build psychological esteem, and as a result these two types of mentoring are linked.

Philanthropic Mentoring

A third way of preparing others to take the wheel is through philanthropic mentoring. "The first responsibility of parents is to raise charitable, community-minded, socially responsible children," says Ginny Esposito, president of the National Center for Family Philanthropy. "So you create opportunities for children at appropriate ages to learn, to experience, to participate in their community, and to develop interests of their own. Secondly you encourage personal accomplishment in your children because one of the most painful things in any foundation is to see a child, or a young adult, or even an older adult who has to turn to the family's name, the family's wealth, the family's philanthropy for a sense of self-esteem.

"If a person comes to the family philanthropy accomplished in their own right, their own education has been respected, their own career has been respected, their own family, their own interests, their own volunteering, they are more likely to be able to participate in a healthy, open way rather than an unhealthy way because they cling too much to the foundation for their own sense of purpose and identity. So personal accomplishment, raising charitable children, these are fundamental to parents. They become more fundamental to the parents of children that are going to have unusual gifts and assets."[5]

Mentoring of philanthropic values can start early as well by empowering children to give, even if it involves small amounts of money. The active part of philanthropy is very powerful. Having a child actually hand over money to a person, say, raising funds for the Salvation Army or personally delivering a gift to a disadvantaged person has a great impact. The conversations around philanthropy can be equally valuable. And just as with financial parenting, the sooner one can give children responsibility for raising and donating money themselves, the sooner the lessons are learned in a personal way.

Doug Mellinger is a technology entrepreneur. He is currently vice chairman of Foundation Source, the software company he founded to help make charitable giving through foundations easier. He is a thought leader on the subject of children, families, and philanthropy. He discussed his process of parenting his children philanthropically.

"I've always wanted to have philanthropy as a key element in my children's lives because it was a big part of my life since my first fund-raiser at age 10. I figured that I even started too late, that philanthropy was one of the greatest education life experience and family building tools, and I wanted to start my kids talking about it and acting at four and five and six years old. And so my kids are now ten, eight, and three and a half, and I've been doing that since they were very, very young and will continue to do so.

"The first thing, since the kids were about three or four, we got them involved with all of our charitable activities. Each year we do the simple things like cook for this one children's home for troubled youth where they can go and live for awhile to get out of a troubled household. And my family, including the kids, cook the meal and bring the food as a gift to the family. Just the experience of delivering it during the Christmas period together as a family gave us the opportunity to discuss with the children what others don't have.

"I went with both my daughters to the supermarket during the holiday season. I gave my kids a couple of coins to give to the guy who was ringing the bell for the Salvation Army. They gave the money to him, and as we walked into the supermarket my older daughter asked me: 'What's he going to do with that money?' And it was fascinating to me that a child of just about seven would actually start connecting the action of giving with wanting to know what the outcome of that gift would be.

"When it comes to the foundation, what I've done is to give my children grant certificates through Foundation Source. It's one of the things I built, and I built it so I could give them $25 and $50 electronic certificates that allow them to go into our database of 750,000 charities and pick a charity or two that they want that money to be given to. And I use the opportunity to sit at the computer with them, but let them press the buttons, so that they can explore the database with me and talk about what they care about, what they want to give the money to, and why the organization that they ultimately chose is the one that they chose."[6]

Anita Roddick, who is mentioned earlier as the founder of The Body Shop, has two daughters. She talks about wanting them to be good citizens who look out for the weak and the frail. She discussed her insights about teaching her children values and preparing them for life:

"Here is what I am teaching my children. Number one is the sense of family, and the sense of community, whether it's a geographic community you live in, or the community of your friends, or, for my children, the community of The Body Shop.

"Number two is travel. Travel is like a university without walls. And children will see, the minute they travel, that the biggest disaster facing anybody is poverty.

"Number three is to have them advised by and working alongside good people.

"Number four is ritual. Ritual is really important with young kids, and so we ritualized a lot of things. We ritualized the food, we ritualized the garden. There's a ritual place for the kids—a little storytelling step. And we taught them very early about the morality of storytelling. Storytelling in our life is about what is good and what is bad, what is right and what is wrong.

"Next is communications. A central tool of leadership, either in the business or in a family, is communications, because if you can't communicate effectively you are invisible. And, you tend to forget to communicate to a family because they're like the wallpaper. But it is critically important."[7]

In summary, as is so eloquently described by Doug Mellinger and Anita Roddick, preparing others to take the wheel is about the leadership practices of psychological mentoring to build self-esteem in children, financial mentoring to prepare children to support themselves, and philanthropic mentoring so children grow to be productive members of society. Legacy leaders apply these practices in their own way. They start early. They seek to help their children identify their own areas of passion and then support them on their own journeys.

CHAPTER 18

PRACTICE 7: CONSTRUCTING FAMILY COMMUNICATION LINES AND BRIDGES

The bond that links your true family is not one of blood, but of respect and joy in each other's life. Rarely do members of one family grow up under the same roof.

RICHARD BACH

From Japan, where the Hoshi Ryokan has stood as a family inn since the year 718 to the Antinori family from Italy who has run a winery starting in the fourteenth century to the Molson family in Canada who has run a brewery since 1786, family businesses face similar challenges and opportunities all over the free world. These families and their family businesses have survived for many generations. "Family unity" and "a commitment to continue the family legacy" are two of the most prevalent and enduring traits of families who have survived the generations intact, writes William O'Hara.[1]

Today, the family business is just one manifestation of the family enterprise, which many families hope will endure. There are at least three general types of family enterprises that exist within families: (1) the family business or collectively managed family wealth if the business is sold, (2) the family foundation or charitable giving vehicle, and (3) the family unit itself.

Family Wealth or Business

A family's wealth, either as it exists in the family business or as a common investment pool if the business is sold, is one family enterprise. It might not be immediately evident, but family wealth created through the sale of a business and that supports the family can be invested as a common pool of funds. For instance, let's assume a family owns a plumbing supply business, and different members of the family own shares in that family business. When that business is sold, each family member has cash to do with as he or she wishes. Certain families opt to combine the money that is created and invest it together so they can access the best money managers and investments possible. As a result, wealth itself can act as a family enterprise. Whether a family has an operating business or an investment business with pooled family money, these family enterprises take a great deal of effort to succeed over time.

Protecting the family wealth is the first task of sustaining multigenerational families. As the generations grow, the assets must grow proportionally if they are to support an increasing number of family members. Whether to maintain the family business and involve family members or sell the business and invest the assets is one key decision families must make. For some it is important for family members to pass down operating control of the family business. This may have to do more with tradition than with other factors. For others, no family members are actively involved with the business operations, but instead they sit on the boards and provide strategic oversight. Still others have sold the original business, and now they are investing the assets as a pool of investments as mentioned earlier.

Any of these structures can work depending on the family and its dynamics and values. What seems most important for a family member who might participate in an operating role, on the board, or in an investment company is that this individual should have the bona fide qualifications to serve successfully in the position. It is quite uncomfortable when this is not the case. No family member wants to risk the family fortune as a result of a family member who lacks the skill or competence to fulfill his or her duties. It can create insecurities or, worse, a rift within the family. On the other hand, individuals at the start of their careers need to be placed in positions that give them the opportunity to grow.

Many families seek the best talent from the outside that they can find to help ensure that their investments are secure. They are diligent about posting positions along with the background requirements to fill them. The survival of the company and the successful growth of assets take precedence over the goals or objectives of any one individual in the family.

Ivan Lansberg, cofounder of Lansberg, Gersick & Associates in New Haven, Connecticut, is a thought leader on succession and continuity in family enterprises. In an article he published on continuity in family businesses, he points to 12 specific tasks required for successful continuity in family businesses:

1. Decide whether you want to continue family ownership.
2. Assess whether the family can withstand the stresses that continuity planning inevitably generates.
3. Get the owner-manager(s) to agree to actively manage the development of a continuity plan and the transition in leadership to the next generation.
4. Consult and actively involve other major stakeholders in the process.
5. Set up appropriate forums for reaching consensus on key issues.
6. Develop a clear vision for the future of the business that all key family members can enthusiastically share and that spell out the role each will play.
7. Choose a successor and other candidates for the future top management team, and plan a course of training for each.
8. Help the successor build authority both in the family and in the business.
9. Design an estate plan stating that specifics of ownership of the enterprise will eventually be distributed among members of the next generation.
10. Make sure that family members understand the rights and responsibilities that come with various roles they will assume.
11. Inform important stakeholders—customers, suppliers, creditors—about the firm's continuity plan.
12. Develop a contingency succession plan, just in case.[2]

These tasks seem straightforward on paper, but when it comes to gaining consensus and executing on them, it is quite difficult. There is little that prepares a family for continuity planning, and often little preparation made by family leaders. In fact, often the opposite is the case. Family wealth builders who have run the family business for years often find it difficult to give up control. Or if they want to give up control, there is no one natural successor. Or maybe there are a number of successors, and no clear way to decide who should fill what role.

It is precisely because of the complexity of continuity in family enterprises that outside consultants are often required and critical to success. Just as a company can go to arbitration if there is a dispute between two parties, at a minimum an outside expert within a family can provide an objective sounding board.

It is this area of continuity planning and communications within a family where trust can break down, which is the most common reason for the failure of wealth transfers.

Family Foundations

A family foundation can be another family enterprise if it truly is a collaborative charitable giving vehicle that includes a number of family members. For many the family foundation is just an extension of their checkbook. The foundation may be created for tax reasons or with a mission that gives the founder an excuse not to give to certain causes. When it is just an extension of personal giving, the foundation is not truly a family foundation, but an individual foundation.

A true family foundation involves multiple family members and has a democratic governance structure. There is a board of directors that often includes family and outside members, each member having an equal vote on decisions related to the foundation. There is a process as well in fully functioning family foundations to prevent the patriarch or matriarch from dominating. Often a pool of money is set aside so that certain family members can give to what they passionately care about. However, the majority of the assets of a true family foundation are given through a consensus process.

For well-functioning family foundations that operate in a collaborative manner, studies have found that they offer real potential benefits for improving family communications and dynamics. In a study of hundreds of multigenerational family foundations, Kelin Gersick found that a well-functioning family foundation, "Can heal a troubled family."[3] In part, well-functioning family foundations open up communications within a family. Children can collaborate with parents as peers. Together they can tackle problems in the outside world, learning and investing in charitable causes together.

Certain families convene generations around their foundation to discuss where and how to give back to their community, and in so doing support the family dynamics as well as the communities and causes they hope to serve. So in many ways a family foundation has two missions. One is to serve the community through philanthropic means. The other is to serve the family. Those family foundations that take their philanthropic missions most seriously are also the most successful in improving family dynamics.

Mark Leslie, who is mentioned earlier, spoke to me in an interview about the role of the family foundation in the life of his family. "My wife felt strongly that we should do philanthropy. My principal interest initially in philanthropy was as a mechanism that creates family magnetism. So we created a foundation to include my wife and myself, my two sons, and both of their wives. It is an opportunity to do good together which is kind of the way we think about it."

Leslie continues, "I spend a lot of time as a leader not as a manager, and I really want to have a shared ownership of that philanthropic activity. So we move at the pace of the organization rather than at the pace you could move at if you wanted to just make a lot of decisions. We've got a little grant committee, and they've been out figuring out how and where we should give."

The founders of family foundations who have been most successful in making their foundations work for the family and across generations utilize a leadership style of collaboration. For them it is about making the process work rather than controlling the process and the money. In addition, just as with family businesses, there is a need to prepare new generations for the responsibilities of sitting on the family foundation board, to learn the requirements of board governance and fiduciary responsibility, and to invest resources wisely. The likelihood of continuity among family foundations is highest, concludes Kelin Gersick in his study, when there is clarity of the mission, quality control of the philanthropic process, and grant-making vitality.[4]

Clarity of mission often involves generations of family members convening around the family foundation table to develop one common mission and focus for the family. This process brings out the individual values of each family member, and then attempts to find common ground between family members. One family foundation with which I am very familiar was granting to environmental causes because this was the interest of the patriarch. As the children became older and developed philanthropic interests of their own, their father suggested that the next generation should decide on one common area of interest. Because the patriarch was willing to give up control, the mission of the foundation changed to a focus on economic justice. The process created buy-in from all family members. There was quality control of the philanthropic process so that no one family member dominated. And the family moved forward together with a new grant-making vitality.

The Family Unit

Another family enterprise is the family unit itself. Take for example the Laird Norton family mentioned earlier in this book. Family members recognize the family as an institution, much as we might recognize the Rotary Club as an institution. For them keeping the family together as an entity is important as a goal in and of itself. They have taken the concepts that James Hughes outlines in his book, *Family Wealth, Keeping It in the Family*, about building human, intellectual, social, and financial capital, to its logical extreme.[5] In many ways they have had to put the systems in place for communication and governance the way any institution would. Although it seems cold and impassive, institutionalizing communications and governance within a family is often required when the numbers of generations and family members grow.

In an interview with Peter Evans of the Laird Norton family, it became evident how intricate and complex this family enterprise has become over the years. "The family enterprise today is a holding company. This month we have our 150th annual meeting. We currently have 23 members of the seventh generation who are owners, and all together I think 406 related family members who are owners in the company. Over our history we have owned, created, or invested in 43 companies.

"The organization as a whole has two foundations both of which at this date are fairly small. One foundation channels money back into the community where we first built our business, in a town in Minnesota, and the other one, which for many years channeled money into sustainable forestry and forestry education, has now just recently turned its focus to water quality issues."

Large, multigenerational families are much like institutions. The planning and processes required to keep them together, to ensure communications, to take on a new initiative, to divide the work and responsibility, and to govern the entity are massive undertakings. Yet, just as a foundation will not withstand the generations without good governance and communication systems, a multigenerational family faces the same needs Much like institutions, multigenerational families like the Laird Norton family find ways to communicate and strengthen their family community. Often this includes the creation of family reports, meetings, and even Web sites.

"One of the big things we did four years ago," said Peter Evans, "is to expand our annual report. It was capturing the financial stuff, but that is only one slice of the family. So we took it from a two-page bifold and made it a 24-page report."

Evans continued, "There are the traditional financial pieces in this report, which you would see in a traditional annual report. In addition, there is the social section that consolidates all of the philanthropic giving in the whole family. When you add it all up this is a really big number. Then we have a whole section on the human side. We track the number of babies that were born, and make those human things as valuable as the numbers. Our annual report has become a memory book of sorts.

"In addition, we've built an internal Web site that is a password protected Web site only available to family members. It has discussion boards, a whole archive of photographs, and all sorts of other information. . . . And we have a quarterly newsletter that is usually about 25 pages."

As this one family shows, governance and communication practices within large family dynasties can appear much like those of institutions. For instance, there may be a written family mission statement and values. There may be a system of joint decision-making (governance) as well that is equally well thought out. Peter Evans provides insights into the system of governance at the Laird Norton family.

"There is a holding company board of directors, which is composed today of eight family members and three outsiders. On that board we have two presidents. One is what we call the family president, and the other one is a business president. The business president oversees all of the investments in the businesses and sits on all the subsidiary boards. The family president is the chairman of the family council, which is a decision-making group, and it is formally a committee of the holding company board. The family council is made up of mostly family members, and a couple of outsiders. It deliberates on all of the family issues. The family council decides on everything from how we address needs for liquidity and what kind of programs we put in place to support our goals to educational programs for generations of family members, including the five-day annual meeting we hold each year."

Creating communications and governance structures and proactively putting in place a plan for succession and continuity are key tools for constructing family communication lines and bridges. They offer keys to making family wealth and values last.

CHAPTER 19

PRACTICE 8: BUILDING A BRAIN TRUST

If I have seen further than others, it is by standing upon the shoulders of giants.

ISAAC NEWTON

The 1998 movie *Pleasantville* depicts the perfect family in the perfect neighborhood where all the residents do what they are "supposed to do." The movie is shot in black and white because everyone conforms. The movie is based on TV shows from the 1950s and 1960s like *Father Knows Best*, *Leave It to Beaver*, *The Andy Griffith Show*, *Dennis the Menace*, and others. These shows were about all-American families in which the father went off to work, the mother stayed home and took care of the kids, and the children lived in a cohesive household. Life was good and simple back then, or so it seemed.

In *Pleasantville*, when Jennifer and David Wagner, sister and brother from the 1990s, are transported into Pleasantville, and back to the 1950s, life begins to change. The picture takes on color. Individual hopes and desires come to the forefront, and life becomes much more complicated.

Most families do not live in Pleasantville (although I grew up there, really). Individuals by and large are not conformists, and families are very complex. Families are made up of members each of whom has his or her own dreams, emotional makeup, and financial circumstances. The family members have family units of their own that include blood and nonblood relatives. Over time circumstances for the family as a whole, and individual family units and members, change. As their circumstances change, their relationships with other family members also change. This creates a complex and evolving system of family communications, expectations, and relationships. The norm in families is complexity and change.

Into this complex web of relationships, well-meaning patriarchs and matriarchs attempt to strengthen their families. Some hope to give their children a better life than they had, which often translates into providing the advantages of money and freedom that they did not have as children. Others hope to keep generations of families together and to enrich their families. Legacy leaders do this by building communication lines and bridges. Still others are focused more on the individual family members than on the family as a whole, attempting to support and mentor them through life.

For individuals to be successful in nourishing the myriad human, financial, psychological, and social needs of their individual family members and of their families overall, they often require the support of trusted advisers. Trust is the key ingredient when it comes to advisers. Outside advisers are brought into the family and come to know the family's secrets. They soon learn that everything is not *Pleasantville*. Outside experts play critical roles to support the family's current needs, as well as the desires of patriarchs and matriarchs after they are gone. These advisers are guardians of children, trustees of estates, managers of a family's wealth, and emotional support systems for families.

Building a brain trust is about assembling an advisory team that works with the family to record its history, nourish its values, support individual family members, and help the family achieve its collective goals. Most individuals of wealth are not effective at building advisory teams and must learn to be the collaborative leaders of their families, not managers or dictators. Most advisers want to control the relationship with the families they advise and must learn to work within a collaborative framework with other family advisers.

The Collaborative Family Leader

There are many types of family leaders just as there are many types of company leaders. There are charismatic leaders out in front and in the news, such as Steve Jobs of Apple Computer. There are visionary leaders such as Bill Gates, who saw the computer revolution coming and understood before others what would be needed by businesses and consumers. There are also leaders whose focus is on execution, and through their execution create an advantage, such as Michael Dell of Dell Computer. Dell built one of the leading computer businesses through superior execution, which led to high quality and relatively low costs. Family leaders, however, who create an enduring family legacy are more like the "Level 5 leaders" described by Jim Collins in his book, *Good to Great.*

"Level 5 leaders channel their ego needs away from themselves and into the larger goal of building a great company. It's not that Level 5 leaders have no ego or self-interest. Indeed, they are incredibly ambitious—but their ambition is first and foremost for the institution, not themselves."[1]

Mark Leslie, the CEO of Veritas in Silicon Valley, describes the type of collaborative leadership he uses with his family.

"What I subscribe to here is actually a leadership style that I evolved to as I got more sophisticated as a leader. I believe the more you trust people, the more trustworthy they become. The more power you give away, the more power you have. Those are principles that I exercised while I was running a big company. It's not about me. It's about the entity, and the mission, and people feeling a sense of personal accomplishment in the work they do. My job is to go help create the environment for that."

Legacy family leaders put the family first, want the family to endure, give up a measure of control, and help to foster collaboration among family members. Successful family leaders also move from being active doers and experts in the financial, social, and emotional aspects of family, to effectively supporting others. They become the CEO providing a common vision and set of values, and they enrich the family by incorporating outside experts into the family. A typical scenario of how family leaders move from active to collaborative leaders follows.

Family leaders often are doers. They sometimes get personally involved in investing their own money and even selecting money managers. When they turn to philanthropy, they can also get personally involved researching nonprofit groups themselves, talking with peers, and spending time figuring out where to give the money. Over time, they realize that they do not want to spend so much personal time on their finances. They don't want to spend so much time immersed in the day-to-day process of sorting out nonprofits and grants either. They may really enjoy the personal involvement, but it often takes time away from other priorities.

As a result, they begin to move away from the operating role to the CEO role. So they hire a financial adviser for their wealth, and manage the financial adviser. They find another person to manage their philanthropy as well. Some hire an outside director. Others "hire" a family member to serve in this role. They realize that by having a financial adviser or foundation director that they are not ceding control but are exponentially increasing their potential to make an impact with their time.

A good example of a person who moved from an operator to a collaborative leader is Paul Brainerd with his philanthropy and the management of his foundation. As Brainerd recounts in our interview, "One of the very key decisions I made early on was that I did not want to manage or run the foundation on a day-in and day-out basis. I wanted to hire people to do that who had more experience than I had in these particular issue areas. Instead, I would participate at the board level as a board member and set the direction in policy for the foundation along with others."

Brainerd continues, "It's being clear about a whole bunch of things: what your focus is going to be on the issues you want to work on; being clear about what your role is going to be, and about what impact you can have given your resources. I defined the focus of the foundation and the underlying values of how we would operate. I believed in hiring people who had experience running nonprofits as well because they know what it is like to be the recipient of a grant."

As Paul Brainerd demonstrated with the way he delegated the management of his philanthropy, managing family wealth and family philanthropy requires special domains of knowledge. Successful legacy builders draw upon advisers whom they can leverage in each specialized area of legacy leaving. Just as a leader would do in business, building a team of advisers and holding team members accountable is important when it comes to the broader context of wealth. Many are not effective at using advisers or creating a cohesive advisory team. Conversely, the wealth advisory industry has not found a way to collaborate with other advisers because of the hope of controlling the relationship with the client—although this is changing.

The Collaborative Adviser

Scott Fithian, now deceased, wrote a thoughtful book for wealth advisers on values-based estate planning. In his book he described the tendency for advisers to want to control the relationship with their clients and how important it is for advisers to work with other advisers in "virtual teams" with complementary skills that come together to solve specific issues for families.

"Generally, people have more than one professional adviser," writes Fithian. "Typically these advisers compete for the client's love and affection, each wanting to control the planning process. Each adviser likely has a different opinion of what the client is trying to accomplish. Not surprisingly, that opinion usually is based on the adviser's perspective, not necessarily the client's.

"In the virtual planning environment, advisers function as a team. They respect each other's ideas. They understand that they must reach consensus prior to presenting any idea to the client for consideration. . . . Virtual planning advisory teams are less permanent and less formal than typical teams of the past. They band together to meet a specific market opportunity—to solve a client's particular planning needs. . . . The very best advisers rely on other advisers. Each trusts that the unique abilities of the others will contribute toward the best possible outcome."[2]

Recently I was asked to participate in a meeting of a group of advisers to families of means to discuss the issue of collaboration. In the meeting was the head of a large trust and estate law firm, a partner in an accounting firm with a family office practice, a philanthropic adviser with a national practice, an executive at a large private bank, among others. The topic was how we could encourage others to work together for the collective good of our clients. The meeting itself was a recognition that the advisory industry is not adequately meeting the needs of its clients and that it requires a number of different areas of expertise and services.

Over the coming years, the advisory industry will grow exponentially. New advisory models will be created, and advisory firms will begin to provide services required by their clients in a more collaborative manner. Wealth advisory firms are already beginning to create boot camps and training programs for the children of their wealthy clients. They are starting to find creative ways to provide philanthropic and other services as well, but they have a long way to go.

A number of legacy leaders have themselves recognized the dearth of trained family, philanthropic, and collaborative wealth advisers and have founded organizations to institutionalize the lessons they have learned as well as attract and capture the brain trust that exists.

Take for instance John C. Whitehead, who grew up during the Great Depression in a middle-class family from New Jersey to become the CEO of Goldman Sachs, and then to head the 9/11 commission in New York City. He became very interested in the gap that exists in nonprofit management and how business executives become involved on the boards of nonprofit organizations. His solution was to create a lasting initiative at Harvard Business School to provide nonprofit leaders with business skills.

John Whitehead recounts, "What I found being chairman of 10 organizations ranging from the Harvard Board of Overseers to the National Gallery of Art in Washington, to Haverford College, which I had attended, to the Mellon Foundation, to the United Nations Association, is that nonprofits are almost always dominated by the chief executive, the chief staff person, who is a dedicated person, very committed to the cause of the organization, but also as a general rule knew very little about management or how to run the organization as an institution. I realized that if you're going to be a lawyer, there's a law school to go to; if you're going to be a businessman, there is a business school to go to; but if you're going to be a nonprofit leader, there's no place to go."

Whitehead continues, "So I helped establish a program at Harvard Business School for teaching young people at the business school, who instead of wanting to make a million dollars in the first year, might want to go into a nonprofit organization in a position of leadership. The influence that this school at Harvard has had on educating other younger people to go into nonprofit careers, not just those that went to Harvard but those that went elsewhere where there are similar kinds of courses now, maybe has as much lasting value as anything I have done."[3]

One other legacy leader who helped to fill an advisory gap for wealth holders is Peter Karoff. Peter had a career as a successful insurance executive and real estate investor in the Boston area and then turned his attention to founding a firm called The Philanthropic Initiative (TPI). TPI advises hundreds of wealthy people on their philanthropy. Peter discussed how TPI was founded to fill a gap in the advisory landscape. Its objective is to mentor those who wish to achieve joy and fulfillment through philanthropy. In addition, TPI helps families with their philanthropy and the creation of productive family foundations.

Said Karoff in our interview, "When Dr. King died, it was the seminal moment for me, and it was a very emotional time. From then on I always had this immense sense of wanting to give back, wanting to find a way to resolve issues of equity, issues of racism. TPI came out of this desire and a fascination that I'd had for years to understand why some people are generous and others are not; and why some companies do the right thing, and others don't. I came to the conclusion that there were few places around that were really providing straight objective advice to donors. TPI allowed me to find a way to mentor others as someone who has fairly strong relationship management skills, customer skills, marketing sense, and a fascination with social issues."

Peter Karoff continued, "At TPI we have a blueprint, and the blueprint is really built around the language of strategic philanthropy. When we started using certain terms 16 years ago, they were not common in the field. Now they're normative. They were common in the halls of the Ford Foundation, or Rockefeller, or somebody who thought that way, but for the average donor the notion of being thoughtful in this way was not really currency."

Recently I learned about an organization called Advisors In Philanthropy (AIP), whose mission is to integrate generational family and philanthropy practices with wealth practices. AIP was established because advisers wanted to learn from other advisers how to incorporate philanthropy into their advisory businesses. Some AIP members are advisers in the insurance business, but as part of selling insurance they have the opportunity to help individuals direct their estates to their children and and to philanthropy. Some are from the estate planning profession and have a similar philanthropic objective. Still others are private bankers or wealth advisers who, as part of providing financial advice, would like to help their clients with a broader set of objectives.

AIP is helping advisers learn legacy practices from each other and from experts in the field so they in turn can educate their clients. They are meeting without clients in the room so they can begin to have honest conversations about collaborative practices that will benefit their customers. They are learning as well that being a collaborative adviser, and taking a broader, legacy approach to their advisory practices, can help them start to build trust with their clients, and this in turn is good for their businesses.

Legacy leadership is about finding the appropriate knowledge experts and incorporating them into the family to enrich the financial, social, human, and intellectual capital of the family. When this is done well, it can have monumentally positive results. Legacy advisory services are becoming more prevalent in mainstream wealth advisory firms, as well as in specialized firms, and will continue to expand to fill the expanding requirements of individuals and families as the great wealth transfer approaches.

CHAPTER 20

BUILDING A PLAN FOR GENERATIONS

It's not enough to make time for your children. There are certain stages in their lives when you have to give them the time when they want it. You can't run your family like a company. It doesn't work.

ANDREW GROVE

The process of preparing generations for wealth, creating alignment within families, and sustaining a cohesive family requires a unique set of leadership skills. In particular it requires the ability to maximize the potential of each family member in the areas he or she selects, to make the family as an institution an ongoing enterprise by strengthening its collective knowledge and values, and to facilitate generational alignment by building communication and trust within the family.

Building a plan for generations is complex because it is so diverse. It deals with future generations of children and how to help them become motivated and successful. It addresses the family unit and how to create family harmony and open communications within the family. The third major area related to families concerns generational family enterprises, such as family businesses, foundations, and trusts, and how to build continuity from generation to generation within these family institutions. (See Table 4.)

Building a generational family plan is the domain of experts such as Lee Hausner, who came out of the Los Angeles school system as a counselor to then advise Goldman Sachs partners as well as their clients about creating motivated children, and Joline

	Children and future generations	Family unit	Generational family enterprises
Principles	Successful, motivated children	Family harmony and open communication	Successful generational family businesses, foundations, and trusts
Priorities	• Transferring and communicating values • Mentoring financial competence • Visioning their purpose	• Family history and mission • Family retreats and enrichment	• Succession planning • Governance planning and skills-based teams • Peer groups
Plan	Goals, actions, review	Goals, actions, review	Goals, actions, review

TABLE 4: *Generational Family Plan Elements*

Godfrey from Independent Means, which provides financial education programs to kids, parents, and mentors. It is the domain of individuals such as Charles Collier of Harvard University, Jay Hughes, an esteemed estate planner, and Roy Williams, a family consultant, who all work to strengthen and enrich the family. Finally, it is the domain of experts who work to make generational transfers of family businesses and foundations successful, such as Ivan Lansberg and Kelin Gersick who run Lansberg, Gersick & Associates, a consulting firm working with families on succession planning and continuity, and Ginny Esposito of the National Center for Family Philanthropy, who works with generations of families on family philanthropy and foundations. They and many others make up the broad field of family wealth advisers.

In this chapter we synthesize the information from these advisers and others in the field into a framework for thinking through the principles, priorities, and planning elements that are effective with children of wealth, family units, and generational family enterprises.

Raising Successful, Motivated Children

How do you raise motivated children when they know they will receive a trust fund? How do you infuse your children with the values and competencies that you feel are important for them to be successful in life? How do you give your children the financial skills to support themselves and to build the confidence of knowing that they can live on their own if need be without the financial support of their parents? How do you help your children vision their purpose so that they find their own area of passion to build a successful career of their choosing? Although there are many books written on parenting children with wealth, we focus here on three essential elements: (1) transferring and communicating values; (2) mentoring financial competency; and (3) helping children vision their purpose.

Transferring and Communicating Values

People often ask me to identify the most important action they can take to raise well-adjusted children, transfer constructive values to them, and not ruin their motivation. My answer is always the same—to model the values by which you want your children to live. Children are incredibly perceptive. They see what you do, even if it conflicts with what you say.

I am reminded of a conversation I had with an accountant who helps individuals run their family offices, manage their bills, and take the drudgery out of dealing with the complexity of multiple homes and obligations. She talked to me about one client who she said didn't feel her children were aware that they had wealth. Her response to her client was, "I think the fact that you own an island in the Caribbean and take your G5 to get there may be a give-away!" Children are usually much more aware than we realize.

It is little wonder that wealth dissipates between the third and fourth generations. The first generation is modeling the value of work and of risk taking. The conversations in those households usually center around being prudent with money, saving for college, making trade-offs, and budgeting. It is typically the third or fourth generation where these conversations happen less, and the connection between work and the value of money is lost.

Being clear about what you value, and acting according to your values, will be perceived by your children as your living value system. Think about what your actions say to your children about what you value. Talk to your children about the values you care about. Help them to understand how your work supports your lifestyle and how your philanthropy is a way to thank the community for supporting you. Be thoughtful about what you discuss around your dinner table or in front of your children. If your discussions are about valuing money and the things money can buy, what does it say to your children? Talk with your children about the role money plays in your life and in your family and what you plan to do with your money based on your values.

At one of many presentations I attended, I was introduced to Joline Godfrey who works with Independent Means. She advises children, parents and mentors on how to raise financially fit kids. She presented a chart to us that is designed to start the conversation between parents and children about values concerning money. It is a simple and powerful tool which I also believe can be expanded to discussions of values beyond money. The exercise goes like this: Individuals are asked to fill in a box expressing their own values with respect to money, such as earning (work), spending, saving, investing, and philanthropy (community). I might add to this list values concerning success (career), relationships (family, friends, other), personal values (integrity, honesty, hard work, etc.), and spirituality. Separately, spouses and children are asked to fill out the same list. The objective is then to discuss where and why various answers differ. Through an exercise such as this, individuals can learn about their children's values and open up a direct dialogue with them. It is the modeling of values, and the opportunities to create meaningful discussions about them, that hold one key to transferring values and raising motivated children.

Mentoring Financial Competency

Preparing others to take the wheel is in part about mentoring. Mentoring children with wealth requires creating competencies in a number of areas. One of the most important areas is financial mentoring, which helps children learn to support themselves independently of their parents. This in turn builds their self-esteem.

So what are the key financial skills that are required to be successful with money, and how proficient are your children with these skills? This was another question that was posed to Joline Godfrey of Independent Means. Again she had a simple and useful exercise for assessing your children's skills in various important financial skills areas.

The skill competencies she asked us to assess for our children were in the following areas: how to save; how to keep track of money; how to get paid what you are worth; how to spend wisely; how to talk about money; how to live within a budget; how to invest; how to exercise the entrepreneurial spirit; how to handle credit; and how to use money to change the world. She asked each of us to rate our children on a scale from 1 (clueless) to 5 (financially fit). Interestingly, she asked us to also rate these areas by age range with the range starting at 5 to 8 years of age and the oldest range being 16 to 18 years of age, although I am sure that mentoring financial competency does not stop at 18. This trademarked exercise and many others are part of Joline Godfrey's book called *Raising Financially Fit Kids*,[1] where she provides many other useful exercises to build financial competency in children.

Traditional education in schools often involves math but not budgeting, saving, or managing money. The tools to build financial competency outside the traditional classroom range from using allowance as a learning tool, to after-school classroom study of financial basics. Budgeting turns out to be one of the key skills for a child or an adult in learning to live within his or her means. It is important to identify opportunities for your children to budget. Early on you can have them budget their lunch money by giving them money for the week or month. You can use an allowance to teach them the importance of earning and savings, and to open an account at a bank so that they can learn about earning interest. You can work with them to buy some shares of a stock in order to teach them about investing.

For older children who may be receiving trust payments, incentives can be part of those payments as well. With an incentive trust, a wealth holder can provide a dollar to his or her child for every dollar earned and/or saved, for instance, or provide other incentives. Certain families make a pool of money available to loan to children to start businesses that may not be funded by financial institutions. In part, the money is considered education money.

As part of financial mentoring, creating an open dialogue about money, as well as a joint plan, is critically important. Take the time to discuss a financial competency plan with your children. For instance, if you offer them an allowance, have them come up with an amount that they think is fair and have them justify the amount to you. You will be amazed at their negotiation skills at a young age, and it will teach them to budget. Discuss with them what is appropriate at different ages. For instance, when they are of driving age, what can they expect when it comes to a car? Will you buy it for them? Should they pay for half or all of their first car? How will they come up with the money to pay for it if that is the choice? Contemplate how your choices communicate expectations to your children.

Next, determine what you are willing to give to your kids. Start with the basics such as food, shelter, education, and transportation. Maybe you want to pay for their education all along the way. As long as they are in school, you will foot the bill. Maybe you want to help them with a down payment on their first house. These are individual decisions that are best made explicit to your children. Then there is the issue of an inheritance and of trusts. Transferring money to children in any significant amount through trusts or other vehicles is not recommended until children are through their career-building years, say the experts.

Discussing expectations related to money and trusts with children is a difficult task, but it is recommended when children reach their twenties. Again the objective is to involve kids as much as possible in the discussion of trusts, how the decisions were made about inheritance, and one's values that were the foundation for those decisions. The important message is that along with money come obligations and expectations. These are the values that are imparted along with the money.

Mentoring children with wealth requires a plan. The plan will differ from family to family since all families have different values and priorities. The plan should be revisited regularly. It should be age-appropriate. The activities that make sense to kids at ages 6–12 are different from those in the teenage years, which are different again from the young adult years. It is important to start when kids are young and when values and personality are being formed. The plan should be developed with your children and communicated to them. It should be implemented consistently as well.

Take the time to assess the competency of your children in various financial areas by completing a skills assessment exercise.

Consider what activities this year you will put in place to teach financial skills to your children in the various categories of financial competency. Develop a financial education plan for your children at different ages by considering the age-appropriate options available. Determine the discussions that you want to have with your children concerning money. Make sure you and your significant other are on the same page. Communicate this together and involve your children in a two-way discussion.

Visioning Their Purpose

How do you help your children find their purpose?

Some children find their calling early. Their purpose is revealed, and their career path is set at a young age. Many more are trying to fulfill the dream of what they think their parents want them to achieve. For many this turns out not to be their own path. Just like adults who are visioning their own purpose, children of wealthy families have a great many choices, which is a blessing and a curse. So how do you enable your children to pursue their own path and find their own passion?

Let me state that I found little research in this area, just as I could not find research that would help adults with this objective. There are personality and skills tests that individuals can take to understand what general skills they possess and the professions for which they might be suited. There is no manual, however, for helping them find their calling. My theory in this area relates to my personal experience and transition. I found my calling in life in my late 40s. It seems as though I could have discovered it earlier.

As I mention in the introduction, I spent many years as an executive in high-tech companies before I lost my passion for this path. If I had been honest with myself and had listened to my instincts, I would have realized from the outset this was not my path. I was picking the most prestigious and growing profession I could think of when I graduated from school, just as I was attending the most prestigious universities. I was hoping to fulfill the desires of my parents, but I had not identified my own purpose.

When I left the high-tech industry, I began an internal search. I had always been interested in finance and social entrepreneurism, so I took a job at Bank of America and began to consult with some incredible social entrepreneurs. At Bank of America I started to look at best practices not only for investing, but for philanthropy. Outside of work, I was allowed to delve deep into the area of legacy. I liked certain things about the investment business and not others. What I liked was dealing with clients who were thinking through their philanthropy and who were on their own personal search as I had been.

The study that led to this book allowed me to research the terrain of legacy, and I found that business models of doing well and doing good were really exciting. (We discuss these in part III of the book). I began to consult with individuals and companies that had both a business and social mission. I began to interview anybody in this field who would talk to me. Some were in academia, some were founding social enterprises, and some were legacy leaders. My excitement grew. My research intensified. I began to write. I began to consult. I began to contemplate how to find my own way of doing well and doing good.

Others came to understand what I was doing, and they added to my knowledge base. A couple of ideas developed about what might be interesting social enterprises for me to launch. I started to wake up in the morning with total excitement. I began to pursue these business ideas with passion. I became an evangelist of sorts because I truly believed that I had found something that could help others.

My lessons in this area for children have similarities to those for adults and are discussed in the section on self-actualization: First, your task is to help your children find their purpose, not your purpose for them. To do this, you must expose them to various career opportunities early. For most people schools do not provide this exposure. Schools are designed to teach broad liberal arts skills through high school. So you must help kids intern in various professions with individuals you feel might be good mentors. This is much like helping them research the terrain.

Second, you must give them permission and enable them to develop their own route map. They need to know that they have the freedom to pursue their passion in whatever profession they choose and that you will support them. Along with their ability to choose their own career is the obligation to ensure that they understand the consequences of various career choices. They may want to work in the Peace Corps for instance, but they will not earn the same living as if they chose a different profession. They will be making a lifestyle choice as well as a career choice. With that understood, they may be perfectly happy to live more modestly in a vocation for which they have passion than to live with greater financial security in a vocation for which they do not have passion.

Third, once your children have identified an area they think would be fulfilling, your job is to advocate for them, mentor them as they hit the unavoidable bumps in the road, and ensure that the communication lines stay open. At this point it is their road that is being traveled, and you are just helping them with the journey.

Supporting children to be successful and motivated is complex. It involves transferring and communicating values. It involves helping them to develop financial competency to support themselves. In addition, it involves helping them to vision their own purpose and find a career that is fulfilling.

Creating Family Harmony

Now let's turn from supporting children with wealth to building a strong family unit. The lessons concerning the family unit and family harmony come from generational families who have made the broader family unit a priority and who are working to create a cohesive family across the generations. When it comes to strengthening the family, it is important to identify ways to capture the family's history, values, and ethos in a collaborative manner that opens up communications. There are a number of ways that this is done including: (1) collaboratively developing the family's mission; (2) convening family members and enriching the family with family retreats; (3) and sharing best practices with other, similar families.

Family History and Mission

Many families have found it helpful to create a shared mission statement for their family to begin the process of bringing the family together around a set of values. As one strolls through the heart of New York City and comes to the famous skating rink at Rockefeller Center, that person will come upon a plaque that has preserved the values for which John D. Rockefeller stood. The plaque is inscribed as follows:

I believe in the supreme will of the individual and in his right to life, liberty and the pursuit of happiness. I believe that every right implies a responsibility, every opportunity, an obligation; every possession a duty. I believe that the law was made for man and not man for the law; that government is the servant of the people and not their master. I believe in the dignity of labor, whether with head or hand; that the world owes no man a living but it owes every man an opportunity to make a living. I believe that thrift is essential to well-ordered living and that economy is a prime request of a sound financial structure, whether in government, business or personal affairs. I believe in the sacredness of a promise, that a man's word should be as good as his bond; that character—not wealth or power or position—is of supreme worth. I believe that the rendering of useful service is the common duty of mankind and that only in the purifying fire of sacrifice is the dross [waste matter] of selfishness consumed and the greatness of the human soul set free. I believe in all-wise-and all-loving God, named by whatever name, and that the individuals highest fulfillment, greatest happiness, and widest usefulness are to be found in living in harmony with His will. I believe that love is the greatest thing in the world; that it alone can overcome hate; that right can and will triumph over might.

This may be the most public and eloquent family mission statement ever preserved. It outlines the values for which John D. Rockefeller stood and the expectations he had for his family, as well as for his country. Creating a shared set of values and a mission statement for a family has in many respects a similar galvanizing effect as it would for a company. If all participate and reaffirm these values from generation to generation, then it has magnificent bonding power. This process is best followed with other family members and can be greatly enhanced with the support of a facilitator who can make sure all members of the family are heard.

As part of the family values, vision, and mission process, there is often an activity involving the capturing of the family's history—where the values and wealth came from. Many families will capture the family's history, stories about their ancestors and their struggles, how the family wealth was created, and who helped to support the family from inside and outside. In this way the family's history can be passed along from generation to generation, captured once, and enhanced as new family history is written.

Take the time to interview those in your family who hold the keys to your family's history. Put together a book, a video, or create some other way to share the family history with existing and new family members. Although this might sound contrived, take the time to involve your family in the process of capturing the family history and creating a mission and values statement for your family. Whenever there is a generational change, revisit the family mission statement and gain the buy-in of new generations to the vision, mission, values, and history of the family.

Family Retreats and Enrichment

Communication and trust are keys to family harmony, as mentioned earlier. And yet many families do not communicate well at a peer level or between generations. One method for breaking down barriers to communication is to create forums for communications, such as family retreats, which are becoming more and more popular.

Many families hold family retreats that can last from a couple of days to a week. Often they will have speakers or educators attend so that the family can learn together. A family may take a week at a different location each year or at the same family retreat. It is part organized learning and shared experiences and part free time to connect with others. Family retreats are becoming more and more common and may involve greater numbers of family members than just the immediate family. Family retreats take a great deal of planning but can build bridges and trust between family members while removing barriers.

Creating communication opportunities within families, to air grievances, builds trust, says Amy Braden, who heads JPMorgan Private Bank's Family Wealth Centre. In an interview with Reuters she points out, "It is normal for families owning businesses or other large assets to squabble over priorities, plans and visions. Conflict is not a bad thing. Conflict is natural. The family's ability to manage those conflicts and arrive at good decisions is absolutely essential."

Family retreats are another way to open up communication within a family and build trust among family members.

Peer Groups

One phenomenon that we observed during our research is that family leaders would like to gain the benefit of knowledge from others like them. In response to this desire wealth groups have been established in various cities around the United States for peers to share their experiences and support one another with the difficult decisions they have to make related to their children and families. From the CCC alliance in Boston, which is tied to Wharton University, to the Met Circle and Tiger 21 in New York, to LIDO in San Francisco and Los Angeles, peers are convening to share their experience as investors, philanthropists, and family leaders.

In Seattle, where no such peer group existed, we started one. We called together colleagues, some of whom were first generation wealth, and others who were heirs. We met at a club and talked about the issues they wanted to address. Anything and everything was on the table. We could discuss finding top investments, shared experiences in philanthropy, or family wealth issues. We identified topics of common interest and ranked them. At the top of the list were topics of self-actualization and of preparing children to deal with wealth.

In truth, in our monthly breakfast meetings we started by focusing a great deal on self-worth and net worth, to dive deeply into the events and people who shaped our values. Next on our agenda was to discuss what we wanted our legacy to be. Top-of-the-list of goals for most of the peers in our group is to ensure that their children have self-esteem and can live productive lives.

It is possible to create a peer group of individuals within your community who are wrestling with similar issues so that you can discuss family wealth practices on a regular basis in a confidential setting. It is one of the best ways to tap into the common wisdom of peers concerning family matters. This is a third opportunity to strengthen the family unit.

Generational Family Enterprises

Another family discipline concerns family enterprises. Families are collections of individuals with a very special bond that is both physical and emotional. When it comes to family enterprises, however, be they family businesses, pooled investments, or family foundations, a plan for succession and system of governance are keys to achieving continuity and generational success. This section is by no means meant to be a detailed "how to" related to succession planning and governance. The area of generational continuity is far too complex for that and often requires a group of experts to help families achieve the results they desire. Instead, this is meant to raise some of the key considerations in terms of succession planning and family governance that families should contemplate when it comes to generational family enterprises.

Succession Planning

With the large number of family businesses expected to transfer to the next generation, or to new owners, in the next several decades, succession and continuity in families continue to be important topics. For many families, ownership of the family business is complex. There may be multiple generations involved in the business or multiple family units with cousins and in-laws in roles of responsibility. Families handle leadership in family businesses differently. Some work collaboratively with siblings and parents in key operating roles, such as the Nordstrom family, founders of the Nordstrom department store chain. Other families we spoke with have chosen not to have family members in operating roles in the family business because of the difficulties that are created, especially if family members are not performing as expected. Rather, they choose to play board roles and to bring outside experts into operating roles. Still others find that there are no apparent heirs who choose to take over leadership of the family business, and as a result the family sells the business and distributes or collectively manages the money.

So the first and most important decision it seems is whether the generation in control of the family business wants to pass it along to the next generation and whether there is someone in the next generation who chooses to be actively involved in leadership or on the board of the family business. On the heels of this decision is whether there are individuals in the next generation who have the training to take on leadership positions, and, if not, what the plan would be to train them in order for them to become qualified.

Since preparing heirs to participate in a family enterprise is a two-way street, Roy Williams and Vic Preisser came up with a readiness self-checklist for heirs, to ensure that the next generation buys in to the roles they will play. The checklist they developed follows:

1. *Have I worked with my parent (s) and other family members to define a clear long-term mission for the family wealth?*
2. *Have I actively worked with my family to develop the strategy for achieving the mission of the family wealth?*
3. *Have the various roles for the management of the family assets been identified, and do I support filling those roles with fully competent individuals?*
4. *Do I know what my personal interests are and understand my abilities well enough to identify a specific role for myself?*
5. *In preparing for a particular role, am I willing to be evaluated against specific observable and measurable standards?*
6. *Have I selected a mentor whom I respect?*
7. *Have I developed with my mentor a specific plan to become competent for the family mission role that satisfies my interests and talents, within the mission staffing timeframe?*
8. *Am I emotionally open to the communications requirements and the continuing learning and evaluation that are required of each role-occupying individual within the family wealth mission structure?*
9. *Do I clearly understand the difference between knowing (what needs to be done) versus doing (what needs to be done) and to discipline myself to act in the best interests of the mission?*

10. Have I assumed personal responsibility for learning from the unavoidable "bumps in the road . . . ?"[2]

The family business is not the only family enterprise in which there is a need for continuity. In fact, many family foundations are set up legally as perpetual entities. As a result, they continue to be passed on to the next generation until there are no assets left. As with family businesses, some families choose to have a family member as director of their foundation while others choose to have outside directors. Again, having a family member in a direct operating role can lead to uncomfortable discussions and performance reviews. With that said, the central issue remains how to include family members and then to transition control of the foundation to new generations when appropriate.

Whether you are dealing with a family business or foundation, proactively develop a plan for succession and continuity if that is the choice of the owners and of their heirs. Make the succession criteria and standards as concrete as possible. Develop a plan for preparing heirs, and make sure there is a buy-in from heirs. Consult an expert to assist with the process who has been through this before with other families.

Developing a Governance Plan and Skills-Based Teams

Governance within families and family enterprises includes the rules that "govern" how decisions will be made. Some of the keys to family governance are to determine a process of decision making and who will be involved in the process; to select and monitor family advisers, mentors, and fiduciaries; and to develop objective standards for roles within family governance and family enterprises. The ultimate objective is for there to be objectivity in decision making and in selecting family members to represent the rest of the family in the decisions being made.

As with other areas of planning, the first step is to assess what you currently have in place. What planning have you done so far? What family enterprises exist, and what roles are in place? What financial, legal, tax-related, and other essential personal and family documents have been executed, and are they easily accessible to family members who might need them? How often do you review your essential documents to make sure they are up to date? The answer to these questions for most of us is that although we have done some planning, our documents are usually out of date, and often the parties affected by the documents do not know of their existence or are not prepared for their consequences until it is too late.

After you assess your current planning, consider the leadership and advisory roles that are required within the family enterprise to fill various roles. Often these could include: board and management positions in the family business; board and operating director positions in the family foundation; leadership positions in family governance councils; trustees of various trust structures for family members; custodians of family assets; guardians of children; legal, financial, insurance, accounting, philanthropy, and other family experts.

Next determine the skills required to fill each of the key roles and whether they ideally should come from within the family or from the outside. Consider that these key roles very well might span a number of generations. Who, for instance, will be responsible for seeing that your desires for your family are taken care of after you are gone? What happens to the governance structure of your family business or other family enterprises if you are out of the picture? The selection of family leaders and trusted advisers in key roles is less a legal issue than a matter of fit with the family. It is also a matter of trust—that a selected person or group of individuals will be looking out for the best interests of your family.

The selection process for key leaders from outside the family is critical. There are few people that a family will trust enough to show the whole family picture. This person is typically a close family friend, or a trusted adviser. Often this person is a trust and estate lawyer because this job requires an understanding of the family's overall picture. The family office executive, accountant, or wealth adviser can also serve in this role. An adviser comes to a point of trust within a family that makes him or her very valuable to a family's continuity.

In addition to the trusted adviser, there is a second set of advisers that often is hired to serve a specific purpose, to enhance the family in some way. These advisers may not be permanent fixtures, but they can be called upon when a certain issue arises. An investment banker skilled in mergers and acquisitions for instance might be hired to help a family sell a family asset. An outside trustee might be hired to watch over a certain number of family trusts. A family psychologist might be called upon to deal with a particularly difficult situation within the family. A philanthropic adviser might be called on to help develop a family foundation mission statement. There are many roles that an adviser needs to fill— including those of a fiduciary, trustee, educator, skilled practitioner, manager, or board member.

More and more it is becoming common and accepted to have a team approach to wealth and legacy. The wealth holder and other family members are the leaders of this team. The key permanent members of this team might be the family lawyer, accountant, and/or wealth adviser. Other members might include a foundation director, an insurance adviser or planner, or a family coach. To make a team work does not only require that the wealth holder serve as a true leader, but it also requires an integrated process.

Creating an effective team is about identifying the skills that a family needs to succeed and then finding people with those skills. Consider the following activities related to creating an effective advisory team. Create a grid delineating the major activities, programs, or enterprises of the family. They can be investment-related, philanthropy-related, or family-related. Determine the optimal skills required to support these activities. In the next column list the current family members and the advisers associated with this activity and the skills they possess. Where there is a gap, there is an opportunity to bring in a knowledgeable person to fill the gap. Develop a process for assessing team members, and have a formal review process, as you would with business executives, on a regular basis.

KEY SECTION OBSERVATIONS

GENERATIONAL FAMILY PRACTICES

- Legacy leaders play a critical role in establishing values in their children and systems in their families. These shared values and systems allow families to survive and thrive throughout the generations.
- Preparing others to take the wheel is about raising successful, motivated children with money. Legacy leaders who are successful in this area transfer values by modeling and communicating values; mentor financial competency so children can support themselves; and help their children vision and identify their own purpose.
- Constructing family communication lines and bridges is required to create family harmony with wealth. Legacy leaders who are successful in this area are effective at facilitating open communication and collaboration within the family. They do this by capturing the family history, developing a collaborative family mission, and establishing annual family retreats and enrichment, among other activities. Some also share best family practices in confidential peer groups with other similar families.
- Building a brain trust is about governance within the family required for successful continuity of family enterprises. Legacy leaders who are successful in this area make generational transitions successful by developing a thoughtful succession plan and carefully selecting skills-based teams of family leaders and advisers to represent the family on key decisions.

PART III

DOING WELL AND DOING GOOD—INDUSTRY TRANSFORMATIONS

If something comes to life in others because of you, then you have made an approach to immortality.

NORMAN COUSINS

Just yesterday a good friend of mine passed away. I was on an airplane heading back to New York from Seattle to see him because I knew that he was breathing his last breaths, and I wanted to say good-bye. When I landed in New York, I found out that he had died already. I went to his home anyway and spent time with his wife; we looked through photographs and remembered Charles. He touched many lives. He lived life fully. He was not wealthy; however, he left a great legacy.

Charles was a visionary person and a loyal person. He would latch on to a company and jump in with both feet. He would raise the leadership to a new level with his high level of energy—his incredible, positive energy. He would swing into action, not letting anything stand in his way. He would call on the titans of government and industry because they needed to hear the story of the companies he adopted. He got results. Charles reminded me that a great part of legacy is the personal journey of leadership.

In a very real sense birth is a beginning, death a destination, and life is a journey. We all start and end in the same way. It is what we do in between that counts. The lesson from Charles is that legacy is in large part about the quality of interactions one has with others in everyday life. It is about touching people. The only way to truly extend a life is through the memories one leaves through others. It is the journey with others that makes the personal trip worthwhile.

As such, the legacy journey is not only for the fortunate few with great wealth, but for mere mortals as well. It is not only the wealthy who benefit from the lessons of legacy leaders. The opportunity to leave something behind of lasting value is open to just about everyone. The lessons of leadership and of summiting practices can be practiced by anyone with the desire and commitment.

The legacy journey is in part an internal journey of discovery and alignment. Legacy leaders must navigate the valleys that lead to misalignments. They must connect with their passions. They must realign their objectives with those of other stakeholders at key junctions during the journey. They must adapt their leadership skills, developed in business, to family and social endeavors.

The legacy journey is in part an external journey about impact. The internal journeys of individuals intersect with family and society. Individuals must climb the wealth/philanthropy/family mountains to create impact. They must learn and apply summiting practices that lead to lasting institutions. They must teach others to take the wheel as well, so that other generations can continue on.

Ultimately, legacies are about leadership. In certain generations great leaders emerge. Back in the days of the railroad Carnegie and Rockefeller emerged. Today, Bill Gates and others have started to put their minds and souls into improving the world with the same leadership skills they used in business.

Yet the impact of these icons does not compare with the sum of the deeds of mere mortals who are legacy leaders in their own right. There are legacy leaders in your church or synagogue. They are on community boards and in the trenches doing the hard work of improving the lives of the disadvantaged. They are heads of families. They are inventors, and they are regular people just taking time out during their day to provide a helping hand.

The largest numbers of legacy leaders in the history of the United States, the baby boomers, are now reaching an age in their journeys where many have crossed the wealth divide and are contemplating their legacies. The wave of money transferring from the baby boom generation to the next generation is beginning. What will be the impact of this great wealth transfer? What will the baby boomer generation, that has created so much change in society already, leave as its last chapter? How will the members of this generation again change the world and the industries that support them on their journeys? If history is a guide, they face great challenges, as does society.

As one peers into the future, it seems clear that the baby boomers and the newly wealthy will innovate again. The greatest innovation will not be in their music, their dress, or in their experimentation with mind-altering substances. Their greatest innovation will be in the discovery of new models of doing well and doing good, which is referred to today as *social entrepreneurship*. In the process they will transform two large and powerful industries. In fact, they are already doing so.

First, they are transforming philanthropy by casting off the traditional ways of thinking about the nonprofit industry and by bringing innovation born from the creativity they learned in business. Second, they are transforming the wealth advisory industry by requiring that their advisers provide more than just financial advice. They are demanding insights related to philanthropy and wealth in their families. As a result, the largest wealth advisory firms and trust companies are evaluating opportunities to differentiate their offerings and support their customers, with more than just financial advice. It is the megatrend of the trillion-dollar baby-boomer wealth transfer that is at the heart of these two monumental transformations.

CHAPTER 21

THE TRANSFORMATION OF PHILANTHROPY

I choose to rise up out of that storm and see that in moments of desperation, fear, and helplessness, each of us can be a rainbow of hope, doing what we can to extend ourselves in kindness and grace to one another. And I know for sure that there is no them . . . there's only us.

OPRAH WINFREY

In October 2003, a group of researchers finished, within a five-month time period, a most aggressive task—to map the new philanthropic world. The study, called "The Blended Value Map," attempted to categorize the players and business models that make up the growing area referred to as *social entrepreneurship*. This new map sought to find organizations that provide a blending of economic and social value, which is at the heart of social entrepreneurship.

The study was supported by a number of new world philanthropy players such as the William and Flora Hewlett Foundation, the David and Lucile Packard Foundation, Omidyar Foundation, Skoll Foundation, Surdna Foundation, and the Center for Social Innovation at Stanford University. They ended up creating five categories of blended value organizations, all with a business model underpinning them and all providing various degrees of social value.[1] The five categories they identified are:

- *Corporate social responsibility.* Companies and business leaders who fall under this category are consciously seeking to integrate strategies for the creation of social and environmental value within their core business models, operations, and supply chains. They range from Starbucks with its strategy to support CARE and raise awareness of its consumers of the needs of the developing world from which it sources its coffee beans, to The Body Shop and Value Village, two retailers that support local charities through their business practices.

- *Social enterprise.* Companies that fall under this category are for-profit and nonprofit businesses including social purpose enterprises, nonprofit business ventures, and mission-based for-profit ventures whose core business model is to create blended economic and social value. Examples here include Newman's Own, an enterprise that donates 100 percent of its profits to charity, and Magic Johnson who, after a career in basketball, has partnered with major companies like Starbucks to bring businesses to the inner city.

- *Social investing.* Investment firms in this category attempt to create both economic and social value and returns. They range from Domini Social Investments, an investment firm that screens investments to ensure that the underlying companies are socially responsible, to the whole area of microfinance, which makes loans to underprivileged individuals in developing countries to start businesses and raise their standard of living.

- *Strategic/effective philanthropy.* Philanthropists and foundations in this category take a businesslike approach to philanthropy with the objective of creating social value rather than just charitable giving. In his book, *The Foundation*, Joel Fleishman identifies foundations that are taking a strategic approach to philanthropy through "creating and disseminating knowledge, building human capital, supporting public policy advocacy, changing public attitudes, and changing the law." One of the clearest examples of strategic philanthropy is the growth of community foundations, which have risen to provide informed and strategic philanthropy in cities around the United States and the world.

- *Sustainable development.* This category of blended value includes organizations with sustainable consumption and production practices. Examples range from the Rockefeller Foundation which invests in sustainable agriculture in developing countries that grow food in efficient and sustainable ways, to construction and development companies that are implementing the latest environmental and conservation technologies in their buildings.

Social entrepreneurship and blended value enterprises are approaches that philanthropists, business leaders, nonprofit leaders, and entrepreneurs are implementing to transform philanthropy and the nonprofit sector. There is something inherently appealing about giving in a sustainable way, to know that your gift continues to make a difference, and to receive a social and financial return on that investment so you can give again. This is true whether the gift is a microloan to fund an impoverished woman to start a business in Africa, an investment in a venture fund that develops new medical technologies to save lives, or capital to grow a company that takes corporate social responsibility seriously.

There is something appealing as well to know that as young adults graduate from college, law school, business school, or various professional universities, there are opportunities for them to go to work for companies and nonprofits where they can do good and make a good living for their families. In fact, this need to work for an enterprise that has a social mission is part of the DNA of many Gen21 young adults ages 15 to 40. They are looking for more than just to make a living; they want to have meaning in their work.

Although a great deal of philanthropy is simply from the heart, and goes to support destitute people and causes in important and meaningful ways, there are more and more examples today of individuals and companies that are implementing strategies as part of this blended value map. Companies are discussing their obligations as corporate citizens to society because their employees and customers are demanding it. There are increasing examples as well of nonprofits that have a money-making component to their enterprise and appear in many respects to act more like businesses. Sustainable development is fast becoming an important buying criterion for consumers as well, demanding that the environment be part of a company's agenda.

People may not be fully aware of the fact that social entrepreneurism is so pervasive, but it is part of everyday life. Here are a number of examples of how the new philanthropists are transforming the industry of philanthropy and creating blended social and financial value.

Newman's Own, a Social Enterprise at Your Local Supermarket

As you walk down the aisle of your favorite supermarket, it is almost impossible to miss the famous likeness of Paul Newman on popcorn boxes, spaghetti sauce, organic chocolate bars, and more. Paul Newman, the famous screen actor, is the founder of a well-known philanthropic venture called Newman's Own.

Newman's Own was conceived by Paul Newman and his good friend A. E. Hotchner. Their idea was to sell commercially the homemade salad dressing that the Newmans originally gave out as holiday gifts. The company was named Newman's Own, and the proceeds of sales after taxes were given to educational and charitable organizations. The original product, Newman's Own Salad Dressing, has grown into a whole product line of dressings, salsa, popcorn, steak sauce, pasta sauce, fruit cocktail juice, and lemonade. Newman's Own also partners with a number of companies to further market its products. Recently, McDonald's fast food chain and Newman's Own entered into a partnership. Newman's Own salad dressing will be packaged and used for the new salad product line McDonald's is introducing to its franchise.

The combination of Newman's popular name recognition and a good product allowed the company to give away approximately $150 million dollars over the years. The proceeds from Newman's Own go to charitable organizations like the "Hole in the Wall Gang" camps, which support families of terminally ill children and which were initiated and funded by Newman's Own contributions. The Scott Newman Center, also founded by Mr. Newman, works to prevent substance abuse through education and short films on drug abuse.

The early social enterprises like Ben & Jerry's, The Body Shop, and Patagonia seemed to be on the fringe, pushing the edge of the envelope with social activist leaders. Today they seem like visionaries as companies like Starbucks are creating a culture with a soul that permeates the company all the way through to the employees and customers.

Most social enterprises reflect the values of their leaders. Howard Schultz cares about giving back. Paul Newman desires to make a difference. One family whose company I advise has gone one step further to create social enterprises around the world through its charitable foundation. This family has billions of dollars in assets. The majority of their assets are in a charitable foundation. The foundation for the most part does not invest these assets in stocks and bonds, but in the creation of social enterprises. It has done this anonymously. The family owns 100 or so companies that all have the same mission, "To transform lives." The companies it owns range from manufacturing companies to industrial and technology companies. All these companies have incredible cultures that empower their workers and improve their communities. Best of all, when these companies create profits or have a liquidity event, the profits from the companies go into the foundation, where they support additional works of charity.

Whether it is Newman's Own selling consumer items in supermarkets with the profits going to charity, or social enterprises created from foundation investments, new models of blended value social enterprises are emerging. With their success others are also finding ways to do well and do good with their companies.

Magic Johnson, Social Investing in the Inner City

Earvin "Magic" Johnson, after retiring from basketball, parlayed his celebrity status into building for-profit companies in the inner city. In doing so, he helped revitalize these once decaying communities. Magic Johnson was a household name in the 1980s as one of the top players in the National Basketball Association, leading the Los Angeles Lakers to five national championships and winning three MVP awards. After retiring from an illustrious career in basketball in 1996, Magic dedicated himself to investing in and revitalizing inner cities in the United States.

Magic grew up in the inner city and knew there was an opportunity to create profitable business enterprises in some of the worst neighborhoods in the country. He also believed that he could improve the lives of many inner city people along the way. Magic's vision was to help bring major retailers to the inner city by combining his knowledge of inner city consumers with the appeal of popular retailers. With this vision Magic began to strike deals with popular retailers such as TGI Fridays in Atlanta and Los Angeles, and Starbucks, where as a joint venture partner he has opened 70 stores. Magic also struck deals with Loews Cineplex theaters, which he owns, and eight 24-hour fitness centers. In addition, Magic has a partnership with Washington Mutual to educate people on how to buy a home and to provide home loans in the inner city.

Magic has implemented his vision with solid results. In part because of his financial success, he has been able to raise a $300 million dollar real estate fund for development in the inner city.[2] It was the social impact of his investments in the inner city, however, that held the most value for Magic.

The net result of Magic's efforts has been a renewed confidence in the inner city as a place to invest. New retailers in the inner city have created new job opportunities for people who live in those neighborhoods. The landscape of the inner city in some instances has been revitalized and has given people hope. And this has been done in a profitable way that has created real returns on investment, some of which Magic has plowed back into his foundation for education, AIDS charities, and computer centers in the inner city.

Magic Johnson has created social business enterprises with a mission that goes beyond the bottom line to enhance life in the inner city. Through his visionary leadership, he has been able to do a great deal of good, while building profitable businesses in the inner city, demonstrating another aspect of blended value investing.

Microfinance: Solving Poverty through a Blended Value Investment Model

There are few investment models that have had as great an impact as microfinance has on the poorest individuals in the world who live on $2 a day. Microfinance has grown from a cottage industry in 1976 when professor Muhammad Yunus founded Grameen Bank in Bangladesh, to 7,000 microfinance institutions funding over 13 million borrowers in 2005 with outstanding loans of $13 billion dollars.

The idea behind microfinance or microlending is to nurture 1,000 flowers from planting small seeds. Microloans are small loans of several hundred dollars to several thousand dollars that are provided often to women in developing countries like India or the Philippines or in certain other Asian or Central American countries. The men and women use these loans to start small businesses such as basket weaving, clothes making, or other similar enterprises. As they grow their businesses, they make money for their families and are also able to pay back the loans with interest. As the borrowers prove their business skills, they are then offered larger loans.

Take, for example, the microloan that was provided to a poor woman in Africa to buy a cow. With the cow, her plan was to sell milk to other villagers. The money to buy the first cow was successful, so she bought another cow. She sold the milk from these two cows, and continued to invest until she had more than a dozen cows. She used the money from the milk she sold to support her family in a new way, and to pay for the education of her children.

The benefit of this approach is that people receiving the loans have the ability to support their families and in some cases earn their way out of poverty. The benefits to the lenders are the ability to do good by supporting families in poverty while receiving a return on their investment. As microlending has proven itself, it has attracted more and more institutions and wealthy individuals to open up their funds and provide capital. Investors range from Citigroup, which has announced a fund of microfinance funds, to Pierre Omidyar, the founder of eBay and a new philanthropist.

Pierre Omidyar's net worth in 2004, at the age of 37, and after the public offering of eBay, was over $10 billion. Pierre and his wife, Pam, are among the new role models for philanthropy, leveraging their wealth in unique and impactful ways. Pierre Omidyar has been a big proponent of microlending and recently donated $100 million to Tufts University for a program to loan small amounts of money to individuals in developing countries to help them out of poverty and to build sustainable businesses on their own.

The gift from Omidyar to Tufts has numerous benefits, not only for the recipients of the microloans. It allowed Mr. Omidyar to give to an institution he cares about, Tufts, and in an area for which he has passion. If invested wisely, the returns from the microloans will help to provide a continuing stream of support for the university as well.

Some people believe that microfinance could be a solution to poverty in the developing world. At a minimum it is one successful model of blended value that addresses global poverty, with a tangible and sustainable return.

The Rise of Community Foundations: Strategic Philanthropy at Work

The nonprofit sector in the United States is large and growing. There are estimated to be over 1.3 million charities tracked by the IRS, and the nonprofit sector represents approximately 7 to 10 percent of GDP depending on how you measure it. With so much diversity of nonprofits, it has become somewhat unwieldy for individuals to find and connect with a nonprofit in the issue area they care about. It is also difficult for nonprofits to identify the donors who care about their issue area. Enter the community foundation.

The first community foundation was established in Cleveland, Ohio, in 1914 by Frederick Goff, a Cleveland banker and attorney. Within five years, community foundations formed in many other places. In 1931, the first donor-advised fund was established by a community foundation in Winston-Salem, North Carolina. Community foundations grew rapidly in the 1960s and beyond as the Tax Reform Act of 1969 increased restrictions on private foundations and provided more advantages for community foundations. Today there are over 700 community foundations in the United States with over $38 billion in assets.

The growth in community foundations is an example of social entrepreneurism and strategic philanthropy at work. Community foundations fill an information gap that has resulted from the explosion of nonprofits and of charitable giving. They are encouraged by the government through tax laws that have made it more favorable to give to a community foundation than to private foundations. Community foundations are also social enterprises because they are often supported by fees they receive through the management of donor funds. In this way they are self-sustaining.

Just as microfinance is changing the landscape of giving in the developing world, community foundations are accomplishing similar objectives at the local level. Community foundations have expanded their role to train new philanthropists, to educate children in philanthropy, and to support high-impact nonprofits at the local level. They are connectors between donors and nonprofits with a business model that supports their existence. They guide donors to community needs in the arts, homelessness, environmental organizations, transportation, health and wellness, education, and elsewhere.

Over time, community foundations have expanded globally, and there are now over 1,175 community foundations in 46 countries.[3] They are organizations that promote strategic philanthropy, and they fill a gap that has existed for donors and nonprofits in local communities around the world.

The Rockefeller Foundation: Building Sustainable Food Production in the Developing World through Strategic Philanthropy

There are many examples of strategic philanthropy, where wealthy individuals have seeded worthy causes. Few have had the impact of the Rockefeller and Ford Foundations in the area of sustainable agriculture, which was written about in detail by Joel Fleishman in his book, *The Foundation*.

In the 1960s there were quite a number of developing nations whose population outstripped the supply of food they were able to cultivate. The Rockefeller Foundation's initial focus was on Mexico. Through an initial grant, the foundation began to work with the Mexican ministry of agriculture to identify new technologies and strategies to improve agricultural output in that region. The idea was to make Mexico self-sufficient in resolving its own food issues and then to move on to other areas of the world.

Over time the Rockefeller Foundation took what it learned in Mexico to Colombia, Chile, and developing countries in Asia. It often partnered with government agencies, such as USAID and the U.S Department of Agriculture, as well as foreign governments. In addition, in 1959 the Ford Foundation partnered with the Rockefeller Foundation to create international food institutes in various countries to apply the best agricultural techniques to the production of rice, wheat, and other crops.

The results of the Green Revolution ". . . is credited with saving at least a billion lives since the mid-1960s."[4] The Rockefeller Foundation's involvement in the Green Revolution is an example as well of strategic philanthropy at work. The Rockefeller Foundation, working with governments and other foundations, made an investment that ultimately created sustainable humanitarian assistance to save lives. In the process, one of the architects of this plan at Rockefeller, Norman Borlaug, won a Nobel Prize.

Strategic philanthropy is about applying knowledge and leverage to solve social issues. This is often done in public/private partnerships, where the government may work with a nonprofit, a private foundation, and even a for-profit business to attack a problem in multiple ways to achieve an outcome. With success, the objective of strategic philanthropy is to disseminate information, and to replicate its success in other areas. It is like proving a business model works first, and then expanding it.

Strategic philanthropy has been around for years, and in some ways it is philanthropy at its best, where multiple parties get together with a common agenda to make something significant happen to improve the world.

The Transformation of Philanthropy through Blended Value

The blended value map is a window into the future of philanthropy. It demonstrates how the nonprofit sector is beginning to innovate. It reveals the acceleration of change that is taking place as well. In the past, philanthropy was about giving from the heart alone. Often the wealthy did this through the creation of private foundations that were formed as perpetual organizations to give away a government-mandated minimum amount of money, 5 percent of assets, on an annual basis. Many individuals and foundations took this task seriously, but with little innovation. Today foundations are not just giving away money, but are more and more looking at the whole balance sheet of a foundation to invest the corpus in new ways.

Some foundations are investing their financial assets in companies where as shareholders they are demanding environmental and employee-friendly practices. Sometimes they are choosing to invest only in companies with positive social practices, as is demonstrated by the growth of socially screened investment funds. These are funds that screen companies for their environmental, social, and employee practices, and foundations won't invest in certain companies unless they meet a certain minimum screen. These types of socially screened funds now have multiple trillions of dollars invested in them.

Philanthropy in the future will change in other fundamental ways as well. First, there have already been changes in giving vehicles, supported by the government. Not only are there private foundations today, but donor advised funds have grown in popularity, as have community foundations. There are donor collaboratives as well, where multiple donors give together within an issue area. There is likely to be additional creativity and innovation in this area.

Second, individuals are recipients of wealth earlier, and many are choosing to be actively involved in their philanthropy rather than leaving it to future generations. As a result, they are not necessarily looking to create a perpetual foundation run by family members and directors after they are gone. Instead, they are applying their energy and skills to their philanthropy today. As part of this trend, individuals are increasingly taking their business backgrounds and applying them to philanthropy, demanding accountability and attempting to track the results of their charitable giving.

Third, there is a recognition that social issues are global in nature. With new technologies, however, individuals are enabled to attack social issues on a global basis. There are greater amounts of information available and readily accessible by individuals wishing to research issues, and new technologies are allowing for collaboration on a global scale with participants in multiple countries. Most of all, there is creativity around new blended value models to solve social problems. Blended value social investing is one major trend that is being driven by new philanthropists and fueled by the trillions of dollars of wealth that has been created around the world in recent years. It is also being fueled by the growing number of philanthropists who are involved in social enterprises, from microfinance to community foundations, which are transforming the private sector. The rise of social entrepreneurism is one example of personal legacies meeting society to create a revolution. The other area is the wealth advisory industry.

THE TRANSFORMATION OF THE WEALTH ADVISORY INDUSTRY

Put not your trust in money, but put your money in trust.

OLIVER WENDELL HOLMES

The next best thing to being wise oneself is to live in a circle of those who are.

C.S. LEWIS

I n an article that appeared in the *International Herald Tribune* on February 26, 2007, it was announced that Goldman Sachs, KKR, and Texas Pacific Group would buy out TXU, the largest power producer in Texas, for $45 billion. This was news not for the magnitude of the deal, but because the combined buyout group had announced a plan to put on hold 11 new coal plants planned by TXU, adhering to a strict code of environmental conduct. At face value this move appeared to be motivated as much by environmental concerns as by business ones.[1]

Skeptics will say that by not building these coal plants the investment firms were able to free up additional cash to fund the buyout. They will also argue that the stock price of TXU had been negatively affected by the move to build these new coal plants in the first place. With that said, Goldman Sachs has been a longtime proponent of reducing carbon emissions. Under the leadership of its former chief executive, Henry Paulson, Jr., who was also chairman of the Nature Conservancy, an environmental advocacy group, Goldman had been very conscious of its environmental role as a financial company.

Large financial institutions are not noted for their altruism, and people have every reason to be skeptical of these behemoth organizations. In many ways these large institutions are the poster children for greed. It is this industry, however, that has the potential more than any other to guide the legacies of its clients, and as a result to determine the outcome of the $100 trillion baby boomer wealth transfer.

Major financial institutions such as Goldman Sachs, Citigroup, and Bank of America support the financial requirements of the baby boomers with their retirement, their estates, their foundations, and their heirs; it is the major banks and insurance companies that manage money within trusts, foundations, and donor-advised funds. They provide loans for the growth of family enterprises. They help a family with the sale of its business and with the management of its businesses and real estate in trust. They can provide guidance for estate planning purposes and for many other purposes as well. They are fiduciaries, trust officers, money managers, philanthropic specialists, planners, lenders, investment bankers, and more.

Although these large financial institutions touch families in many ways, they have not found a way to integrate their many services into a road map that is easily digestible by a family. They employ individuals with the expertise to help families with their legacies; however, they have not created many tools for this or an integrated process to do so. That is changing.

Another revolution is under way, which will lead to the transformation of the wealth advisory industry. This revolution is being driven by the needs of the baby boomers, as well as the very real requirements of the industry itself to differentiate its offerings from those of its competitors. New, integrated wealth advisory firms, or legacy firms if you will, are responding to the needs for integrated advice. They see the opportunity that is coming of the great wealth transfer, and they want their piece of the pie.

Today there are greater numbers of wealthy people than ever before. There are now 691 billionaires worldwide according to *The Economist*. In addition there are over 77,500 families with over $30 million in assets and 8.3 million people with $1 million or more in assets worldwide.[2] Industry players are aware of the coming tidal wave and are beginning to put their plans in place. They are positioning to serve one or more sectors of this population.

The traditional picture of the money-hungry investment banker depicted by Michael Douglas as Gordon Gekko in *Wall Street* is evolving. This change is not coming easily, however, in part because public wealth advisory firms have real financial pressures and quarterly earnings goals, while wealthy families often have long-term, multigenerational goals. There is a divergence of goals that is creating unease at these exclusive financial establishments in part because advisers are often not meeting the expectations of their wealthiest clients. It is also creating dissatisfaction among many wealth holders who question the motivation of their advisers.

What Wealthy Clients Want and Advisory Firms Need

The Spectrum Group, a consulting firm that analyzes the needs of high-net-worth clients, found in its 2004 study that trust was eroding between such clients and their primary investment advisers. The study found that "the advice offered to clients is often investment based and does not solve the greater holistic need" of these clients.[3]

Individuals want integrated advice from someone who understands their goals and issues. They also want independent advice from firms that have their best interests in mind rather than the best interests of the firm. Up to 50 percent of ultra-high-net-worth individuals say that independent advice is one of their most important criteria. Clients of independent wealth advisory firms that offer consulting services, but sell no investment products, are much more satisfied than are those of advisers that also offer their own investment products. Trust and objectivity, which is greatly enhanced by firms that are independent, have become key selection criteria for wealthy individuals when choosing a wealth adviser.[4]

If that is what families want, then the question remains why these needs are not being met to the satisfaction of wealth holders. One answer is that the wealth advisory industry faces a dilemma, which is increased commoditization, compression of fees, and lower profitability from customers who are less loyal than they used to be.

Historically, financial advisory firms primarily sold their own investment products and funds to very loyal customers. Over time, with technological advances that have made it easier to compare products, customers became more aware of their exposure to the markets and volatility of returns. This was exacerbated by the technology crash in 2000. Customers came to realize that they weren't really diversified at all, but instead were invested in a limited set of products, primarily U.S. equities, bonds, and cash, which performed quite poorly compared with the standard U.S. equity indexes. In fact, a large percentage of large cap equity managers, those who invest for a living in U.S. companies, consistently underperformed the S&P 500.[5]

In order to retain clients, advisory firms switched from selling their own products to being consultants. Like the major university endowments, they started to spend a great deal of time on determining which asset classes to be in, called asset allocation, and less on their own products. They also began to look outside their own firms for the best managers worldwide that could manage money in each asset class. This more open way of doing business, of finding the best managers and not selling their own products exclusively, became known as an "open architecture" model.

The benefit to a firm of an open architecture model is that the firm is able to retain clients longer. It is hard to fire an investment adviser who is looking at the same set of managers you are and is willing to fire them along with you and replace that manager with another one they have researched. The challenge at open architecture firms that focus on asset allocation is that they are less profitable than firms that sell investment products. In addition, it has also become more and more difficult to differentiate one firm from another because they are now all doing the same thing.

The Rise of the Legacy Advisory Firm

This progression from investment product firms to wealth advisers and asset allocators is likely to continue to the point where the largest wealth advisory firms, from Citigroup to Bank of America to Goldman Sachs and others, will continue to add services to differentiate their offerings. In the process they will move from financial consultants to legacy advisers.

The full-service model is being offered by the largest, often public, financial institutions that have been consolidators in the industry and that have been assembling a broad array of financial products and services. Their offerings include investment banking services (to help individuals sell or restructure family businesses), investment services, trust services, estate and tax planning, foundation services, insurance, financial boot camps for kids, and much, much more. They provide great value for the services they offer because they are able to bundle their offerings and reap multiple revenue streams from a single customer.

The trend toward the bundling of services will continue for large, full-service firms, and they will begin to assist individuals not only with their financial needs but also with their philanthropy and family enterprises. As mostly public companies, these firms will have to do this in creative ways that combine additional services with a profitable business model. This is happening already, and as a result wealth advisory firms are creating new products and services that combine doing well and doing good.

For example, I was recently invited to attend a dinner with a senior executive of one of the largest financial institutions in the world. The executive had come to Seattle on one stop of a fact-finding trip. He was not there to preach insights on investing or buyouts. He was there because he perceived that his clients' priorities and needs had gone beyond the financial management of their assets. He, and others in the executive ranks of this global financial company, feel that this is a time in history that requires new ways of serving clients. He was there to ask how his firm might serve the philanthropic and family needs of his clients in a profitable way that also fit into his company's businesses and corporate strategy.

This executive pointed out that his firm was touching its wealthy clients in multiple ways, through the management of their money, their foundation assets, their kids' trusts, and financing for their family businesses. In addition, this firm was getting into the now popular area of microfinance, mentioned earlier, and providing loans to the world's poorest inhabitants, living on $2 a day. What this firm wasn't doing was to make its myriad services available to clients in an integrated or digestible manner.

Large financial firms are not the first to innovate, however, when they see proven demand for products and services, they move in to fill that demand. For instance, Citigroup announced the creation of its microfinance business division in 2005. It was not the first to jump in; the microfinance industry having been in existence since 1976, some would argue. The demand for microfinance, however, has proven itself to be a sound investment model with increasing customer demand. As a result, Citigroup jumped in.

Another example of financial institutions jumping in to a blended value business opportunity after it had been established is the area of socially screened investment funds. Socially screened investment funds do not invest in companies that negatively affect the health of individuals, such as tobacco companies, or that have poor environmental, employee, or consumer practices. As a result the investments are not supporting companies whose practices detract from society. Wayne Silby and John Guffy founded one of the earliest socially screened investment funds, the Calvert Fund, in 1976. Today there are over $2 trillion in socially screened funds, including exchange traded funds and traditional stock funds, which are offered by a wide variety of financial institutions.

The largest financial firms are seeking ways to provide these services profitably and in a bundled manner to individuals. Because they receive revenue from customers in a variety of ways, these large firms are the ones most likely to provide legacy types of services to support those revenue streams. They are being pulled into this new realm because a growing number of their wealthy customers are demanding these services. Ultimately these firms will need to wrestle with how to develop an integrated process for dealing with wealth and legacy more broadly, and to do this in a profitable way.

Legacy Advisory Firms, Doing Well and Doing Good

As the sheer numbers of wealthy people increase and as they seek to achieve significance beyond money, wealth advisory firms will need to find new models for doing business. Already a number of wealth advisory firms are integrating a values-based estate planning model to their processes. My prediction is that this will become the norm precisely because a values-based process creates an opportunity for firms to have different discussions with their clients—conversations that build trust. A values-based planning model also allows wealth advisers to understand the needs of their clients at a deeper level. These needs can lead to multiple product sales. The values analysis comes first, however, and the sale of multiple products and services results from the analysis.

A second legacy opportunity for investment banks is to take their capital formation arms and raise capital for funds that invest in new health-care technologies or new alternative energy technologies or microfinance, where the money that is put to work can yield a real return. This is a win/win scenario because smart people out of the top business and law schools will be attracted to these funds. These graduates will be able to make real money while doing good for society. The banks win because they get their fees from raising capital. Society wins because new environmentally friendly technologies and health-care treatments are created.

Ultimately, there will be a virtuous meeting of individual creativity and investor capital raised for the social good. In the process, wealth advisory firms will move to become legacy advisory firms. They will support their clients' needs or lose their clients. They may accomplish this end result by partnering with firms that fill gaps in their service offerings, as many are doing today. However, if they are going to succeed, they will need to embrace the goal of becoming world legacy leaders. They will need to develop a model of doing well and doing good. Some will. The rest will follow.

KEY SECTION OBSERVATIONS

DOING WELL AND DOING GOOD

- The trillion dollar wealth tranfer has begun and will over time transform two large and established industries: (1) the philanthopy industry and nonprofit sector and (2) the wealth advisory industry.
- The transformation of philanthropy and the nonprofit sector will in part result from new business models that blend financial and social values. These blended value models include corporate social responsibility, social enterprises, social investing, strategic/effective philanthropy, and sustainable development.
- The transformation of the wealth advisory industry is resulting from the expressed needs of wealthy clients for more services and the requirement that the wealth advisory firms differentiate their offerings. Over time wealth advisory firms will need to identify blended value products and services that fit within their corporate strategy, support their customers, and enhance their bottom lines.
- A missing element to advance these industry transformations is an integrated process that helps individuals clarify their goals and brings together what today are fragmented services. When this is done effectively, wealth advisory firms will become legacy advisory firms, and their offerings will become blended value offerings.

ENDNOTES

Introduction

1. Paul G. Schervish and John J. Havens, Boston College study, Social Welfare Research Institute, "Wealth and Commonwealth: New Findings on the Trends in Wealth and Philanthropy," *Nonprofit and Voluntary Sector Quarterly*, vol. 30, no.1, March 2001, pp. 5–25.
2. Gary Onks, *Sold on Seniors: How You Can Reach and Sell the $20 Trillion Senior Marketplace*, Fredericksburg, VA: Sold on Seniors, Inc., 2001.
3. Roy Williams and Vic Preisser, *Preparing Heirs: Five Steps to a Successful Transition of Family Wealth and Values*, San Francisco: Robert D. Reed Publishers, 2003, p. 17.
4. Spectrum Group's Ultra High-Net-Worth Executive Presentation, June 17, 2004.
5. Thought leaders interview by Randall Ottinger, April 2005.
6. Interview by Randall Ottinger with Page Snow of Foundation Source, April 2005.
7. Joel. L. Fleishman, *The Foundation*, New York: PublicAffairs (a member of the Perseus Books Group), 2007, p. 15.
8. Ibid.

Section—Crossing the Wealth Divide: The Challenges after Success

1. "Jay Gould," accessed on Wikipedia in 2005.
2. Stuart E. Lucas, *Wealth: Grow It, Protect It, Spend It, and Share It*, Upper Saddle River, NJ: Wharton School Publishing, 2006.

Chapter 1

1. Thayer Cheatham Willis, *Navigating the Dark Side of Wealth: A Life Guide for Inheritors*, Portland, OR: New Concord Press, 2005, p. 24.
2. Howard Stevenson and Laura Nash, *Just Enough: Tools for Creating Success in Your Work and Life*, Hoboken, NJ: John Wiley & Sons, 2004.
3. Presentation by Vin Cipolla, "The High-Net–Worth Landscape and Opportunity," *HNW WealthPulse*, March 2002.

Chapter 2

1. Carol J. Loomis, "Warren Buffett Gives It Away," *Fortune*, (Europe edition), vol. 154, July 10, 2006.
2. Bob Buford, *Half Time: Changing Your Game Plan from Success to Significance*, Grand Rapids, MI: Zondervan, 1994.

Chapter 3

1. Harold James, "A Family Affair," *The Financial Times*, March 25, 2006.
2. Roy Williams and Vic Preisser, *Preparing Heirs*, p. 31.

Section—Navigating the Valleys: Where Things Go Wrong

1. Daniel Kahneman, "Would You Be Happier If You Were Richer? A Focusing Illusion," *Science*, vol. 312, no. 5782, June 30, 2006, p. 1908.
2. Ibid.
3. Roy Williams and Vic Preisser, *Preparing Heirs*, p. 1.
4. Eric Schmitt, "For the First Time, Nuclear Families Drop below 25% of Households," *New York Times*, May 15, 2001.

5. Jay L. Zagorsky, "Marriage and Divorce's Impact on Wealth," *Journal of Sociology*, vol. 41, no. 4, (2005), pp. 406–424.

Chapter 4

1. "Howard Robard Hughes, Jr.," accessed on Wikipedia in 2006.
2. Ibid.
3. "Many Americans Leave Loved Ones Vulnerable, Due to Lack of Estate Planning," Lawers.com, accessed May 24, 2006.
4. Thayer Cheatham Willis, *Navigating the Dark Side of Wealth*, p. 24.

Chapter 5

1. Walter Kirn, "Dad's Empire," *New York Times*, section 6, December 26, 2004, p. 53.
2. Roy Williams and Vic Preisser, *Preparing Heirs*, p. 49.
3. Lee Hausner, *Children of Paradise: Successful Parenting for Prosperous Families*, Los Angeles: Jeremy P. Tarcher, Inc., 1990.
4. Ibid., p. 123.
5. Ibid.

Chapter 6

1. Timothy O'Brien, "Fortune's Fools: Why the Rich Go Broke," *New York Times*, September 17, 2006.
2. Presentation by Vin Cipolla, "The High-Net-Worth Landscape and Opportunity," p. 17.
3. Spectrum Group's Ultra High-Net-Worth Executive Presentation, June 17, 2004, p. 12.
4. Interview by Randall Ottinger with Charles Collier, 2006.

Section—Climbing the Mountains: Learned Legacy Excellence

1. "S&P Releases Latest Index Versus Active Fund Scorecard," press release, New York, April 13, 2006.
2. Gary P. Brinson, Brian D. Singer, and Gilbert L. Beebower, "Determinants of Portfolio Performance II: An Update," *Financial Analysts Journal*, vol. 47, no. 3, May–June 1991, pp. 40–48.

Chapter 7

1. Marc Gunther, "Yale's $8 Billion Man," *The Yale Alumni Magazine*, 2007.
2. Yale University, "The Yale Endowment 2005."
3. David F. Swensen, *Pioneering Portfolio Management: An Unconventional Approach to Institutional Investment*, New York: The Free Press (a division of Simon & Schuster), 2000.
4. Yale University, "The Yale Endowment 2006."

Chapter 8

1. Geoffrey E. Moore, *A Call to Action*, Santa Monica, CA: The Prostate Cancer Foundation, 2004.
2. Joel. L. Fleishman, *The Foundation*, p. 59.
3. Cora Daniels, "The Man Who Changed Cancer," *Fortune*, November 29, 2004, p. 92.
4. "Foundation Growth and Giving Estimates," study by The Foundation Center, 2005 edition.

Section—Self-Actualization Practices

1. Janet A. Simons, Donald B. Irwin, and Beverly A. Drinnien, *Psychology—The Search for Understanding*, New York: West Publishing Company, 1987.

Chapter 10

1. Paul G. Schervish, "Today's Wealth Holder and Tomorrow's Giving: The New Dynamics of Wealth and Philanthropy," *Journal of Gift Planning*, vol. 9, no. 3, 3rd quarter 2005, p. 18.
2. "Annual U.S. Charitable Giving Exceeds $260 Billion," American Association of Fundraising Counsel and Giving USA, Glenville, IL, June 19, 2006.

Chapter 11

1. Mary Maxwell Gates (1929–1994) and family, David Wilma, HistoryLink, accessed January 1, 2005.
2. Hoover Online profile, Bill and Melinda Gates Foundation, Web site reference to *New York Times Magazine*, April 16, 2000.
3. Amanda Ripley, "From Riches to Rags," *Time*, December 18, 2005, p. 5.
4. Ibid.
5. Ibid.
6. Hoover Online profile, Bill and Melinda Gates Foundation, Web site reference to FundingUniverse, Bill and Melinda Gates Foundation.
7. Amanda Cantrell, "Gates to Leave Day-to-Day Role at Microsoft," *CNNMoney*, June 16, 2006.
8. Ian Wilhelm, "Gates Foundation Announces It Does Not Plan to Operate Forever," *Chronicle of Philanthropy*, November 29, 2006.
9. www.gatesfoundation.org/AboutUs/OurValues/GuidingPrinciples/.
10. Ralph Smith, "Many Happy Returns," *Robb Report Worth*, August 2, 2004.

Chapter 12

1. Stephen R. Covey, *The 7 Habits of Highly Effective People*, New York: The Free Press, 1989, 2004, p. 287.
2. Scott Fithian, *Values-Based Estate Planning*, New York: John Wiley and Sons, 2000, pp. 202–228.

Section—Social Impact Practices

1. "2004 Indian Ocean Earthquake," accessed on Wikipedia.
2. Eric Weiner, "Donations to Tsunami Relief Dwarf Other Disasters," *NPR*, December 26, 2005.

Chapter 13

1. Interview with Bob Geldof, BBC, October 21, 1999.
2. Center for Venture Philanthropy Web site.
3. Ibid.
4. Sandy Weill and Judah Kraushaar, *The Real Deal*, New York: Warner Business Books, 2006, p. 482.
5. Carol Tice, "Getting Results, Business Support Makes King County Affiliate No. 1 in Nation," *Puget Sound Business Journal*, May 13–19, 2005, p. 12A.

Chapter 14

1. Anita Roddick, *Body and Soul*, London: Ebury Press, 1991, pp. 109–110.
2. "Rock Star with a Cause," speech by Bono transcribed in *Grids, the TNT Logistics Benelux Magazine for Logistics and Supply Chain Excellence*, spring/summer 2005, pp. 4-5.
3. Skoll Foundation Web site.

Chapter 15

1. "Holocaust Denial on Trial: Truth Triumphs in 2000 Court Victory," Emory University, Rabbi Donald Tam Institute for Jewish Studies. Taken from Web site by the same name.
2. Ibid.
3. Interview by Randall Ottinger with Les Wexner, 2006.
4. "Paul Tudor Jones," accessed on Wikipedia in 2006.

Section—Generational Family Practices

1. William T. O'Hara, *Centuries of Success*, Avon, MA: Adams Media, 2004, p. 3.
2. Ibid., p. 7.

Chapter 17

1. Interview by Randall Ottinger with Mario Morino in 2005.
2. Interview by Randall Ottinger with Les Wexner in 2005.
3. Barbara Blouin, Katherine Gibson, and Margaret Kiersted, *Coming into Money: Preparing Your Children for an Inheritance*, Halifax, NS: Trio Press, 2001.
4. Interview by Randall Ottinger with Mark Leslie in 2005.
5. Interview by Randall Ottinger with Ginny Esposito in 2005.
6. Interview by Randall Ottinger with Doug Mellinger in 2005.
7. Interview by Randall Ottinger with Anita Roddick in 2005.

Chapter 18

1. William T. O'Hara, *Centuries of Success*.
2. Ian Lansberg, "Twelve Tasks in Succession," *Family Business Magazine*, Summer 1993.

3. Kelin Gersick, *Generations of Givin*, Lanham, MD, Lexington Books, 2004, p. 206.
4. Ibid., Table D4.
5. James E. Hughes, Jr., *Family Wealth—Keeping It in the Family: How Family Members and Their Advisers Preserve Human, Intellectual, and Financial Assets for Generations*, Princeton, NJ: Bloomberg Press, 2004.

Chapter 19

1. Jim Collins, *Good to Great*, New York: HarperCollins, 2001, p. 21.
2. Scott Fithian, *Values-Based Estate Planning, A Step-by-Step Approach to Wealth Transfer for Professional Advisors*, New York: John Wiley and Sons, 2000, pp. 87–88.
3. Interview by Randall Ottinger with John Whitehead in 2005.

Chapter 20

1. Joline Godfrey, *Raising Financially Fit Kids*, Berkeley, CA: Ten Speed Press, 2003.
2. Roy Williams and Vic Preisser, *Preparing Heirs*, p. 138.

Chapter 21

1. Jed Emerson, "The Blended Value Map, Tracking the Intersects and Opportunities of Economic, Social, and Environmental Value Creation," Blendedvalue.org, October, 2003.
2. Eston Kimani, MIT-AITI Entrepreneurship, Lecture 6, Social Entrepreneurship, 2004.
3. Community Foundations Global Status Report, Worldwide Initiatives for Grantmaker Support, 2005.
4. Joel. L. Fleishman, *The Foundation*, p. 122.

Chapter 22

1. Andrew Ross Sorkin, "$45 Billion TXU Deal Is an Environmental Watershed," *International Herald Tribune*, February 26, 2007.
2. "The Business of Giving," *The Economist*, February 25, 2006.
3. Spectrum Group's Ultra High-Net-Worth Executive Presentation, June 17, 2004, p. 7.
4. Ibid., p. 50.
5. "S&P Releases Latest Index Versus Active Fund Scorecard," Press release, New York, April 13, 2006.

INDEX

ABOUT THE AUTHOR

Randall J. Ottinger has been involved in business, social entre-preneurship, and philanthropy for over 25 years. He is cofounder of LMR Advisors, which provides strategic philanthropy and legacy advisory services to individuals, wealth advisory firms, and social enterprises. Prior to starting LMR Advisors, Mr. Ottinger was involved in the private bank of Bank of America advising large family offices, and spent more than 20 years as an executive in high-tech companies. Mr. Ottinger is also a key investment executive in the Ottinger-Heath family office, and cochairman of the Ottinger Foundation. Recently, Mr. Ottinger has founded a social enterprise called the Wealth Impact Network (WIN), which is developing a market-based approach to philanthropy based on Mr. Ottinger's research into the application of portfolio theory to philanthropy. Mr. Ottinger has a BA from Cornell University and an MBA from Harvard Business School. He is a member of Young President's Organization, Social Venture Partners, and Advisors in Philanthropy. For more information please go to www.beyondsuccesslegacy.com.